I0010359

Java 9 with JShell

Introducing the full range of Java 9's new features via JShell

Gastón C. Hillar

BIRMINGHAM - MUMBAI

Java 9 with JShell

Copyright © 2017 Packt Publishing

All rights reserved. No part of this book may be reproduced, stored in a retrieval system, or transmitted in any form or by any means, without the prior written permission of the publisher, except in the case of brief quotations embedded in critical articles or reviews.

Every effort has been made in the preparation of this book to ensure the accuracy of the information presented. However, the information contained in this book is sold without warranty, either express or implied. Neither the author, nor Packt Publishing, and its dealers and distributors will be held liable for any damages caused or alleged to be caused directly or indirectly by this book.

Packt Publishing has endeavored to provide trademark information about all of the companies and products mentioned in this book by the appropriate use of capitals. However, Packt Publishing cannot guarantee the accuracy of this information.

First published: March 2017

Production reference: 1250317

Published by Packt Publishing Ltd.
Livery Place
35 Livery Street
Birmingham B3 2PB, UK.

ISBN 978-1-78728-284-1

www.packtpub.com

Credits

Author
Gastón C. Hillar

Reviewer
Daniel Mühlbachler

Acquisition Editor
Frank Pohlmann

Content Development Editor
Radhika Atitkar

Technical Editor
Bhagyashree Rai

Copy Editor
Tom Jacob

Project Coordinator
Remzil Nisha Dcruz

Proofreader
Safis Editing

Indexer
Tejal Daruwale Soni

Graphics
Kirk D'Penha

Production Coordinator
Melwyn Dsa

About the Author

Gastón C. Hillar is Italian and has been working with computers since he was 8 years old. In the early 80s, he began programming with the legendary Texas TI-99/4A and Commodore 64 home computers. Gastón has a bachelor's degree in computer science (he graduated with honors). He also holds an MBA (he graduated with an outstanding thesis). At present, Gastón is an independent IT consultant and a freelance author who is always looking for new adventures around the world.

He was a senior contributing editor at Dr. Dobb's and has written more than a hundred articles on software development topics. He has received the prestigious Intel® Black Belt Software Developer award eight times. He has written many articles about Java for Oracle Java Magazine. Gastón was also a former Microsoft MVP in technical computing.

He is a guest blogger at Intel® Software Network (http://software.intel.com). You can reach him at gastonhillar@hotmail.com and follow him on Twitter at http://twitter.com/gastonhillar. Gastón's blog is http://csharpmulticore.blogspot.com.

He lives with his wife, Vanesa, and his two sons, Kevin and Brandon.

Acknowledgement

At the time of writing this book, I was fortunate enough to work with an excellent team at Packt Publishing, whose contributions vastly improved the presentation of this book. Dominic Shakeshaft and Frank Pohlmann allowed me to provide ideas to develop this book, and I jumped into the exciting project of teaching object-oriented and functional programming with Java 9 using JShell as the main tool. My conversations with Frank helped me realize my vision for this book and create a robust table of contents. Radhika Atitkar provided many sensible suggestions regarding the text, the format, and the flow. The reader will notice her great work. I would like to thank my technical reviewers and proofreaders for their thorough reviews and insightful comments. I was able to incorporate some of the knowledge and wisdom they have gained in their many years in the software development industry. This book was possible because they gave valuable feedback.

The process of writing a book requires a huge amount of lonely hours. I wouldn't be able to write a book without dedicating some time to play soccer against my sons, Kevin and Brandon, and my nephew, Nicolas. Of course, I never won a match. However, I did score a few goals.

About the Reviewer

Daniel Mühlbachler got interested in computer science shortly after entering high school, where he later developed web applications as part of a scholarship system for outstanding pupils.

He has a profound knowledge of web development (PHP, HTML, CSS/LESS, and AngularJS), and he has worked with a variety of other programming languages and systems, such as Java/Groovy, Grails, Objective-C and Swift, Matlab, Julia, C (with Cilk), Node.js, and Linux servers.

Furthermore, he works with some database management systems based on SQL and also some NoSQL systems, such as MongoDB and SOLR; this is also reflected in several projects that he is currently involved in at Catalysts GmbH.

After studying abroad as an exchange student in the United Kingdom, he completed his bachelor's degree at the Johannes Kepler University in Linz, Austria, with a thesis on aerosol satellite data processing for mobile visualization; this is where he also became familiar with processing large amounts of data.

Daniel enjoys solving challenging problems and is always keen on working with new technologies, especially those related to the fields of big data, functional programming, optimization, and NoSQL databases.

More detailed information about his experience, as well as his contact details, can be found at www.muehlbachler.org and www.linkedin.com/in/danielmuehlbachler.

www.PacktPub.com

eBooks, discount offers, and more

Did you know that Packt offers eBook versions of every book published, with PDF and ePub files available? You can upgrade to the eBook version at www.PacktPub.com and as a print book customer, you are entitled to a discount on the eBook copy. Get in touch with us at customercare@packtpub.com for more details.

At www.PacktPub.com, you can also read a collection of free technical articles, sign up for a range of free newsletters and receive exclusive discounts and offers on Packt books and eBooks.

https://www.packtpub.com/mapt

Get the most in-demand software skills with Mapt. Mapt gives you full access to all Packt books and video courses, as well as industry-leading tools to help you plan your personal development and advance your career.

Why subscribe?

- Fully searchable across every book published by Packt
- Copy and paste, print, and bookmark content
- On demand and accessible via a web browser

Customer Feedback

Thanks for purchasing this Packt book. At Packt, quality is at the heart of our editorial process. To help us improve, please leave us an honest review on this book's Amazon page at https://www.amazon.com/dp/1787282848. If you'd like to join our team of regular reviewers, you can e-mail us at customerreviews@packtpub.com. We award our regular reviewers with free eBooks and videos in exchange for their valuable feedback. Help us be relentless in improving our products!

I dedicate this book to my sons, Kevin and Brandon, and my wife, Vanesa

Table of Contents

Preface

Java is definitely one of the most popular programming languages of this century. However, whenever we had to quickly explore new algorithms or new application domains, Java didn't provide us with a simple way of executing code snippets and print the results. As a result of this limitation, many developers started working with other programming languages that offered a REPL (Read-Evaluate-Print-Loop) utility, such as Scala and Python. However, many times, it was necessary to go back to Java after the exploratory phase finished and the requirements and the algorithms were clear.

Java 9 introduces JShell, a new utility that allows us to easily run Java 9 code snippets and print the results. This utility is a REPL, and makes it easy for us to work with Java as developers do with Scala and Python. JShell makes it easier to learn Java 9 and its most important features.

Object-oriented programming, also known as OOP, is a required skill in absolutely every modern software developer job. It makes a lot of sense because OOP allows you to maximize code reuse and minimize maintenance costs. However, learning object-oriented programming is challenging because it includes too many abstract concepts that require real-life examples to be easy to understand. In addition, object-oriented code that doesn't follow best practices can easily become a maintenance nightmare.

Java is a multi-paradigm programming language, and one of its most important paradigms is OOP. If you want to work with Java 9, you need to master OOP in Java. In addition, as Java 9 also grabs nice features found in functional programming languages, it is convenient to know how to mix OOP code with functional programing code.

This book will allow you to develop high-quality reusable object-oriented code in Java 9 with JShell. You will learn the object-oriented programming principles and how Java 9 implements them, combined with modern functional programming techniques. You will learn how to capture objects from real-world elements and create object-oriented code that represents them. You will understand Java's approach towards object-oriented code. You will maximize code reuse and reduce maintenance costs. Your code will be easy to understand and it will work with representations of real-life elements.

In addition, you will learn how to organize code using the new modularity feature introduced in Java 9, and you will be ready to create complex applications.

What this book covers

Chapter 1, JShell – A Read-Evaluate-Print-Loop for Java 9, starts our journey towards object-oriented programming with Java 9. We will learn how to launch and work with a new utility introduced with Java 9 that will allow us to easily run Java 9 code snippets and print its results: JShell. This utility will make it easy for us to learn object-oriented programming.

Chapter 2, Real-World Objects to UML Diagrams and Java 9 via JShell, teaches how to recognize objects from real-life situations. We will understand that working with objects makes it easier to write code that is easier to understand and reuse. We will learn how to recognize real-world elements and translate them into the different components of the object-oriented paradigm supported in Java. We will start organizing classes with UML (Unified Modeling Language) diagrams.

Chapter 3, Classes and Instances, shows that classes represent blueprints or templates to generate the objects, which are also known as instances. We will design a few classes that represent blueprints of real-life objects. We will learn about an object's life cycle. We will work with many examples to understand how initialization works. We will declare our first class to generate a blueprint for objects. We will customize its initialization and test its personalized behavior in action with live examples in the JShell. We will understand how the garbage collection works.

Chapter 4, Encapsulation of Data, teaches you the different members of a class in Java 9 and how they are reflected in members of the instances generated from a class. We will work with instance fields, class fields, setters, getters, instance methods, and class methods. We will generate computed properties with setters and getters. We will take advantage of access modifiers to hide data. We will use static fields to create values shared by all the instances of a class.

Chapter 5, Mutable and Immutable Classes, introduces the differences between mutating and non-mutating objects. First, we will create a mutable class, and then we will build an immutable version of this class. We will learn the advantages of non-mutating objects when writing concurrent code.

Chapter 6, Inheritance, Abstraction, Extension, and Specialization, discusses how to take advantage of simple inheritance to specialize or extend a base class. We will design many classes from top to bottom and we will use chained constructors. We will use UML diagrams to design classes that inherit from another class. We will code the classes in the interactive JShell. We will override and overload methods. We will run code to understand how all the things we code work.

Chapter 7, Members Inheritance and Polymorphism, teaches you how to control whether subclasses can or cannot override members. We will take advantage of one of the most exciting object-oriented features: polymorphism. We will take advantage of JShell to easily understand typecasting. We will declare methods that perform operations with instances of classes.

Chapter 8, Contract Programming with Interfaces, introduces how interfaces work in combination with classes in Java 9. The only way to have multiple inheritance in Java 9 is through the usage of interfaces. We will learn about the declaration and combination of multiple blueprints to generate a single instance. We will declare interfaces with different types of requirements. Then, we will declare many classes that implement the created interfaces. We will combine interfaces with classes to take advantage of multiple inheritance in Java 9. We will combine inheritance for interfaces and inheritance for classes.

Chapter 9, Advanced Contract Programming with Interfaces, dives deeper in to contract programming with interfaces. We will work with methods that receive interfaces as arguments. We will understand how downcasting works with interfaces and classes and we will treat instances of an interface type as a different subclass. JShell will allow us to easily understand the complexities of typecasting and downcasting. We will work with more complex scenarios in which we will combine class inheritance with interface inheritance.

Chapter 10, Maximization of Code Reuse with Generics, introduces you to working with parametric polymorphism. We will learn how to maximize code reuse by writing code capable of working with objects of different types, that is, instances of classes that implement specific interfaces or whose class hierarchy includes specific superclasses. We will work with interfaces and generics. We will create a class that works with a constrained generic type. We will use a generic class for multiple types, thanks to generics.

Chapter 11, Advanced Generics, dives deeper in parametric polymorphism. We will declare a class that works with two constrained generic types. We will use a generic class with two generic type parameters in JShell. We will generalize existing classes by taking advantage of generics in Java 9.

Chapter 12, Object-Oriented, Functional Programming, and Lambda Expressions, discusses that functions are first-class citizens in Java 9. We will work with functional interfaces within classes. We will use many functional programming features included in Java 9 and combine them with everything we learned in the previous chapters about object-oriented programming. This way, we will be able to use the best of both worlds. We will analyze the differences between the imperative and functional programming approach for many algorithms. We will take advantage of lambda expressions and combine map operations with reduce.

Chapter 13, Modularity in Java 9, puts together all the pieces of the object-oriented puzzle. We will refactor existing code to take advantage of object-oriented programming. We will understand the usage of modular source code in Java 9. We will work with modules to create a new Java 9 solution, organize object-oriented code with the new modularity in Java 9, and learn many techniques of debugging object-oriented code.

What you need for this book

You will need a computer with a dual-core CPU and at least 4 GB RAM, capable of running JDK 9 Windows Vista SP2, Windows 7, Windows 8.x, Windows 10 or higher, or macOS 10.9 or higher, and any Linux distribution supported by JDK 9. Any IoT device capable of running JDK 9 will also be useful.

Who this book is for

This book can be understood by anyone who is a graduate of computer science or someone who has just begun working as a software engineer. Basically, an understanding of an object-oriented programming language such as Python, C++, or indeed, an earlier Java version, is sufficient. It would be helpful to have participated in the full product cycle of a software engineering project.

Conventions

In this book, you will find a number of styles of text that distinguish between different kinds of information. Here are some examples of these styles, and an explanation of their meaning.

Code words in text, database table names, folder names, filenames, file extensions, pathnames, dummy URLs, user input, and Twitter handles are shown as follows: Code words in text are shown as follows: "JShell allows us to call the `System.out.printf` method to easily format output we want to print."

A block of code is set as follows:

```
double getGeneratedRectangleHeight() {
    final Rectangle rectangle = new Rectangle(37, 87);
    return rectangle.height;
}
```

When we wish to draw your attention to a particular part of a code block, the relevant lines or items are set in bold:

```
double getGeneratedRectangleHeight() {
    final Rectangle rectangle = new Rectangle(37, 87);
    return rectangle.height;
}
```

Any command-line input or output is written as follows:

```
javac -version
```

New terms and **important words** are shown in bold. Words that you see on the screen, in menus or dialog boxes for example, appear in the text like this: "Click on **Accept** and then click on **Exit**."

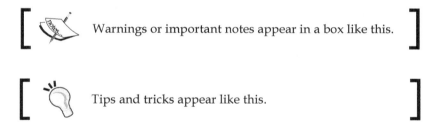

> Warnings or important notes appear in a box like this.

> Tips and tricks appear like this.

Reader feedback

Feedback from our readers is always welcome. Let us know what you think about this book—what you liked or may have disliked. Reader feedback is important for us to develop titles that you really get the most out of.

To send us general feedback, simply send an e-mail to `feedback@packtpub.com`, and mention the book title via the subject of your message.

If there is a topic that you have expertise in and you are interested in either writing or contributing to a book, see our author guide on www.packtpub.com/authors.

Customer support

Now that you are the proud owner of a Packt book, we have a number of things to help you to get the most from your purchase.

Downloading the example code

You can download the example code files for this book from your account at http://www.packtpub.com. If you purchased this book elsewhere, you can visit http://www.packtpub.com/support and register to have the files e-mailed directly to you.

You can download the code files by following these steps:

1. Log in or register to our website using your e-mail address and password.
2. Hover the mouse pointer on the **SUPPORT** tab at the top.
3. Click on **Code Downloads & Errata**.
4. Enter the name of the book in the **Search** box.
5. Select the book for which you're looking to download the code files.
6. Choose from the drop-down menu where you purchased this book from.
7. Click on **Code Download**.

You can also download the code files by clicking on the **Code Files** button on the book's webpage at the Packt Publishing website. This page can be accessed by entering the book's name in the **Search** box. Please note that you need to be logged in to your Packt account.

Once the file is downloaded, please make sure that you unzip or extract the folder using the latest version of:

- WinRAR / 7-Zip for Windows
- Zipeg / iZip / UnRarX for Mac
- 7-Zip / PeaZip for Linux

The code bundle for the book is also hosted on GitHub at https://github.com/PacktPublishing/Java-9-with-JShell. We also have other code bundles from our rich catalog of books and videos available at https://github.com/PacktPublishing/. Check them out!

Downloading the color images of this book

We also provide you with a PDF file that has color images of the screenshots/ diagrams used in this book. The color images will help you better understand the changes in the output. You can download this file from `https://www.packtpub.com/sites/default/files/downloads/Java9withJShell_ColorImages.pdf`.

Errata

Although we have taken every care to ensure the accuracy of our content, mistakes do happen. If you find a mistake in one of our books — maybe a mistake in the text or the code — we would be grateful if you could report this to us. By doing so, you can save other readers from frustration and help us improve subsequent versions of this book. If you find any errata, please report them by visiting `http://www.packtpub.com/submit-errata`, selecting your book, clicking on the **Errata Submission Form** link, and entering the details of your errata. Once your errata are verified, your submission will be accepted and the errata will be uploaded to our website or added to any list of existing errata under the Errata section of that title.

To view the previously submitted errata, go to `https://www.packtpub.com/books/content/support` and enter the name of the book in the search field. The required information will appear under the **Errata** section.

Piracy

Piracy of copyrighted material on the Internet is an ongoing problem across all media. At Packt, we take the protection of our copyright and licenses very seriously. If you come across any illegal copies of our works in any form on the Internet, please provide us with the location address or website name immediately so that we can pursue a remedy.

Please contact us at `copyright@packtpub.com` with a link to the suspected pirated material.

We appreciate your help in protecting our authors and our ability to bring you valuable content.

Questions

If you have a problem with any aspect of this book, you can contact us at `questions@packtpub.com`, and we will do our best to address the problem.

1
JShell – A Read-Evaluate-Print-Loop for Java 9

In this chapter, we will start our journey toward object-oriented programming with Java 9. You will learn how to launch and work with a new utility introduced with Java 9 that will allow us to easily run Java 9 code snippets and print their results: JShell. This utility will make it easy for you to learn object-oriented programming. We will do the following:

- Get ready for our journey toward **OOP (Object-Oriented Programming)** with Java 9
- Install the required software on Windows, macOS, or Linux
- Understand the benefits of working with a **REPL (Read-Evaluate-Print-Loop)** utility
- Check default imports and use auto-complete features
- Run Java 9 code in JShell
- Evaluate expressions
- Work with variables, methods, and sources
- Edit the source code in our favorite external code editor
- Load source code

Getting ready for our journey toward OOP with Java 9

In this book, you will learn to take advantage of all the object-oriented features included in the Java programming language version 9, known as Java 9. Some of the examples might be compatible with previous Java versions, such as Java 8, Java 7, and Java 6, but it is essential to use Java 9 or later because this version is not backwards compatible. We won't write code that is backwards compatible with previous Java versions because our main goal is to work with Java 9 or later and to use its syntax and all of its new features.

Most of the time, we won't use any **IDE (Integrated Development Environment)**, and we will take advantage of JShell and many other utilities included in the JDK. However, you can use any IDE that provides a Java 9 REPL to work with all the examples. You will understand the benefits of working with a REPL in the next sections. You will definitely benefit from an IDE in the last chapter where you will explore the new modularity features introduced with Java 9.

You don't need any previous experience with the Java programming language to work with the examples in the book and learn how to model and create object-oriented code with Java 9. If you have some experience with C#, C++, Python, Swift, Objective-C, Ruby, or JavaScript, you will be able to easily learn Java's syntax and understand the examples. Many modern programming languages have been borrowing features from Java and vice versa. Therefore, any knowledge of these languages will be extremely useful.

In this chapter, we will install the required software on Windows, macOS, or Linux. We will understand the benefits of working with a REPL, specifically, JShell, to learn object-oriented programming. We will learn how to run Java 9 code in the JShell and how to load the source code samples in the REPL. Finally, we will learn how to run Java code on Windows, macOS, and Linux from the command line or terminal.

Installing the required software on Windows, macOS, or Linux

We must download and install the latest version of **JDK 9 (Java Development Kit 9)** for our operating system from `https://jdk9.java.net/download/`. We must accept the license agreement for Java to download the software.

As happened with previous versions, JDK 9 is available on many different platforms, including but not limited to the following:

- Windows 32-bit
- Windows 64-bit
- macOS 64-bit (formerly known as Mac OS X or simply OS X)
- Linux 32-bit
- Linux 64-bit
- Linux on ARM 32-bit
- Linux on ARM 64-bit

Once we have completed the installation for the appropriate version of JDK 9 based on our operating system, we can add the `bin` sub-folder of the folder in which JDK 9 has been installed to the `PATH` environment variable. This way, we would be able to launch the different utilities from any folder in which we are located.

 If we don't add the `bin` sub-folder of the folder in which JDK 9 has been installed to the `PATH` environment variable in our operating system, we will always have to use the full path to the `bin` sub-folder when executing the commands. In the next instructions to launch the different Java command-line utilities, we will assume that we are located in this `bin` sub-folder or that the `PATH` environment variable includes it.

Once we have installed JDK 9, and added the `bin` folder to the `PATH` environment variable, we can run the following command in Windows Command Prompt or in macOS or Linux Terminal:

```
javac -version
```

The previous command will display the current version for the primary Java compiler included in the JDK that compiles Java source code into Java bytecodes. The version number should start with 9, as shown in the next sample output:

```
javac 9-ea
```

If the results of the previous command display a version number that doesn't start with 9, we must check whether the installation completed successfully. In addition, we have to make sure that the `PATH` environment variable doesn't include paths to previous versions of the JDK and that it includes the `bin` folder for the recently installed JDK 9.

Now, we are ready to launch JShell. Run the following command in Windows Command Prompt or in macOS or Linux Terminal:

`jshell`

The previous command will launch JShell, display a welcome message that includes the JDK version being used, and the prompt will change to `jshell>`. Whenever we see this prompt, it means we are still in JShell. The following screenshot shows JShell running in a Terminal window on macOS.

```
                                   bin — java • jshell — 78×24
Gastons-MacBook-Pro:~ gaston$ cd $(/usr/libexec/java_home)/bin
Gastons-MacBook-Pro:bin gaston$ pwd
/Library/Java/JavaVirtualMachines/jdk-9.jdk/Contents/Home/bin
Gastons-MacBook-Pro:bin gaston$ javac -version
javac 9-ea
Gastons-MacBook-Pro:bin gaston$ ./jshell
|   Welcome to JShell -- Version 9-ea
|   For an introduction type: /help intro

jshell>
```

 If we want to leave JShell at any time, we just need to press *Ctrl + D* in a Mac. Another option is to enter `/exit` and press *Enter*.

Understanding the benefits of working with a REPL

Java 9 introduced an interactive REPL command-line environment named JShell. This tool allows us to execute Java code snippets and get immediate results. We can easily write code and see the results of its execution without having to create a solution or project. We don't have to wait for the project to finish the build process to check the results of executing many lines of code. JShell, as any other REPL, facilitates exploratory programming, that is, we can easily and interactively try and debug different algorithms and structures.

If you have worked with other programming languages that provide a REPL or an interactive shell such as Python, Scala, Clojure, F#, Ruby, Smalltalk, and Swift among many others, you already know the benefits of working with a REPL.

For example, imagine that we have to interact with an **IoT** (**Internet of Things**) library that provides Java bindings. We have to write Java code to use the library to control a drone, also known as a **UAV** (**Unmanned Aerial Vehicle**). The drone is an IoT device that interacts with many sensors and actuators, including digital electronic speed controllers linked to engines, propellers, and servomotors.

We want to be able to write a few lines of code to retrieve data from sensors and control the actuators. We just need to make sure things work as explained in the documentation. We want to make sure that the values read from the altimeter change when we move the drone. JShell provides us with the appropriate tool to start interacting with the library in a few seconds. We just need to launch JShell, load the library, and start writing Java 9 code in the REPL. With previous Java versions, we would have needed to create a new project from scratch and write some boilerplate code before we could start writing the first lines of code that interacted with the library. JShell allows us to start working faster and reduces the need to create an entire skeleton to start running Java 9 code. JShell allows interactive exploration of **APIs** (**Application Programming Interfaces**) from a REPL.

We can enter any Java 9 definition in JShell. For example, we can declare methods, classes, and variables. We can also enter Java expressions, statements, or imports. Once we have entered the code to declare a method, we can enter a statement that uses the previously defined method and see the results of the execution.

JShell allows us to load source code from a file, and therefore, you will be able to load the source code samples included in this book and evaluate them in JShell. Whenever we have to work with source code, you will know the folder and the file from which you can load it. In addition, JShell allows us to execute JShell commands. We will learn about the most useful commands later, in this chapter.

JShell allows us to call the `System.out.printf` method to easily format output we want to print. We will take advantage of this method in our sample code.

 JShell disables some features from Java 9 that aren't useful in the interactive REPL. Whenever we have to work with these features in JShell, we will make it clear that JShell will disable them and we will explain their effects.

The semicolon (;) is optional at the end of a statement in JShell. However, we will always use a semicolon at the end of each statement because we don't want to forget that we must use semicolons when we write real-life Java 9 code in projects and solutions. We will only omit the semicolon at the end of a statement when we enter expressions to be evaluated by JShell.

For example, the following two lines are equivalent and both of them will print `"Object-Oriented Programming rocks with Java 9!"` as a result of their execution in JShell. The first line doesn't include a semicolon (;) at the end of the statement and the second line includes the semicolon (;). We will always use the semicolon (;) as in the second line, to keep consistency.

```
System.out.printf("Object-Oriented Programming rocks with Java 9!\n")
System.out.printf("Object-Oriented Programming rocks with Java 9!\n");
```

The following screenshot shows the results of executing the two lines in JShell running on Windows 10:

```
Command Prompt - jshell                                          —    □    ×

C:\Users\gaston>jshell
|  Welcome to JShell -- Version 9-ea
|  For an introduction type: /help intro

jshell> System.out.printf("Object-Oriented Programming rocks with Java 9!\n")
Object-Oriented Programming rocks with Java 9!
$1 ==> java.io.PrintStream@4c70fda8

jshell> System.out.printf("Object-Oriented Programming rocks with Java 9!\n");
Object-Oriented Programming rocks with Java 9!
$2 ==> java.io.PrintStream@4c70fda8

jshell>
```

In some examples, we will take advantage of the fact that JShell provides us networking access. This feature is extremely useful to interact with Web Services. However, you have to make sure that you don't have JShell blocked in your firewall configuration.

 Unluckily, at the time I was writing this book, JShell didn't include syntax highlighting features. However, you will learn how to use our favorite editor to write and edit code that we can then execute in JShell.

Checking default imports and using auto-complete features

By default, JShell provides a set of common imports and we can use the `import` statement to import the necessary types from any additional package we might need to run our code snippets. We can enter the following command in JShell to list all the imports:

```
/imports
```

The following lines show the results of the previous command:

```
|    import java.io.*
|    import java.math.*
|    import java.net.*
|    import java.nio.file.*
|    import java.util.*
|    import java.util.concurrent.*
|    import java.util.function.*
|    import java.util.prefs.*
|    import java.util.regex.*
|    import java.util.stream.*
```

As happens when we write Java code outside of JShell, we don't need to import the types from the `java.lang` package because they are imported by default and they aren't listed when we run the `/imports` command in JShell. Thus, by default, JShell provides us access to all the types in the following packages:

- `java.lang`
- `java.io`
- `java.math`
- `java.net`
- `java.nio.file`
- `java.util`
- `java.util.concurrent`
- `java.util.function`
- `java.util.prefs`
- `java.util.regex`
- `java.util.stream`

JShell provides auto-completion features. We just need to press the *Tab* key whenever we want to have assistance from the auto-complete feature, as done when we work with the Windows Command Prompt or the Terminal in macOS or Linux.

Sometimes, there are too many options that start with the first characters we entered. In these cases, JShell provides us with a list of all the available options to provide us help. For example, we can enter S and press the *Tab* key. JShell will list all the types imported from the previously listed packages that start with an S. The following screenshot shows the results in JShell:

We want to enter System. Considering the previous list, we will just enter Sys to make sure that System is the only option that starts with Sys. Basically, we are cheating to understand how auto-completion works in JShell. Enter Sys and press the *Tab* key. JShell will display System.

Now, enter a dot (`.`) followed by an o (you will have `System.o`) and press the *Tab* key. JShell will display `System.out`.

Next, enter a dot (`.`) and press the *Tab* key. JShell will display all the public methods declared in `System.out`. After the list, JShell will include `System.out.` again to allow us to continue entering our code. The following screenshot shows the results in JShell:

```
Command Prompt - jshell                                               —    □    ×
StringJoiner                    StringReader
StringTokenizer                 StringWriter
SubmissionPublisher             Supplier
SuppressWarnings                SyncFailedException
SynchronousQueue                System

jshell> System.out.
append(          checkError()    close()         equals(
flush()          format(         getClass()      hashCode()
notify()         notifyAll()     print(          printf(
println(         toString()      wait(           write(

jshell> System.out.
```

Enter `print1` and press the *Tab* key. JShell will complete to `System.out.println(`, that is, it will add an n and open parenthesis (`(`). This way, we just have to enter the arguments for the method because there was just one method that started with `print1`. Enter `"Auto-complete is helpful in JShell");` and press *Enter*. The following line shows the complete statement:

```
System.out.println("Auto-complete is helpful in JShell");
```

The following screenshot shows the results in JShell after running the previous line:

```
Command Prompt - jshell                                               —    □    ×
notify()         notifyAll()     print(          printf(
println(         toString()      wait(           write(

jshell> System.out.println(
println(

jshell> System.out.println("Auto-complete is helpful in JShell");
Auto-complete is helpful in JShell

jshell>
```

Running Java 9 code in JShell

Now, we want to run Java 9 code in JShell and understand what happens after we enter each code snippet. Press *Ctrl + D* to exit the current JShell session. Run the following command in the Windows Command Prompt or in a macOS or Linux Terminal to launch JShell with a verbose feedback:

```
jshell -v
```

The verbose feedback will provide us additional details about what JShell does after it executes or evaluates each code snippet. Enter the following code in JShell to create a new method named `calculateRectangleArea`. The method receives a `width` and a `height` for a rectangle and returns the result of the multiplication of both values of type `float`:

```
float calculateRectangleArea(float width, float height) {
    return width * height;
}
```

After we enter the previous lines, JShell will display the next message indicating it has created a method named `calculateRectangleArea` with two arguments of `float` type:

```
|  created method calculateRectangleArea(float,float)
```

 Notice that all the messages written by JShell start with a pipe symbol (|).

Enter the following command in JShell to list the current active snippets of code that we have typed and executed so far in the current session:

```
/list
```

The following lines show the results. Notice that JShell prefaces the code snippet with the snippet id, that is, a unique number that identifies each code snippet. JShell will display the following lines as a result of the previous command. The code snippet that created the `calculateRectangleArea` method has been assigned 1 as the snippet id.

```
1 : float calculateRectangleArea(float width, float height) {
        return width * height;
    }
```

Enter the following code in JShell to create a new `float` variable named `width` and initialize it with `50`:

```
float width = 50;
```

After we enter the previous line, JShell will display the next message indicating it has created a variable named `width` of `float` type and it assigned the value `50.0` to this variable:

width ==> 50.0

| created variable width : float

Enter the following code in JShell to create a new `float` variable named `height` and initialize it with `25`:

```
float height = 25;
```

After we enter the previous line, JShell will display the next message indicating it has created a variable named `height` of the `float` type and it assigned the value `25.0` to this variable:

height ==> 25.0

| created variable height : float

Enter `float area = ca` and press the *Tab* key. JShell will complete to `float area = calculateRectangleArea(`, that is, it will add `lculateRectangleArea` and open parenthesis (`(`). This way, we just have to enter the two arguments for the method because there was just one method that started with `ca`. Enter `width, height);` and press *Enter*. The following line shows the complete statement:

```
float area = calculateRectangleArea(width, height);
```

After we enter the previous line, JShell will display the next message indicating it has created a variable named `area` of the `float` type and it assigned the result of calling the `calculateRectangleArea` method with the previously declared `width` and `height` variables as arguments. The method returns `1250.0` as a result and it is assigned to the `area` variable.

area ==> 1250.0

| created variable area : float

Enter the following command in JShell to list the current active snippets of code that we have typed and executed so far in the current session:

/list

The following lines show the results. Notice that JShell prefaces the code snippet with the snippet id, that is, a unique number that identifies each code snippet. JShell will display the following lines as a result of the previous command:

```
1 : float calculateRectangleArea(float width, float height) {
        return width * height;
    }
2 : float width = 50;
3 : float height = 25;
4 : float area = calculateRectangleArea(width, height);
```

Enter the following code in JShell to display the values for the width, height, and area variables with a call to System.out.printf. The first %.2f in the string we pass as a first argument to System.out.printf makes the next argument after the string (width) to be displayed as a floating point number with two decimal places. We repeat %.2f twice to display the height and area variables as floating point numbers with two decimal places.

```
System.out.printf("Width: %.2f, Height: %.2f, Area: %.2f\n", width,
height, area);
```

After we enter the previous line, JShell will format the output with System.out. printf and will print the next message followed by the name of a scratch variable:

```
Width: 50.00, Height: 25.00, Area: 1250.00

$5 ==> java.io.PrintStream@68c4039c

|  created scratch variable $5 : PrintStream
```

Evaluating expressions

JShell allows us to evaluate any valid Java 9 expression, as we might do when we use an IDE and the typical expression evaluation dialog box. Enter the following expression in JShell:

```
width * height;
```

After we enter the previous line, JShell will evaluate the expression and it will assign the results to a scratch variable whose name starts with $ and continues with a number. JShell displays the scratch variable name, $6, the value assigned to the variable that indicates the result of evaluating the expression, 1250.0, and the type for the scratch variable, float. The next lines show the message displayed in JShell after we enter the previous expression:

```
$6 ==> 1250.0
|  created scratch variable $6 : float
```

Notice that the name for the scratch variable might be different. For example, instead of $6, it might be $7 or $8. We can run a code snippet that uses the previously created scratch variable as we do with any other variable created in the current JShell session. Enter the following code in JShell to display the value for the $6 variable as a floating point number with two decimal places. Make sure you replace $6 with the scratch variable name that JShell generated.

```
System.out.printf("The calculated area is %.2f", $6);
```

After we enter the previous line, JShell will format the output with `System.out.printf` and will print the next message:

The calculated area is 1250.00

We can also use the previously created scratch variable in another expression. Enter the following code in JShell to add `10.5` (`float`) to the value of the $6 variable. Make sure you replace $6 with the scratch variable name that JShell generated.

```
$6 + 10.5f;
```

After we enter the previous line, JShell will evaluate the expression and it will assign the results to a new scratch variable whose name starts with $ and continues with a number. JShell displays the scratch variable name, $8, the value assigned to the variable that indicates the result of evaluating the expression, `1260.5`, and the type for the scratch variable, `float`. The next lines show the message displayed in JShell after we enter the previous expression:

$8 ==> 1250.5
| created scratch variable $8 : float

As happened before, the name for the scratch variable might be different. For example, instead of $8, it might be $9 or $10.

Working with variables, methods, and sources

So far, we have been creating many variables, and JShell created a few scratch variables after we entered expressions and they were successfully evaluated. Enter the following command in JShell to list the type, name, and value of the current active variables that have been created so far in the current session:

/vars

The following lines show the results:

```
|    float width = 50.0
|    float height = 25.0
|    float area = 1250.0
|    PrintStream $5 = java.io.PrintStream@68c4039c
|    float $6 = 1250.0
|    float $8 = 1260.5
```

Enter the following code in JShell to assign 80.25 (float) to the previously created width variable:

```
width = 80.25f;
```

After we enter the previous line, JShell will display the next message indicating it has assigned 80.25 (float) to the existing variable named width of the float type:

```
width ==> 80.25
|  assigned to width : float
```

Enter the following code in JShell to assign 40.5 (float) to the previously created height variable:

```
height = 40.5f;
```

After we enter the previous line, JShell will display the next message indicating it has assigned 40.5 (float) to the existing variable named height of the float type:

```
height ==> 40.5
|  assigned to height : float
```

Enter the following command in JShell again to list the type, name, and value of the current active variables:

```
/vars
```

The following lines show the results that reflect the new values we have assigned to the width and height variables:

```
|    float width = 80.25
|    float height = 40.5
|    float area = 1250.0
|    PrintStream $5 = java.io.PrintStream@68c4039c
|    float $6 = 1250.0
|    float $8 = 1260.5
```

Enter the following code in JShell to create a new method named
calculateRectanglePerimeter. The method receives a width variable and a
height variable for a rectangle and returns the result of the multiplication by 2
of the sum of both values of the float type.

```
float calculateRectanglePerimeter(float width, float height) {
    return 2 * (width + height);
}
```

After we enter the previous lines, JShell will display the next message indicating it
has created a method named calculateRectanglePerimeter with two arguments
of the float type:

```
| created method calculateRectanglePerimeter(float,float)
```

Enter the following command in JShell to list the name, parameter types, and return
the type of the current active methods that have been created so far in the current
session:

```
/methods
```

The following lines show the results.

```
|    calculateRectangleArea (float,float)float
|    calculateRectanglePerimeter (float,float)float
```

Enter the following code in JShell to print the results of calling the recently created
calculateRectanglePerimeter with width and height as the arguments:

```
calculateRectanglePerimeter(width, height);
```

After we enter the previous line, JShell will call the method and it will assign the
results to a scratch variable whose name starts with $ and continues with a number.
JShell displays the scratch variable name, $16, the value assigned to the variable
that indicates the result returned by the method, 241.5, and the type for the scratch
variable, float. The next lines show the message displayed in JShell after we enter
the previous expression that called a method:

```
$16 ==> 241.5
| created scratch variable $16 : float
```

Now, we want to make changes to the recently created
calculateRectanglePerimeter method. We want to add a line to print the
calculated perimeter. Enter the following command in JShell to list the source code
for the method:

```
/list calculateRectanglePerimeter
```

The following lines show the results:

```
15 : float calculateRectanglePerimeter(float width, float height) {
        return 2 * (width + height);
     }
```

Enter the following code in JShell to overwrite the method named calculateRectanglePerimeter with a new code that prints the received width and height values and then prints the calculated perimeter with calls to the System.out. printf method that works in the same way as the built-in printf method. We can copy and paste the pieces from the previously listed source code. The changes are highlighted here:

```
float calculateRectanglePerimeter(float width, float height) {
    float perimeter = 2 * (width + height);
    System.out.printf("Width: %.2f\n", width);
    System.out.printf("Height: %.2f\n", height);
    System.out.printf("Perimeter: %.2f\n", perimeter);
    return perimeter;
}
```

After we enter the previous lines, JShell will display the next messages indicating it has modified and overwritten the method named calculateRectanglePerimeter with two arguments of the float type:

```
|   modified method calculateRectanglePerimeter(float,float)
|     update overwrote method calculateRectanglePerimeter(float,float)
```

Enter the following code in JShell to print out the results of calling the recently modified calculateRectanglePerimeter with width and height as the arguments:

```
calculateRectanglePerimeter(width, height);
```

After we enter the previous line, JShell will call the method and it will assign the results to a scratch variable whose name starts with $ and continues with a number. The first lines display the output generated by the three calls to System.out.printf that we added to the method. Finally, JShell displays the scratch variable name, $19, the value assigned to the variable that indicates the result returned by the method, 241.5, and the type for the scratch variable, float.

The next lines show the messages displayed in JShell after we enter the previous expression that called the new version of the method:

```
Width: 80.25
Height: 40.50
Perimeter: 241.50
$19 ==> 241.5
|  created scratch variable $19 : float
```

Editing the source code in our favorite external code editor

We created a new version of the `calculateRectanglePerimeter` method. Now, we want to make similar changes to the `calculateRectangleArea` method. However, this time, we will take advantage of an editor to make it easier to make changes to the existing code.

Enter the following command in JShell to launch the default JShell Edit Pad editor to edit the source code for the `calculateRectangleArea` method:

/edit calculateRectangleArea

JShell will display a dialog box with JShell Edit Pad and the source code for the `calculateRectangleArea` method, as shown in the following screenshot:

JShell Edit Pad lacks most of the features we enjoy from code editors and we cannot even consider it a decent code editor. In fact, it just allows us to easily edit the source code without having to copy and paste from the previous listing. We will learn how to configure a better editor later.

Enter the following code in the JShell Edit Pad to overwrite the method named calculateRectangleArea with a new code that prints the received width and height values and then prints the calculated area with calls to the Sytem.out.printf method. The changes are highlighted here:

```
float calculateRectangleArea(float width, float height) {
    float area = width * height;
    System.out.printf("Width: %.2f\n", width);
    System.out.printf("Height: %.2f\n", height);
    System.out.printf("Area: %.2f\n", area);
    return area;
}
```

Click on **Accept** and then click on **Exit**. JShell will close the JShell Edit Pad and display the next messages indicating it has modified and overwritten the method named calculateRectangleArea with two arguments of the float type:

```
|   modified method calculateRectangleArea(float,float)
|     update overwrote method calculateRectangleArea(float,float)
```

Enter the following code in JShell to print the results of calling the recently modified calculateRectangleArea method with width and height as the arguments:

```
calculateRectangleArea(width, height);
```

After we enter the previous line, JShell will call the method and it will assign the results to a scratch variable whose name starts with $ and continues with a number. The first lines display the output generated by the three calls to System.out.printf that we added to the method. Finally, JShell displays the scratch variable name, $24, the value assigned to the variable that indicates the result returned by the method, 3250.125, and the type for the scratch variable, float. The next lines show the messages displayed in JShell after we enter the previous expression that called the new version of the method:

```
Width: 80.25
Height: 40.50
Area: 3250.13
$24 ==> 3250.125
|  created scratch variable $24 : float
```

The good news is that JShell allows us to easily configure any external editor to edit the code snippets. We just need to grab the complete path to the editor we want to use and run a command in JShell to configure the editor we want to launch whenever we use the /edit command.

For example, in Windows, the default installation path for the popular Sublime Text 3 code editor is C:\Program Files\Sublime Text 3\sublime_text.exe. If we want to use this editor to edit code snippets in JShell, we must run the /set editor command followed by the path enclosed in double quotes. We have to make sure that we replace the backslash (\) with double backslashes (\\) in the path string. For the previously explained path, we must run the following command:

```
/set editor "C:\\Program Files\\Sublimet Text 3\\sublime_text.exe"
```

After we enter the previous command, JShell will display a message indicating to us that the editor was set to the specified path:

```
| Editor set to: C:\Program Files\Sublime Text 3\sublime_text.exe
```

After we change the editor, we can enter the following command in JShell to launch the new editor to make changes to the source code for the calculateRectangleArea method:

```
/edit calculateRectangleArea
```

JShell will launch Sublime Text 3 or any other editor that we might have specified and will load a temporary file with the source code for the `calculateRectangleArea` method, as shown in the following screenshot:

```
|  The '/set' command requires a sub-command. See: '/help /set'

jshell> /set editor "C:\\Program Files\\Sublime Text 3\\sublime_text.exe"
|  Editor set to: C:\Program Files\Sublime Text 3\sublime_text.exe

jshell> /edit calculateRectangleArea
```

C:\Users\gaston\AppData\Local\Temp\jshelltemp3750194570671083214\4872338378820725526.edit - Sublime Text (UNREGISTERED)   — □ ×
File Edit Selection Find View Goto Tools Project Preferences Help
4872338378820725526.edit ×

```
1  float calculateRectangleArea(float width, float height) {
2      float area = width * height;
3      System.out.printf("Width: %.2f\n", width);
4      System.out.printf("Height: %.2f\n", height);
5      System.out.printf("Area: %.2f\n", area);
6      return area;
7  }
8
```

Line 3, Column 15   Tab Size: 4   Java

> If we save the changes, JShell will automatically overwrite the method as we did when we used the default editor: JShell Edit Pad. After we make the necessary edits, we must close the editor to continue running Java code or JShell commands in JShell.

In any of the platforms, JShell will create a temporary file with the `.edit` extension. Thus, we can configure our favorite editor to use Java syntax highlighting whenever we open files with the `.edit` extension.

In macOS or Linux, paths are different than in Windows, and therefore, the necessary steps are different. For example, in macOS, in order to launch the popular Sublime Text 3 code editor when it is installed in the default path, we must run `/Applications/Sublime Text.app/Contents/SharedSupport/bin/subl`.

If we want to use this editor to edit code snippets in JShell, we must run the `/set editor` command followed by the complete path enclosed in double quotes. For the previously explained path, we must run the following command:

```
/set editor "/Applications/Sublime Text.app/Contents/SharedSupport/bin/
subl"
```

After we enter the previous command, JShell will display a message indicating to us that the editor was set to the specified path:

```
|  Editor set to: /Applications/Sublime Text.app/Contents/SharedSupport/
bin/subl
```

After we change the editor, we can enter the following command in JShell to launch the new editor to make changes to the source code for the `calculateRectangleArea` method:

```
/edit calculateRectangleArea
```

JShell will launch Sublime Text 3 on macOS or any other editor that we might have specified and will load a temporary file with the source code for the `calculateRectangleArea` method, as shown in the following screenshot:

Loading source code

Of course, we don't have to enter the source code for each example. Auto-completion features are useful, but we will take advantage of a command that allows us to load source code from a file in JShell.

Press *Ctrl + D* to exit the current JShell session. Run the following command in the Windows Command Prompt or in a macOS or Linux Terminal to launch JShell again with a verbose feedback:

jshell -v

The following lines show code that declares the latest versions of the calculateRectanglePerimeter and calculateRectangleArea methods. Then, the code declares and initializes two variables of the float type: width and height. Finally, the last two lines call the previously defined methods with width and height as their arguments. The code file for the sample is included in the java_9_ oop_chapter_01_01 folder, in the example01_01.java file.

```
float calculateRectanglePerimeter(float width, float height) {
    float perimeter = 2 * (width + height);
    System.out.printf("Width: %.2f\n", width);
    System.out.printf("Height: %.2f\n", height);
    System.out.printf("Perimeter: %.2f\n", perimeter);
    return perimeter;
}

float calculateRectangleArea(float width, float height) {
    float area = width * height;
    System.out.printf("Width: %.2f\n", width);
    System.out.printf("Height: %.2f\n", height);
    System.out.printf("Area: %.2f\n", area);
    return area;
}

float width = 120.25f;
float height = 35.50f;
calculateRectangleArea(width, height);
calculateRectanglePerimeter(width, height);
```

Once you have downloaded the source code for the book in a folder, you can use the /open command in JShell to load and execute one of the files from the source code. Before each code snippet, we always mention where the source code is located.

If the root folder for the source code in Windows is `C:\Users\Gaston\Java9`, you can run the following command to load and execute the previously shown source code in JShell:

```
/open C:\Users\Gaston\Java9\java_9_oop_chapter_01_01\example01_01.java
```

If the root folder for the source code in macOS or Linux is `~/Documents/Java9`, you can run the following command to load and execute the previously shown source code in JShell:

```
/open ~/Documents/Java9/java_9_oop_chapter_01_01/example01_01.java
```

After we enter the previous command followed by the path based on our configuration and our operating system, JShell will load and execute the previously shown source code and will display the output generated after running the loaded code snippet. The following lines show the output:

```
Width: 120.25
Height: 35.50
Area: 4268.88
Width: 120.25
Height: 35.50
Perimeter: 311.50
```

Now, enter the following command in JShell to list the current, active snippets of code, loaded from the source file, that have been executed in the current session so far:

```
/list
```

The following lines show the results. Notice that JShell prefaces the different method definitions and expressions with different snippet ids because the loaded source code behaves in the same way as if we were entering one snippet after the other:

```
  1 : float calculateRectanglePerimeter(float width, float height) {
        float perimeter = 2 * (width + height);
        System.out.printf("Width: %.2f\n", width);
        System.out.printf("Height: %.2f\n", height);
        System.out.printf("Perimeter: %.2f\n", perimeter);
        return perimeter;
      }
```

```
2 : float calculateRectangleArea(float width, float height) {
        float area = width * height;
        System.out.printf("Width: %.2f\n", width);
        System.out.printf("Height: %.2f\n", height);
        System.out.printf("Area: %.2f\n", area);
        return area;
    }
3 : float width = 120.25f;
4 : float height = 35.50f;
5 : calculateRectangleArea(width, height);
6 : calculateRectanglePerimeter(width, height);
```

Make sure you use the previously explained /open command followed by the path and the file name for the code file that you want to load and execute in JShell whenever you find source code in the book. This way, you won't have to enter each code snippet and you will be able to check the results of executing the code in JShell.

Test your knowledge

1. JShell is:

    1. A Java 9 REPL.

    2. An equivalent of `javac` in previous JDK versions.

    3. A Java 9 bytecode decompiler.

2. REPL means:

    1. Run-Expand-Process-Loop.

    2. Read-Evaluate-Process-Lock.

    3. Read-Evaluate-Print-Loop.

3. Which of the following commands lists all the variables created in the current JShell session:

    1. `/variables`

    2. `/vars`

    3. `/list-all-variables`

4. Which of the following commands lists all the methods created in the current JShell session:

    1. `/methods`
    2. `/meth`
    3. `/list-all-methods`

5. Which of the following commands lists the source code evaluated so far in the current JShell session:

    1. `/source`
    2. `/list`
    3. `/list-source`

Summary

In this chapter, we started our journey toward object-oriented programming with Java 9. We learned how to launch and work with the new utility introduced with Java 9 that allows us to easily run Java 9 code snippets and print its results: JShell.

We learned the necessary steps to install JDK 9 and we understood the benefits of working with a REPL. We learned to use JShell to run Java 9 code and evaluate expressions. We also learned many of its useful commands and features. We will use them in the forthcoming chapters when we will start working with object-oriented code.

Now that we have learned to work with JShell, we will learn how to recognize real-world elements and translate them into the different components of the object-oriented paradigm supported in Java 9, which is what we are going to discuss in the next chapter.

2
Real-World Objects to UML Diagrams and Java 9 via JShell

In this chapter, we will learn how to recognize objects from real-life situations. We will understand that working with objects makes it simpler to write code that is easier to understand and reuse. We will learn how to recognize real-world elements and translate them into the different components of the object-oriented paradigm supported in Java 9. We will:

- Identify objects from applications requirements
- Capture objects from the real world
- Generate classes to create objects
- Recognize variables and constants to create fields
- Identify actions to create methods
- Organize classes with UML diagrams
- Use feedback from domain experts to improve our classes
- Work with Java objects in JShell

Identifying objects from applications requirements

Whenever you have to solve a problem in the real world, you use elements and interact with them. For example, when you are thirsty, you take a glass, fill it up with water, soda, or your favorite juice, and then you drink. Similarly, you can easily recognize elements, known as objects, from real-world scenarios and then translate them into object-oriented code. We will start learning the principles of object-oriented programming to use them in the Java 9 programming language to develop any kind of applications.

Now, we will imagine we have to develop a RESTful Web Service that will be consumed by mobile apps and a web application. These apps and applications will have different user interfaces and diverse user experiences. However, we don't have to worry about these differences because we will be focused on the Web Service, that is, we will be backend developers.

Artists use different combinations of geometric shapes and organic shapes to create art. Of course, creating art is a bit more complex than this simple definition, but our goal is to learn object-oriented programming and not to become experts in art.

Geometric shapes are made of points and lines, and they are precise. The following are examples of geometric shapes: circles, triangles, squares, rectangles.

Organic shapes are shapes that have a natural look and have a curving appearance. These shapes are usually irregular or asymmetrical. We usually associate things from the natural world, such as animals and plants, with organic shapes.

When artists want to create abstract interpretations of things that would normally require organic shapes, they use geometric shapes. Imagine that Vanessa Pitstop is a painter and craftswoman. She started uploading videos about her artwork to Instagram and YouTube a few years ago and reaches a great milestone in her artistic career: San Francisco Museum of Modern Art prepares an exhibition of her most important artwork. This special event generated a huge impact on social networking sites and, as usually happens, there is a new software development task related to this important boost in popularity.

Pitstop is an extremely popular YouTuber and her channel has more than four million followers. Many Hollywood actresses bought their artwork and uploaded selfies on Instagram with her artwork as a background. Her exhibition generated a huge additional interest in her creations and one of the sponsors wants to create mobile apps and a web application that reproduce her artwork based on geometric shapes and provide details about the all the tools and the acrylic paint that the user needs to buy to produce the artwork.

Pitstop sketches basic shapes and then paints them with acrylic paint to build geometric patterns. The mobile app and the web application will use our Web Service to build Pitstop's predefined patterns, based on the canvas size and some predefined color schemes selected by the user. Our Web Service will receive the canvas size and the color scheme to generate the pattern and a bill of materials. Specifically, the Web Service will provide a list of the different tools and the acrylic paint tubes, jars, or bottles that the user must buy to paint the drawn pattern. Finally, the user will be able to place an online order to request all of some of the suggested materials.

The following image shows a first example of Pitstop's artwork with geometric patterns. Let's take a look at the image and extract the objects that compose the pattern.

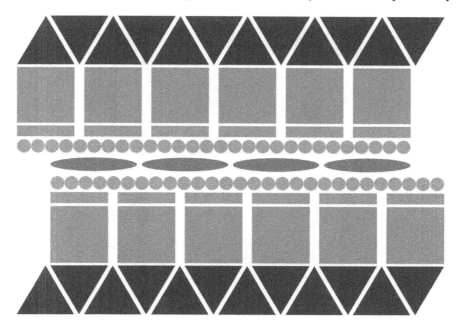

The following objects compose the geometric pattern, specifically, the following 2D shapes from top to bottom:

- 12 equilateral triangles
- 6 squares
- 6 rectangles
- 28 circles
- 4 ellipses
- 28 circles

- 6 rectangles
- 6 squares
- 12 equilateral triangles

It is fairly simple to describe 108 objects or 2D shapes that compose the pattern. We were able to recognize all these objects and to indicate the specific 2D shape for each of them. If we measure each triangle, we will realize they are equilateral triangles.

The following image shows a second example of Pitstop's artwork with geometric patterns. Let's take a look at the image and extract the objects that compose the pattern.

The following objects compose the geometric pattern, specifically, the following 2D shapes from top to bottom:

- 12 equilateral triangles
- 6 regular pentagons
- 6 rectangles
- 24 regular hexagons
- 4 ellipses
- 24 regular hexagons
- 6 rectangles
- 6 regular pentagons
- 12 equilateral triangles

This time, we could describe 100 objects or 2D shapes that compose the pattern. We were able to recognize all these objects and indicate the specific 2D shape for each of them. If we measure each pentagon and hexagon, we will realize they are regular pentagons and hexagons.

The following image shows a third example of Pitstop's artwork with geometric patterns. In this case, we have a huge number of 2D shapes. Let's take a look at the image and just extract the different 2D shapes included in the pattern. This time, we won't count the number of objects.

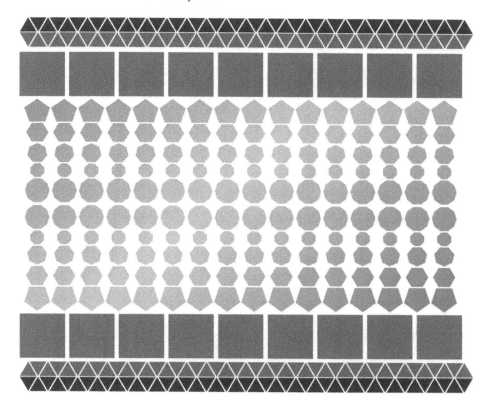

The pattern includes the following 2D shapes:

- Equilateral triangles
- Squares
- Regular pentagons
- Regular hexagons

- Regular heptagons
- Regular octagons
- Regular decagons

The following image shows a fourth example of Pitstop's artwork with geometric patterns. In this case, we also have a huge number of 2D shapes and some of them intersect with each other. However, we will still be able to recognize the different 2D shapes if we pay some attention. Let's take a look at the image and just extract the different 2D shapes included in the pattern. We won't count the number of objects.

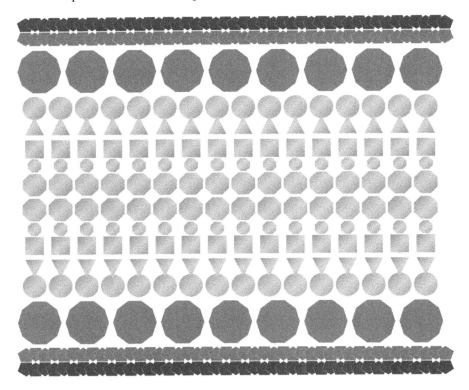

The pattern includes the following 2D shapes:

- Regular pentagons
- Regular decagons
- Circles
- Equilateral triangles
- Squares
- Regular octagons

The following image shows a fifth example of Pitstop's artwork with geometric patterns. In this case, we will recognize the shapes from left to right because the pattern has a different orientation. We have many shapes that intersect with each other. Let's take a look at the image and just extract the different 2D shapes included in the pattern. We won't count the number of objects.

The pattern includes the following 2D shapes:

- Circles
- Regular octagons
- Equilateral triangles
- Squares
- Regular octagons

Capturing real-world objects

We could easily recognize objects from Pitstop's artwork. We understood that each pattern is composed of many 2D geometric shapes and we recognized the different shapes that she used in all the examples we analyzed. Now, let's focus on one of the core requirements for the Web Service, which is calculating the required amounts of acrylic paint to produce the artwork. We must take into account the following data for each 2D shape included in the pattern in order to calculate the required materials and the amount of acrylic paint to produce each shape:

* The line color
* The perimeter
* The fill color
* The area

It is possible to use a specific color for the line that draws the borders of each shape, and therefore, we have to calculate the perimeter to use it as one of the values that will allow us to estimate the amount of acrylic paint that the user must buy to paint the border of each 2D shape. Then, we have to calculate the area to use it as one of the values that will allow us to estimate the amount of acrylic paint that the user must buy to fill the area of each 2D shape.

We have to start working on the backend code for our Web Service that calculates areas and perimeters for the different 2D shapes we have recognized in all the sample artwork we have analyzed so far. We conclude that the Web Service must support patterns with the following nine shapes:

* Circles
* Ellipses
* Equilateral triangles
* Squares
* Rectangles
* Regular pentagons
* Regular hexagons
* Regular octagons
* Regular decagons

After doing some research to refresh our minds about 2D geometry, we can start writing Java 9 code. Specifically, we might write nine methods that calculate the areas of the previously enumerated 2D shapes and another nine to calculate their perimeters. Note that we are talking about methods that would return the calculated value, also known as functions. We stopped thinking about objects, and therefore, we will face some problems with this path, which we will solve with an object-oriented approach.

For example, if we start thinking about methods to solve the problem, one possible solution is to code the following eighteen functions to do the job:

- calculateCircleArea
- calculateEllipseArea
- calculateEquilateralTriangleArea
- calculateSquareArea
- calculateRectangleArea
- calculateRegularPentagonArea
- calculateRegularHexagonArea
- calculateRegularOctagonArea
- calculateRegularDecagonArea
- calculateCirclePerimeter
- calculateEllipsePerimeter
- calculateEquilateralTrianglePerimeter
- calculateSquarePerimeter
- calculateRectanglePerimeter
- calculateRegularPentagonPerimeter
- calculateRegularHexagonPerimeter
- calculateRegularOctagonPerimeter
- calculateRegularDecagonPerimeter

Each of the previously enumerated methods has to receive the necessary parameters of each shape and return either its calculated area or perimeter. These functions do not have side effects, that is, they do not make changes to the parameters they receive and they just return the results of the calculated areas or perimeters.

Now, let's forget about methods or functions for one moment. Let's go back to the real-world objects from the Web Service requirements that we were assigned. We have to calculate the areas and perimeters of nine elements, which are nine nouns in the requirements that represent real-life objects, specifically 2D shapes. We have already built a list with nine real-world objects.

After recognizing the real-life objects and thinking a bit about them, we can start designing our Web Service by following an object-oriented paradigm. Instead of creating a set of methods that perform the required tasks, we can create software objects that represent the state and behavior of each of the enumerated 2D shapes. This way, the different objects mimic the real-world 2D shapes. We can work with the objects to specify the different attributes required to calculate the area and perimeter. Then, we can extend these objects to include the additional data required to calculate other required values, such as the quantity of acrylic paint required to paint the borders.

Now, let's move to the real world and think about each of the previously enumerated nine shapes. Imagine that we have to draw each of the shapes on paper and calculate their areas and perimeters. After we draw each shape, which values will we use to calculate their areas and perimeters? Which formulas will we use?

We started working on an object-oriented design before we started coding, and therefore, we will work as if we didn't know many concepts of geometry. For example, we can easily generalize the formulas that we use to calculate the perimeters and areas of regular polygons. However, in most cases we won't be experts on the subject and we have to gain some knowledge on the application domain before we can generalize behavior with an object-oriented approach. Thus, we will dive deeper into the subject as if we had little knowledge on the topic.

The following figure shows a drawn circle and the formulas that we will use to calculate its perimeter and area. We just need the radius value, usually identified as **r**.

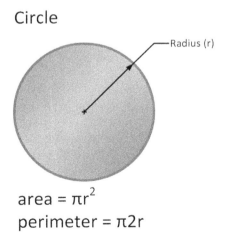

Circle

Radius (r)

$$area = \pi r^2$$
$$perimeter = \pi 2r$$

The following figure shows a drawn ellipse and the formulas that we will use to calculate its perimeter and area. We need the values for the semimajor axis (usually labelled as **a**) and semiminor axis (usually labelled as **b**). Notice that the formula provided for the perimeter provides an approximation that is not very accurate. We will dive deeper on this specific problem later.

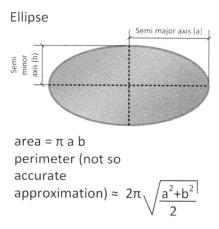

Ellipse

$$area = \pi\, a\, b$$

$$perimeter\ (not\ so\ accurate\ approximation) \approx 2\pi\sqrt{\frac{a^2+b^2}{2}}$$

The following figure shows a drawn equilateral triangle and the formulas that we will use to calculate its perimeter and area. This type of triangle has equal sides, and the three internal angles are equal to 60 degrees. We just need the length of side value, usually identified as **a**.

Equilateral triangle

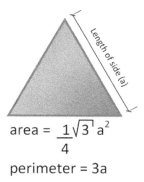

$$area = \frac{1\sqrt{3}\,a^2}{4}$$

$$perimeter = 3a$$

The following figure shows a drawn square and the formulas that we will use to calculate its perimeter and area. We just need the length of side value, usually identified as **a**.

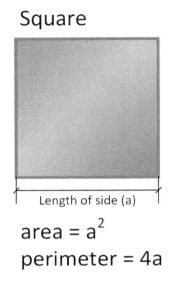

Square

Length of side (a)

$$area = a^2$$
$$perimeter = 4a$$

The following figure shows a drawn rectangle and the formulas that we will use to calculate its perimeter and area. We need the width and height values, usually identified as **w** and **h**.

Rectangle

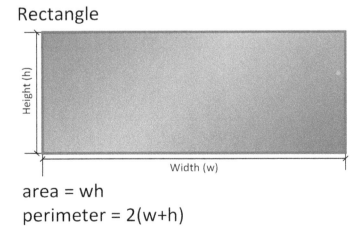

Height (h)

Width (w)

$$area = wh$$
$$perimeter = 2(w+h)$$

The following figure shows a drawn regular pentagon and the formulas that we will use to calculate its perimeter and area. We just need the length of the side value, usually labelled as **a**.

Regular pentagon

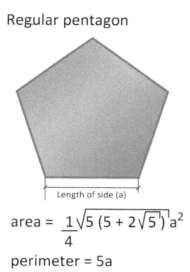

Length of side (a)

$$\text{area} = \frac{1}{4}\sqrt{5\left(5 + 2\sqrt{5}\right)}\,a^2$$

perimeter = 5a

The following figure shows a drawn regular hexagon and the formulas that we will use to calculate its perimeter and area. We just need the length of the side value, usually labelled as **a**.

Regular hexagon

Length of side (a)

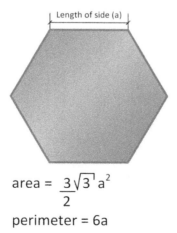

$$\text{area} = \frac{3\sqrt{3}\,a^2}{2}$$

perimeter = 6a

The following figure shows a drawn regular octagon and the formulas that we will use to calculate its perimeter and area. We just need the length of the side value, usually labelled as **a**.

Regular octagon

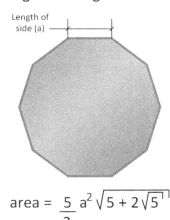

$$\text{area} = 2\,(1 + \sqrt{2}\,)\,a^2$$
$$\text{perimeter} = 8a$$

The following figure shows a drawn regular decagon and the formulas that we will use to calculate its perimeter and area. We just need the length of the side value, usually labelled as **a**.

Regular decagon

$$\text{area} = \frac{5}{2}\,a^2\,\sqrt{5 + 2\sqrt{5}}$$
$$\text{perimeter} = 10a$$

The following table summarizes the data required for each shape to calculate its perimeter and area:

Shape	Required data
Circle	Radius
Ellipse	Semimajor and semiminor axes
Equilateral triangle	Length of a side
Square	Length of a side
Rectangle	Width and height
Regular pentagon	Length of a side
Regular hexagon	Length of a side
Regular octagon	Length of a side
Regular decagon	Length of a side

Each object that represents a specific shape encapsulates the required data that we identified. For example, an object that represents an ellipse will encapsulate the ellipse's semimajor and semiminor axes values, while an object that represents a rectangle will encapsulate the rectangle's width and height values.

 Data encapsulation is one of the major pillars of object-oriented programming.

Generating classes to create objects

Imagine that we have to draw and calculate the perimeters and areas of three different rectangles. You will end up with three rectangles drawn with their widths and height values and their calculated perimeters and areas. It would be great to have a blueprint to simplify the process of drawing each rectangle with their different width and height values.

In object-oriented programming, a **class** is a template definition or blueprint from which objects are created. Classes are models that define the state and behavior of an object. After declaring a class that defines the state and behavior of a rectangle, we can use it to generate objects that represent the state and behavior of each real-world rectangle.

Objects are also known as instances. For example, we can say each rectangle object is an instance of the Rectangle class.

The following picture shows two rectangle instances named rectangle1 and rectangle2. These instances are drawn with their width and height values specified. We can use a Rectangle class as a blueprint to generate the two different Rectangle instances. Note that rectangle1 has the width and height values of 36 and 20, and rectangle2 has the width and height values of 22 and 41. Each instance has different values for their width and height. It is very important to understand the difference between a class and the objects or instances generated through its usage. The object-oriented programming features supported in Java 9 allow us to discover which blueprint we used to generate a specific object. We will use these features in many examples in the upcoming chapters. Thus, we can determine whether each object is an instance of the Rectangle class or not.

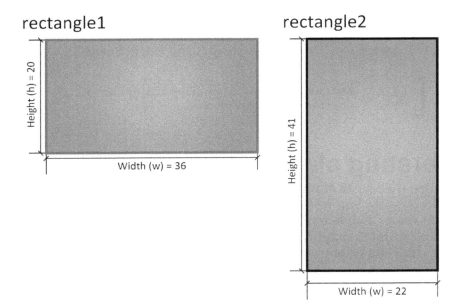

The following picture shows two regular pentagon instances named pentagon1 and pentagon2. These instances are drawn with their length of side values specified. We can use a RegularPentagon class as a blueprint to generate the two different RegularPentagon instances. Note that pentagon1 has the length of a side value of 20, and pentagon2 has the length of a side value of 16. Each instance has different values for its length of a side.

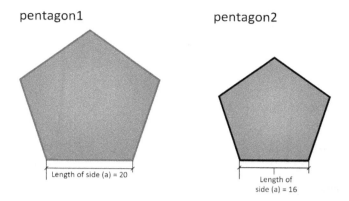

The following picture shows four ellipse instances named `ellipse1`, `ellipse2`, `ellipse3`, and `ellipse4`. These instances are drawn with their semimajor axis and semiminor axis values specified. We can use an `Ellipse` class as a blueprint to generate the four different `Ellipse` instances. Note that each ellipse has its own specific values for the semimajor and semiminor axes.

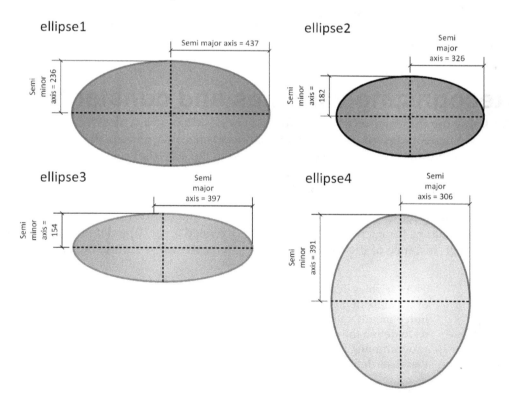

We recognized nine completely different real-world objects from the Web Service requirements, and therefore, we can generate the following nine classes to create the necessary objects:

- `Circle`
- `Ellipse`
- `EquilateralTriangle`
- `Square`
- `Rectangle`
- `RegularPentagon`
- `RegularHexagon`
- `RegularOctagon`
- `RegularDecagon`

Note the usage of **Pascal case** for class names. Pascal case means that the first letter of each word that composes the name is capitalized, while the other letters are in lowercase. This is a coding convention in Java. For example, we use the `EquilateralTriangle` name for the class that will be the blueprint that will allow us to generate multiple equilateral triangles.

Recognizing variables and constants

We know the information required for each of the shapes to achieve our goals. Now, we have to design the classes to include the necessary fields that provide the required data to each instance. We have to make sure that each class has the necessary fields that encapsulate all the data required by the objects to perform all the tasks based on our application domain.

Let's start with the `Circle` class. We need to know the radius for each instance of this class, that is, for each circle object. Thus, we need an encapsulated variable that allows each instance of the `Circle` class to specify the value for the radius.

The variables defined in a class to encapsulate the data for each instance of the class in Java 9 are known as **fields**. Each instance has its own independent value for the fields defined in the class. The fields allow us to define the characteristics for an instance of the class. In other programming languages that support object-oriented principles, these variables defined in a class are known as **attributes**.

The `Circle` class defines a floating point field named `radius`, whose initial value is equal to `0` for any new instance of the class. After we create an instance of the `Circle` class, it is possible to change the value of the `radius` attribute. Thus, our circle can become smaller or larger after we created it.

Note the usage of **Camel case** for field names. Camel case means that the first letter is lowercase, and then, the first letter for each word that composes the name is capitalized, while the other letters are in lowercase. It is a coding convention in Java for both variables and fields. For example, we use the name `radius` for the field that stores the value of the radius and we will use `lengthOfSide` for the property that stores the value of the length of side in other classes that require this data.

Imagine that we create two instances of the `Circle` class. One of the instances is named `circle1` and the other `circle2`. The instance names allow us to access the encapsulated data for each object, and therefore, we can use them to change the values of the exposed fields.

Java 9 uses a dot (`.`) to allow us to access the properties of instances. So, `circle1.radius` provides access to the radius for the `Circle` instance named `circle1`, and `circle2.radius` does the same for the `Circle` instance named `circle2`.

Note that the naming convention makes it easy for us to differentiate an instance name, that is, a variable, from a class name. Whenever we see the first letter in uppercase or capitalized, it means that we are talking about a class, as in `Circle` or `Rectangle`.

We can assign `14` to `circle1.radius` and `39` to `circle2.radius`. This way, each `Circle` instance will have a different value for the `radius` field.

Now, let's move to the `Rectangle` class. We have to define two floating point fields for this class: `width` and `height`. Their initial values will also be `0`. Then, we can create four instances of the `Rectangle` class named `rectangle1`, `rectangle2`, `rectangle3`, and `rectangle4`.

We can assign the values summarized in the following table to the four instances of the `Rectangle` class:

Instance name	width	height
rectangle1	141	281
rectangle2	302	162
rectangle3	283	73
rectangle4	84	214

This way, `rectangle1.width` will be equal to `141`, while `rectangle4.width` will be equal to `84`. The `rectangle1` instance represents a rectangle with `width` of `141` and `height` of `281`.

The following table summarizes the floating point fields defined for each of the nine classes that we need for our Web Service backend code:

Class name	Fields list
`Circle`	`radius`
`Ellipse`	`semiMinorAxis` and `semiMajorAxis`
`EquilateralTriangle`	`lengthOfSide`
`Square`	`lengthOfSide`
`Rectangle`	`width` and `height`
`RegularPentagon`	`lengthOfSide`
`RegularHexagon`	`lengthOfSide`
`RegularOctagon`	`lengthOfSide`
`RegularDecagon`	`lengthOfSide`

 The fields are members of their respective classes. However, fields aren't the only members that classes can have.

Note that six of these classes have the same field: `lengthOfSide`, specifically, the following six classes: `EquilateralTriangle`, `Square`, `RegularPentagon`, `RegularHexagon`, `RegularOctagon`, and `RegularDecagon`. We will dive deep into what these six classes have in common later and take advantage of object-oriented features to reuse code and simplify our Web Service maintenance. However, we are just starting our journey, and we will make improvements as we learn additional object-oriented features included in Java 9. In fact, let's remember we are learning about the application domain and that we are still not experts in 2D shapes.

The following image shows a **UML (Unified Modeling Language)** class diagram with the nine classes and their fields. This diagram is very easy to understand. The class name appears on the top of the rectangle that identifies each class. A rectangle below the same shape that holds the class name displays all the field names exposed by the class with a plus sign (**+**) as a prefix. This prefix indicates that what follows it is an attribute name in UML and a field name in Java 9. Take into account that the next UML diagram doesn't represent the best organization for our classes. It is just the first sketch.

Circle
+radius

Ellipse
+semiMinorAxis
+semiMajorAxis

EquilateralTriangle
+lengthOfSide

Square
+lengthOfSide

Rectangle
+width
+height

RegularPentagon
+lengthOfSide

RegularHexagon
+lengthOfSide

RegularOctagon
+lengthOfSide

RegularDecagon
+lengthOfSide

Identifying actions to create methods

So far, we designed nine classes and identified the necessary fields for each of them. Now, it is time to add the necessary pieces of code that work with the previously defined fields to perform all the necessary tasks, that is, to calculate perimeters and areas. We have to make sure that each class has the necessary encapsulated functions that process the property values specified in the objects to perform all the tasks.

Let's forget a bit about similarities between the different classes. We will work with them individually as if we didn't have the necessary knowledge of geometric formulas. We will start with the Circle class. We need pieces of code that allow each instance of this class to use the value of the radius property to calculate the area and perimeter.

The functions defined in a class to encapsulate the behavior of each instance of the class are known as **methods**. Each instance can access the set of methods exposed by the class. The code specified in a method can work with the fields specified in the class. When we execute a method, it will use the fields of the specific instance. Whenever we define methods, we must make sure that we define them in a logical place, that is, in the place where the required data is kept.

When a method doesn't require parameters, we can say that it is a **parameterless** method. In this case, all the methods we will initially define for the classes will be parameterless methods that just work with the values of the previously defined fields and use the formulas previously shown in the figures when we analyzed each 2D shape in detail. Thus, we will be able to call these methods without arguments. We will start creating methods, but we will be able to explore additional options based on specific Java 9 features later.

The `Circle` class defines the following two parameterless methods. We will declare the code for both methods within the definition of the `Circle` class so that they can access the `radius` property value, as follows:

- `calculateArea`: This method returns a floating point value with the calculated area for the circle. It returns Pi (π) multiplied by the square of the `radius` field value ($\pi * radius^2$ or $\pi * (radius \wedge 2)$).

- `calculatePerimeter`: This method returns a floating point value with the calculated perimeter for the circle. It returns Pi (π) multiplied by 2 times the `radius` field value ($\pi * 2 * radius$).

In Java 9, `Math.PI` provides us with the value for Pi. The `Math.pow` method allows us to calculate the value of a first argument raised to the power of the second argument. We will learn how to code these methods in Java 9 later.

These methods do not have side effects, that is, they do not make changes to the related instance. The methods just return the calculated values, and therefore, we consider them non-mutating methods. Their operation is naturally described by the `calculate` verb.

Java 9 uses a dot (.) to allow us to execute the methods of the instances. Imagine that we have two instances of the `Circle` class: `circle1` with the `radius` property equal to 5 and `circle2` with the `radius` property equal to 10.

If we call `circle1.calculateArea()`, it will return the result of $\pi * 5^2$, which is approximately 78.54. If we call `square2.calculateArea()`, it will return the result of $\pi * 10^2$, which is approximately 314.16. Each instance has a diverse value for the `radius` attribute, and therefore, the results of executing the `calculateArea` method are different for each of them.

If we call `circle1.calculatePerimeter()`, it will return the result of $\pi * 2 * 5$, which is approximately 31.41. On the other hand, if we call `circle2.calculatePerimeter()`, it will return the result of $\pi *2 * 10$, which is approximately 62.83.

Now, let's move to the `Rectangle` class. We need exactly two methods with the same names specified for the `Circle` class: `calculateArea` and `calculatePerimeter`. In addition, the methods return the same type and don't need parameters, so we can declare both of them as parameterless methods, as we did in the `Circle` class. However, these methods have to calculate the results in a different way; that is, they have to use the appropriate formulas for a rectangle and take into account the values for the `width` and `height` fields. The other classes also need the same two methods. However, each of them will use the appropriate formulas for the related shape.

We have a specific problem with the `calculatePerimeter` method that the `Ellipse` class generates. Perimeters are extremely complex to calculate for ellipses, so there are many formulas that provide approximations. An exact formula requires an infinite series of calculations. We will use an initial formula that isn't very accurate but we will find a workaround for this situation later and we will improve the results. The initial formula will allow us to return a floating point value with the calculated approximation of the perimeter for the ellipse.

The following diagram shows an updated version of the UML diagram with the nine classes, their attributes, and their methods. It shows the results of the second round:

Circle
+radius
+calculateArea() +calculatePerimeter()

Ellipse
+semiMinorAxis +semiMajorAxis
+calculateArea() +calculatePerimeter()

EquilateralTriangle
+lengthOfSide
+calculateArea() +calculatePerimeter()

Square
+lengthOfSide
+calculateArea() +calculatePerimeter()

Rectangle
+width +height
+calculateArea() +calculatePerimeter()

RegularPentagon
+lengthOfSide
+calculateArea() +calculatePerimeter()

RegularHexagon
+lengthOfSide
+calculateArea() +calculatePerimeter()

RegularOctagon
+lengthOfSide
+calculateArea() +calculatePerimeter()

RegularDecagon
+lengthOfSide
+calculateArea() +calculatePerimeter()

Organizing classes with UML diagrams

So far, our object-oriented solution includes nine classes with their fields and methods. However, if we take another look at these nine classes, we will notice that all of them have the same two methods: `calculateArea` and `calculatePerimeter`. The code for the methods in each class is different because each shape uses a special formula to calculate either the area or perimeter. However, the declarations, contracts, interfaces, or protocols for the methods are the same. Both methods have the same name, are always parameterless, and return a floating point value. Thus, all of them return the same type.

When we talked about the nine classes, we said we were talking about nine different geometrical 2D shapes or simply shapes. Thus, we can generalize the required behavior, protocol, or interface for these nine shapes. The nine shapes must define the `calculateArea` and `calculatePerimeter` methods with the previously explained declarations. We can create an interface to make sure that the nine classes provide the required behavior.

The interface is a special class named `Shape`, and it generalizes the requirements for the geometrical 2D shapes in our application. In this case, we will work with a special class that we won't use to create instances, but in the future, we will use interfaces for the same goal. The `Shape` class declares two parameterless methods that return a floating point value: `calculateArea` and `calculatePerimeter`. Then, we will declare the nine classes as subclasses of the `Shape` class, which will inherit these definitions, and provide the specific code for each of these methods.

The subclasses of `Shape` (`Circle`, `Ellipse`, `EquilateralTriangle`, `Square`, `Rectangle`, `RegularPentagon`, `RegularHexagon`, `RegularOctagon`, and `RegularDecagon`) implement the methods because they provide code while maintaining the same method declarations specified in the `Shape` superclass. **Abstraction** and **hierarchy** are two major pillars of object-oriented programming. We are just making our first steps in this topic.

Object-oriented programming allows us to discover whether an object is an instance of a specific superclass. After we change the organization of the nine classes and they become subclasses of `Shape`, any instance of `Circle`, `Ellipse`, `EquilateralTriangle`, `Square`, `Rectangle`, `RegularPentagon`, `RegularHexagon`, `RegularOctagon`, or `RegularDecagon` is also an instance of the `Shape` class.

In fact, it isn't difficult to explain the abstraction because we speak the truth about the object-oriented model when we say that it represents the real world.

It makes sense to say that a regular decagon is indeed a shape, and therefore, an instance of `RegularDecagon` is also an instance of the `Shape` class. An instance of `RegularDecagon` is both a `Shape` (the superclass of `RegularDecagon`) and a `RegularDecagon` (the class that we used to create the object).

The following figure shows an updated version of the UML diagram with the superclass or base class (`Shape`), its nine subclasses, and their attributes and methods. Note that the diagram uses a line that ends in an arrow that connects each subclass to its superclass. You can read the line that ends in an arrow as the following: the class where the line begins *is a subclass of* the class that has the line ending with an arrow. For example, `Circle` is a subclass of `Shape`, and `Rectangle` is a subclass of `Shape`. The diagram shows the results of the third round.

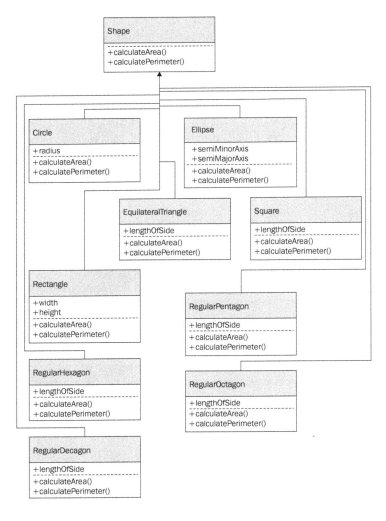

A single class can be the superclass of many subclasses.

Using feedback from domain experts

Now, it is time to have a meeting with our domain expert, that is, someone that has an excellent knowledge of 2D geometry. We can use the UML diagram to explain the object-oriented design for the solution. After we explain the different classes that we will use for abstracting the behavior, the domain expert explains to us that there are many shapes that have something in common and that we can generalize the behavior even further. The following six shapes are regular polygons:

- An equilateral triangle (the EquilateralTriangle class) has three sides
- A square (the Square class) has four sides
- A regular pentagon (the RegularPentagon class) has five sides
- A regular hexagon (the RegularHexagon class) has six sides
- A regular octagon (the RegularOctagon class) has eight sides
- A regular decagon (the RegularDecagon class) has ten sides

Regular polygons are polygons that are both equiangular and equilateral. All the sides that compose a regular polygon have the same length and are placed around a common center. This way, all the angles between any two sides are equal.

The following picture shows the six regular polygons and the generalized formulas that we can use to calculate their perimeters and areas. The generalized formula to calculate the area requires us to calculate a cotangent, which is abbreviated as **cot** in the formula.

Equilateral triangle

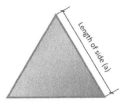

Number of sides (n) = 3

Square

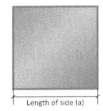

Number of sides (n) = 4

Regular pentagon

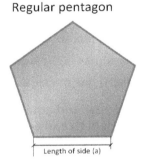

Number of sides (n) = 5

Regular hexagon

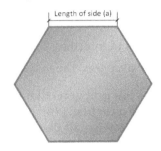

Number of sides (n) = 6

Regular octagon

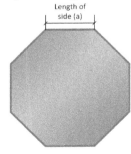

Number of sides (n) = 8

Regular decagon

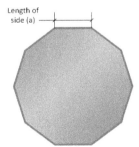

Number of sides (n) = 10

$$area = \frac{1}{4} na^2 \cot\left(\frac{\pi}{n}\right)$$

$$perimeter = na$$

In Java 9, the Math class doesn't provide a method to directly calculate a cotangent. However, it provides a method to calculate a tangent: Math.tan. The cotangent of x is equal to 1 divided by the tangent of x: 1/ Math.tan(x). Thus, we can easily calculate the cotangent with this formula.

As the three shapes use the same formula with just a different value for the number of sides (**n**) parameter, we can generalize the required interface for the six regular polygons. The interface is a special class named RegularPolygon that defines a new getSidesCount method that returns the number of sides with an integer value. The RegularPolygon class is a subclass of the previously defined Shape class. It makes sense because a regular polygon is indeed a shape. The six classes that represent regular polygons become subclasses of RegularPolygon. However, both the calculateArea and calculatePerimeter methods are coded in the RegularPolygon class using the generalized formulas. The subclasses code the getSidesCount method to return the right value, as follows:

- EquilateralTriangle: 3
- Square: 4
- RegularPentagon: 5
- RegularHexagon: 6
- RegularOctagon: 8
- RegularDecagon: 10

The RegularPolygon class also defines the lengthOfSide property that was previously defined in the three classes that represent regular polygons. Now, the six classes become subclasses of RegularPolygon and inherit the lengthOfSide property. The following figure shows an updated version of the UML diagram with the new RegularPolygon class and the changes in the six classes that represent regular polygons. The six classes that represent regular polygons do not declare either the calculateArea or calculatePerimeter methods because these classes inherit them from the RegularPolygon superclass and don't need to make changes to these methods that apply a general formula.

The diagram shows the results of the fourth round.

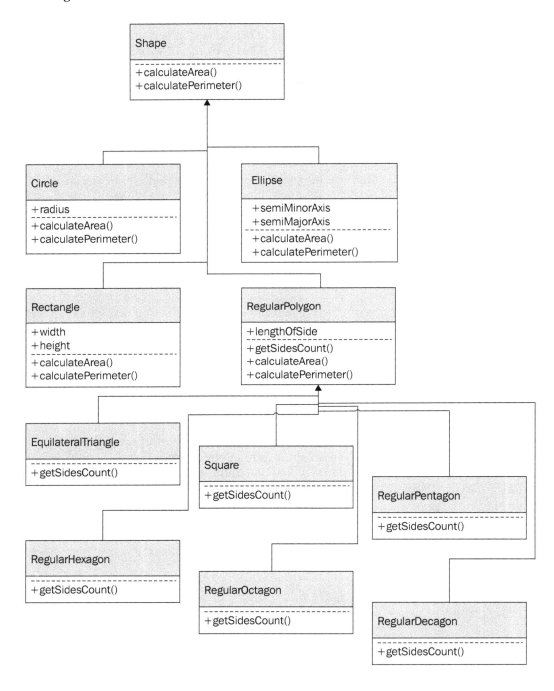

When we analyzed ellipses, we mentioned that there was a problem when calculating its perimeter. We talked with our domain expert and he provided us with detailed information about the issue. There are many formulas that provide approximations of the perimeter value for this shape. It makes sense to add additional methods that calculate the perimeter using other formulas. He suggested us to make it possible to calculate the perimeters with the following formulas:

- A formula proposed by *David W. Cantrell*
- A second version of the formula developed by *Srinivasa Aiyangar Ramanujan*

We will define the following two additional parameterless methods to the `Ellipse` class. The new methods will return a floating point value and solve the specific problem of the ellipse shape:

- `calculatePerimeterWithRamanujanII`
- `calculatePerimeterWithCantrell`

This way, the `Ellipse` class will implement the methods specified in the `Shape` superclass and also add two specific methods that aren't included in any of the other subclasses of `Shape`. The following figure shows an updated version of the UML diagram with the new methods for the `Ellipse` class.

The diagram shows the results of the fifth round:

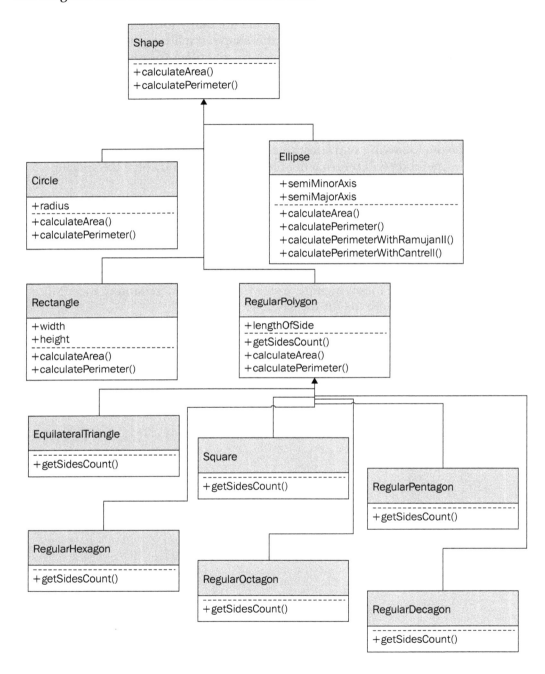

Test your knowledge

1. Objects are also known as:

    1. Subclasses.

    2. Fields.

    3. Instances.

2. Which of the following class names follows the Pascal case convention and would be an appropriate name for a class in Java 9:

    1. `regularDecagon`

    2. `RegularDecagon`

    3. `Regulardecagon`

3. The code specified in a method within a class:

    1. Can access the fields specified in the class.

    2. Cannot interact with other members of the class.

    3. Cannot access the fields specified in the class.

4. The functions defined in a class to encapsulate behavior for each instance of the class are known as:

    1. Subclasses.

    2. Fields.

    3. Methods.

5. A subclass:

    1. Inherits only methods from its superclass.

    2. Inherits only fields from its superclass.

    3. Inherits all members from its superclass.

6. The variables defined in a class to encapsulate data for each instance of the class in Java 9 are known as:

    1. Fields.

    2. Methods.

    3. Subclasses.

7. The variables defined in a class to encapsulate data for each instance of the class in Java 9 are known as:

    1. Fields.

    2. Methods.

    3. Subclasses.

8. Which of the following field names follows the Camel case convention and would be an appropriate name for a field in Java 9:

    1. `SemiMinorAxis`

    2. `semiMinorAxis`

    3. `semiminoraxis`

Summary

In this chapter, you learned how to recognize real-world elements and translate them into the different components of the object-oriented paradigm supported in Java 9: classes, fields, methods, and instances. You understood that the classes represent blueprints or templates to generate the objects, also known as instances.

We designed a few classes with fields and methods that represent blueprints for real-life objects, specifically, 2D shapes. Then, we improved the initial design by taking advantage of the power of abstraction and specialized different classes. We generated many versions of the initial UML diagram as we added superclasses and subclasses. We understood the application domain and we made changes to the original design as our knowledge increased and we realized we were able to generalize behavior.

Now that you have learned some of the basics of the object-oriented paradigm, we are ready to start creating classes and instances in Java 9 with JShell, which is what we are going to discuss in the next chapter. It is time to start object-oriented coding!

3
Classes and Instances

In this chapter, we will start working with examples on how to code classes and customize the initialization of instances in Java 9. We will understand how classes work as blueprints to generate instances and dive deeply into the garbage collection mechanism. We will:

- Understand classes and instances in Java 9
- Work with object initialization and its customization
- Learn about an object's lifecycle
- Introduce garbage collection
- Declare classes
- Customize constructors and initialization
- Understand how garbage collection works
- Create instances of classes and understand their scope

Understanding classes and instances in Java 9

In the previous chapter, we learned some of the basics of the object-oriented paradigm, including classes and objects. We started working on the backend for a Web Service related to 2D shapes. We ended up creating a UML diagram with the structure of many classes, including their hierarchy, fields, and methods. It is time to take advantage of JShell to start coding a basic class and work with its instances in JShell.

In Java 9, a class is always the type and blueprint. The object is the working instance of the class, and therefore, objects are also known as **instances**.

 Classes are first-class citizens in Java 9 and they will be the main building blocks of our object-oriented solutions.

One or more variables can hold a reference to an instance. For example, consider that we have the following three variables of the `Rectangle` type:

- `rectangle1`
- `rectangle2`
- `rectangle10`
- `rectangle20`

Let's consider that the `rectangle1` variable holds a reference to an instance of the `Rectangle` class with its `width` set to `36` and its `height` set to `20`. The `rectangle10` variable holds a reference to the same instance referenced by `rectangle1`. Thus, we have two variables that hold a reference to the same `Rectangle` object.

The `rectangle2` variable holds a reference to an instance of the `Rectangle` class with its `width` set to `22` and its `height` set to `41`. The `rectangle20` variable holds a reference to the same instance referenced by `rectangle2`. We have another two variables that hold a reference to the same `Rectangle` object.

The following picture illustrates the situation where many variables of the `Rectangle` type that hold a reference to a single instance. The variable names are at the left-hand side and the rectangles with their width and height values represent a specific instance of the `Rectangle` class.

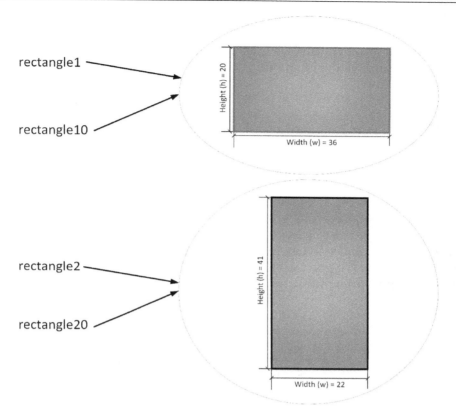

We will work with many variables that hold a reference to a single instance in JShell later in this chapter.

Working with object initialization and its customization

When you ask Java to create an instance of a specific class, something happens under the hood. Java creates a new instance of the specified type, the **JVM (Java Virtual Machine)** allocates the necessary memory, and then executes the code specified in the constructor.

When Java executes the code within the constructor, there is already a live instance of the class. Thus, the code in the constructor has access to the fields and methods defined in the class. Obviously, we must be careful in the code we put within the constructor because we might end up generating huge delays when we create instances of the class.

> Constructors are extremely useful to execute setup code and properly initialize a new instance.

Let's forget about the hierarchy structure in which we were working for the classes that represent 2D shapes. Imagine that we have to code the `Circle` class as a standalone class that doesn't inherit from any other class. Before we can call either the `calculateArea` or `calculatePerimeter` methods, we want the `radius` field for each new `Circle` instance to have a value initialized to the appropriate value that represents the circle. We don't want new `Circle` instances to be created without specifying an appropriate value for the `radius` field.

> Constructors are extremely useful when we want to define the values for the fields of the instances of a class right after their creation and before we can access the variables that reference the created instances. In fact, the only way to create instances of a specific class is to use the constructors we provide.
>
> Whenever we need specific arguments to be available at the time we create an instance, we can declare many different constructors with the necessary arguments and use them to create instances of a class. Constructors allow us to make sure that there is no way of creating specific classes without using the provided constructors that make the necessary arguments required. Thus, if the provided constructor requires a `radius` argument, we won't be able to create an instance of the class without specifying a value for the `radius` argument.

Imagine that we have to code the `Rectangle` class as a standalone class that doesn't inherit from any other class. Before we can call either the `calculateArea` or `calculatePerimeter` methods, we want both the `width` and `height` fields for each new `Rectangle` instance to have their values initialized to the appropriate values that represent each rectangle. We don't want new `Rectangle` instances to be created without specifying an appropriate value for the `width` and `height` fields. Thus, we will declare a constructor for this class that requires values for `width` and `height`.

Introducing garbage collection

At some specific time, your application won't require to work with an instance anymore. For example, once you have calculated the perimeter of a circle and you have returned the necessary data in the Web Service response, you don't need to continue working with the specific `Circle` instance anymore. Some programming languages require you to be careful about leaving live instances alive and you have to explicitly destroy them and deallocate the memory that it was consuming.

Java provides automatic memory management. The JVM runtime uses a garbage collection mechanism that automatically deallocates memory used by instances that aren't referenced anymore. The garbage collection process is extremely complicated, there are many different algorithms with their advantages and disadvantages, and the JVM has specific considerations that should be taken into account to avoid unnecessary huge memory pressure. However, we will keep our focus on the object's life cycle. In Java 9, when the JVM runtime detects you aren't referencing an instance anymore or the last variable that holds a reference to a specific instance has run out of scope, it makes the instance ready to be part of the next garbage collection cycle.

For example, let's consider our previous example where we had four variables that hold references to two instances of the Rectangle class. Consider that both the rectangle1 and the rectangle2 variables run out of scope. The instance that was referenced by rectangle1 is still being referenced by rectangle10, and the instance that was referenced by rectangle2 is still being referenced by rectangle20. Thus, none of the instances can be removed from memory, as they are still being referenced. The following picture illustrates the situation. The variables that are out of scope have a NO sign at the right-hand side.

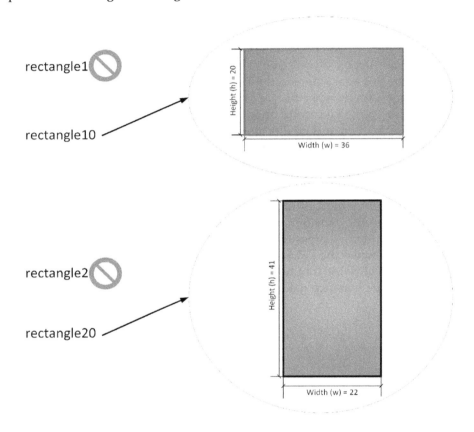

After `rectangle10` runs out of scope, the instance that it referenced becomes disposable, and therefore, it can be safely added to the list of objects that can be removed from memory. The following picture illustrates the situation. The instance that is ready to be removed from memory has a recycle symbol.

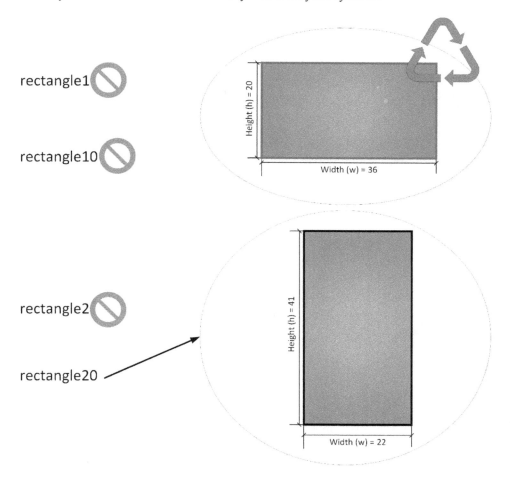

After `rectangle20` runs out of scope, the instance that it referenced becomes disposable, and therefore, it can be safely added to the list of objects that can be removed from memory. The following picture illustrates the situation. The two instances are ready to be removed from memory and both of them have a recycle symbol.

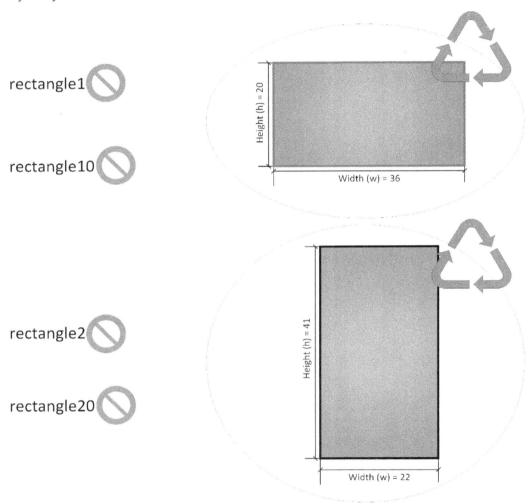

The JVM automatically runs the garbage collection process in the background and automatically claims back the memory consumed by the instances that were ready for garbage collection and aren't referenced anymore. We don't know when the garbage collection process will occur for specific instances and we shouldn't interfere in the process. The garbage collection algorithm has been improved in Java 9.

Imagine that we have to distribute the items that we store in a box. After we distribute all the items, we must throw the box in a recycle bin. We cannot throw the box to the recycle bin when we still have one or more items in it. We definitely don't want to lose the items we have to distribute because they are very expensive.

The problem has a very easy solution: we just need to count the number of items that remain in the box. When the number of items in the box reaches zero, we can get rid of the box, that is, we can throw it to the recycle bin. Then, the garbage collection process will remove all the items that have been thrown to the recycle bin.

Luckily, we don't have to worry about throwing instances to a recycle bin. Java does it automatically for us. It is completely transparent for us.

One or more variables can hold a reference to a single instance of a class. Thus, it is necessary to take into account the number of references to an instance before Java can put an instance into the garbage collection ready list. When the number of references to a specific instance reaches zero, it is considered safe to remove the instance from memory and claim back the memory consumed by the instance because nobody needs this specific instance anymore. At this time, the instance is ready to be removed by the garbage collection process.

For example, we can create an instance of a class and assign it to a variable. Java will know that there is one reference to this instance. Then, we can assign the same instance to another variable. Java will know there are two references to this single instance.

After the first variable runs out of scope, the second variable that holds a reference to the instance will still be accessible. Java will know there is still another variable that holds a reference to this instance, and therefore, the instance won't be ready for garbage collection. At this point, the instance must still be available, that is, we need it alive.

After the second variable runs out of scope, there are no more variables that hold a reference to the instance. At this point, Java will mark the instance as ready for garbage collection because there are no more variables holding a reference to the instance and it can be safely removed from memory.

Declaring classes

The following lines declare a new minimal `Rectangle` class in Java. The code file for the sample is included in the `java_9_oop_chapter_03_01` folder, in the `example03_01.java` file.

```
class Rectangle {
}
```

The `class` keyword, followed by the class name (`Rectangle`), composes the header of the class definition. In this case, we don't specify a parent class or superclass for the `Rectangle` class. A pair of curly braces (`{}`) encloses the class body after the class header. In the forthcoming chapters, we will declare classes that inherit from another class, and therefore, they will have a superclass. In this case, the class body is empty. The `Rectangle` class is the simplest possible class we can declare in Java 9.

 Any new class you create that doesn't specify a superclass will be a subclass of the `java.lang.Object` class. Thus, the `Rectangle` class is a subclass of `java.lang.Object`.

The following lines represent an equivalent way of creating the `Rectangle` class. However, we don't need to specify that the class inherits from `java.lang.Object` because it adds unnecessary boilerplate code. The code file for the sample is included in the `java_9_oop_chapter_03_01` folder, in the `example03_02.java` file.

```
class Rectangle extends java.lang.Object {
}
```

Customizing constructors and initialization

We want to initialize instances of the Rectangle class with the width and height values for the new rectangle. In order to do so, we can take advantage of the previously introduced constructors. Constructors are special class methods that are automatically executed when we create an instance of a given type. Java runs the code within the constructor before any other code within a class.

We can define a constructor that receives both the width and height values as arguments, and use it to initialize the fields with the same names. We can define as many constructors as we want to, and therefore, we can provide many different ways of initializing a class. In this case, we just need one constructor.

The following lines create a Rectangle class and define a constructor within the class body. At this time, we aren't using access modifiers at all because we want to keep the class declaration as simple as possible. We will work with them later. The code file for the sample is included in the java_9_oop_chapter_03_01 folder, in the example03_03.java file.

```
class Rectangle {
    double width;
    double height;

    Rectangle(double width, double height) {
        System.out.printf("Initializing a new Rectangle instance\n");
        System.out.printf("Width: %.2f, Height: %.2f\n",
            width,
            height);
        this.width = width;
        this.height = height;
    }
}
```

The constructor is a class method that uses the same name as the class: Rectangle. In our sample Rectangle class, the constructor receives two arguments of the double type: width and height. The code within the constructor prints a message indicating that the code is initializing a new Rectangle instance and prints the values for the width and height. This way, we will understand when the code within the constructor is executed. Because the constructor has an argument, it is known as a **parameterized constructor**.

Then, the following line assigns the `width` double value received as an argument to the `width` double field. We use `this.width` to access the `width` field for the instance and `width` to reference the argument. The `this` keyword provides access to the instance that has been created and we want to initialize, that is, the object that is being built. We use `this.height` to access the `height` field for the instance and `height` to reference the argument.

The two lines before the constructor declare the `width` and `height` double field. These two fields are member variables that we can access without restrictions after the constructor finishes its execution.

The following lines create four instances of the `Rectangle` class named `rectangle1`, `rectangle2`, `rectangle3`, and `rectangle4`. The code file for the sample is included in the `java_9_oop_chapter_03_01` folder, in the `example03_04.java` file.

```
Rectangle rectangle1 = new Rectangle(31.0, 21.0);
Rectangle rectangle2 = new Rectangle(182.0, 32.0);
Rectangle rectangle3 = new Rectangle(203.0, 23.0);
Rectangle rectangle4 = new Rectangle(404.0, 14.0);
```

Each line that creates an instance specifies the type for the new variable (`Rectangle`) followed by the variable name that will hold the reference to the new instance (`rectangle1`, `rectangle2`, `rectangle3`, or `rectangle4`). Then each line assigns the result of using the `new` keyword followed by the desired value for the `width` and `height` arguments separated by a comma and enclosed in parentheses.

In Java 9, we have to specify the type for the variable in which we want to hold the reference to an instance. In this case, we declare each variable with the `Rectangle` type. In case you have experience with other programming languages that provide a keyword to generate implicitly typed local variables such as the `var` keyword in C#, you must know there is no equivalent in Java 9.

After we enter all the lines that declare the class and create the four instances in JShell, we will see four messages that say "Initializing a new Rectangle instance" followed by the width and height values specified in the call to the constructor of each instance. The following screenshot shows the results of executing the code in JShell:

```
jshell> class Rectangle {
   ...>     double width;
   ...>     double height;
   ...>
   ...>     Rectangle(double width, double height) {
   ...>         System.out.printf("Initializing a new Rectangle instance\n");
   ...>         System.out.printf("Width: %.2f, Height: %.2f\n", width, height);
   ...>         this.width = width;
   ...>         this.height = height;
   ...>     }
   ...> }
|  created class Rectangle

jshell>

jshell> Rectangle rectangle1 = new Rectangle(31.0, 21.0);
Initializing a new Rectangle instance
Width: 31.00, Height: 21.00
rectangle1 ==> Rectangle@551aa95a

jshell> Rectangle rectangle2 = new Rectangle(182.0, 32.0);
Initializing a new Rectangle instance
Width: 182.00, Height: 32.00
rectangle2 ==> Rectangle@1dfe2924

jshell> Rectangle rectangle3 = new Rectangle(203.0, 23.0);
Initializing a new Rectangle instance
Width: 203.00, Height: 23.00
rectangle3 ==> Rectangle@6e6c3152

jshell> Rectangle rectangle4 = new Rectangle(404.0, 14.0);
Initializing a new Rectangle instance
Width: 404.00, Height: 14.00
rectangle4 ==> Rectangle@3cef309d

jshell>
```

After we execute the previous lines, we can check the values for the `width` and `height` fields for each of the instances we have created. The following lines show expressions that JShell can evaluate to display the values for each field. The code file for the sample is included in the `java_9_oop_chapter_03_01` folder, in the `example03_05.java` file.

```
rectangle1.width
rectangle1.height
rectangle2.width
rectangle2.height
rectangle3.width
rectangle3.height
rectangle4.width
rectangle4.height
```

The following screenshot shows the results of evaluating the previous expressions in JShell.

```
jshell>

jshell> rectangle1.width
$6 ==> 31.0

jshell> rectangle1.height
$7 ==> 21.0

jshell> rectangle2.width
$8 ==> 182.0

jshell> rectangle2.height
$9 ==> 32.0

jshell> rectangle3.width
$10 ==> 203.0

jshell> rectangle3.height
$11 ==> 23.0

jshell> rectangle4.width
$12 ==> 404.0

jshell> rectangle4.height
$13 ==> 14.0

jshell>
```

Enter the following expression in JShell. The code file for the sample is included in the `java_9_oop_chapter_03_01` folder, in the `example03_06.java` file.

```
rectangle1 instanceof Rectangle
```

JShell will display `true` as a result of the evaluation of the previous expression because `rectangle1` is an instance of the `Rectangle` class. The `instanceof` keyword allows us to test whether an object is of the specified type. With this keyword, we can determine whether an object is a `Rectangle` object.

As previously explained, `Rectangle` is a subclass of the `java.lang.Object` class. JShell already imported all the types from `java.lang`, and therefore, we can just reference this class as `Object`. Enter the following expression in JShell. The code file for the sample is included in the `java_9_oop_chapter_03_01` folder, in the `example03_07.java` file.

```
rectangle1 instanceof Object
```

JShell will display `true` as a result of the evaluation of the previous expression because `rectangle1` is also an instance of the `java.lang.Object` class.

Enter the following expression in JShell. The code file for the sample is included in the `java_9_oop_chapter_03_01` folder, in the `example03_08.java` file.

```
rectangle1.getClass().getName()
```

JShell will display `"Rectangle"` as a result for the previous line because the `rectangle1` variable holds an instance of the `Rectangle` class. The `getClass` method allows us to retrieve the runtime class of an object. The method is inherited from the `java.lang.Object` class. The `getName` method converts the runtime type to a string.

Now, we will try to create an instance of `Rectangle` without providing arguments. The following line won't allow Java to compile the code and will display a build error in JShell because the compiler cannot find a parameterless constructor declared in the `Rectangle` class. The only constructor declared for this class requires two `double` arguments, and therefore, Java doesn't allow `Rectangle` instances to be created without specifying the values for `width` and `height`. The code file for the sample is included in the `java_9_oop_chapter_03_01` folder, in the `example03_09.java` file.

```
Rectangle rectangleError = new Rectangle();
```

The next screenshot shows the detailed error message:

```
jshell> Rectangle rectangleError = new Rectangle();
|  Error:
|  constructor Rectangle in class Rectangle cannot be applied to given types;
|    required: double,double
|    found: no arguments
|    reason: actual and formal argument lists differ in length
|  Rectangle rectangleError = new Rectangle();
|                             ^-------------^

jshell>
```

Understanding how garbage collection works

We will understand how garbage collection works with a few simple examples. We don't want to code a garbage collection process and we won't dive too deep into all the details about this complex process. Our goal is to create object-oriented code with Java 9 and not to create a new implementation of the JVM.

Now, we will add some code to the previously created Rectangle class to make Java execute some code before the garbage collection removes an instance of this class from memory. We only add this code to have a clear understanding of how garbage collection works. It is not recommended, and usually not necessary at all, to add code to the finalize method as we will do right now. Think about the next code as a code snippet just for educational purposes and not something we should do with our classes. We must take into account that we don't know when the garbage collection process will determine that it is necessary to claim back the memory used by the instances we will create. It is safe to do it but we cannot predict when the garbage collection process will do it. In this case, we are running JShell with the default garbage collection mechanism provided by the JVM.

You can follow best practices to release resources without having to add code to the finalize method. Remember that you don't know exactly when the finalize method is going to be executed. Even when the reference count reaches zero and all the variables that hold a reference have gone out of scope, the garbage collection algorithm implementation might keep the resources until the appropriate garbage collection destroys the instances. Thus, it is never a good idea to use the finalize method to release resources.

The following lines show the new complete code for the `Rectangle` class. The new lines are highlighted. The code file for the sample is included in the `java_9_oop_chapter_03_01` folder, in the `example03_10.java` file.

```java
class Rectangle {
    double width;
    double height;

    Rectangle(double width, double height) {
        System.out.printf("Initializing a new Rectangle
instance\n");
        System.out.printf("Width: %.2f, Height: %.2f\n",
            width,
            height);
        this.width = width;
        this.height = height;
    }

    // The following code doesn't represent a best practice
    // It is included just for educational purposes
    // and to make it easy to understand how the
    // garbage collection process works
    @Override
    protected void finalize() throws Throwable {
        try {
            System.out.printf("Finalizing Rectangle\n");
            System.out.printf("Width: %.2f, Height: %.2f\n", width,
                height);
        } catch(Throwable t){
            throw t;
        } finally{
            super.finalize();
        }
    }
}
```

The new lines declare a `finalize` method that overrides the inherited method from `java.lang.Object` and prints a message indicating that it is finalizing a `Rectangle` instance and displays the width and height values for the instance. Don't worry about the pieces of the code that you don't understand yet because we will learn them in the forthcoming chapters. The goal for the new piece of code included in the class is to let us know when the garbage collection process is going to remove the object from memory.

Avoid writing code that overrides the `finalize` method. Java 9 doesn't promote the usage of the `finalize` method to perform cleanup operations.

The following lines create two instances of the `Rectangle` class named `rectangleToCollect1` and `rectangleToCollect2`. Then, the next lines assign `null` to both variables, and therefore, the reference count for both objects reaches zero and they become ready for garbage collection. The two instances can be safely removed from memory because there are no more variables in scope holding a reference to them. The code file for the sample is included in the `java_9_oop_chapter_03_01` folder, in the `example03_11.java` file.

```
Rectangle rectangleToCollect1 = new Rectangle(51, 121);
Rectangle rectangleToCollect2 = new Rectangle(72, 282);
rectangleToCollect1 = null;
rectangleToCollect2 = null;
```

The following screenshot shows the results of executing the previous lines in JShell:

```
jshell> Rectangle rectangleToCollect1 = new Rectangle(51, 121);
Initializing a new Rectangle instance
Width: 51.00, Height: 121.00
rectangleToCollect1 ==> Rectangle@551aa95a

jshell> Rectangle rectangleToCollect2 = new Rectangle(72, 282);
Initializing a new Rectangle instance
Width: 72.00, Height: 282.00
rectangleToCollect2 ==> Rectangle@1dfe2924

jshell> rectangleToCollect1 = null;
rectangleToCollect1 ==> null

jshell> rectangleToCollect2 = null;
rectangleToCollect2 ==> null

jshell>
```

The two rectangle instances can be safely removed from memory but we don't see the messages indicating that the `finalize` method has been executed for each of these instances. Remember that we don't know when the garbage collection process will determine that it is necessary to claim back the memory used by these instances.

In order to understand how the garbage collection process works, we will force a garbage collection. However, it is very important to understand that we should never force a garbage collection in real-life applications. We must leave the JVM select the most appropriate time to perform a collection.

The next line shows the code that calls the `System.gc` method to force the JVM to perform a garbage collection. The code file for the sample is included in the `java_9_oop_chapter_03_01` folder, in the `example03_12.java` file.

```
System.gc();
```

The following screenshot shows the results of executing the previous line in JShell. We will see the messages that indicate that the `finalize` method for the two instances has been called.

```
jshell> rectangleToCollect1 = null;
rectangleToCollect1 ==> null

jshell> rectangleToCollect2 = null;
rectangleToCollect2 ==> null

jshell> System.gc();
Finalizing Rectangle

jshell> Width: 72.00, Height: 282.00
Finalizing Rectangle
Width: 51.00, Height: 121.00


jshell>
```

The following lines create an instance of the `Rectangle` class named `rectangle5` and then assign a reference to this object to the `referenceToRectangle5` variable. This way, the reference count to the object increases to two. The next line assigns `null` to `rectangle5` and makes the reference count for the object to go down from two to one. The `referenceToRectangle5` variable stills holds a reference to the `Rectangle` instance, and therefore, the next line that forces a garbage collection won't remove the instance from memory and we won't see the results of the execution of the code in the `finalize` method. There is still one variable on scope that holds a reference to the instance. The code file for the sample is included in the `java_9_oop_chapter_03_01` folder, in the `example03_13.java` file.

```
Rectangle rectangle5 = new Rectangle(50, 550);
Rectangle referenceToRectangle5 = rectangle5;
rectangle5 = null;
System.gc();
```

The following screenshot shows the results of executing the previous lines in JShell:

```
jshell> Rectangle rectangle5 = new Rectangle(50, 550);
Initializing a new Rectangle instance
Width: 50.00, Height: 550.00
rectangle5 ==> Rectangle@34c4973

jshell> Rectangle referenceToRectangle5 = rectangle5;
referenceToRectangle5 ==> Rectangle@34c4973

jshell> rectangle5 = null;
rectangle5 ==> null

jshell> System.gc();

jshell>
```

Now, we will execute a line that assigns null to referenceToRectangle5 to force the reference count to reach zero for the referenced instance and we will force the garbage collection process to run in the next line. The code file for the sample is included in the java_9_oop_chapter_03_01 folder, in the example03_14.java file.

```
referenceToRectangle5 = null;
System.gc();
```

The following screenshot shows the results of executing the previous lines in JShell. We will see the messages that indicate that the finalize method for the instance has been called.

```
jshell> System.gc();

jshell> referenceToRectangle5 = null;
referenceToRectangle5 ==> null

jshell> System.gc();
Finalizing Rectangle
Width: 50.00, Height: 550.00
jshell>
```

It is very important to know that you don't need to assign `null` to a reference to force the JVM to claim back the memory from objects. In the previous examples, we wanted to understand how the garbage collection worked. Java will automatically destroy the objects when they aren't referenced anymore in a transparent way.

Creating instances of classes and understanding their scope

We will write a few lines of code that create an instance of the `Rectangle` class named `rectangle` within the scope of a `getGeneratedRectangleHeight` method. The code within the method uses the created instance to access and return the value of its `height` field. In this case, the code uses the `final` keyword as a prefix to the `Rectangle` type to declare an **immutable reference** to the `Rectangle` instance named `rectangle`.

 An immutable reference is also known as a constant reference because we cannot replace the reference held by the `rectangle` constant with another instance of `Rectangle`.

After we define the new method, we will call it and we will force a garbage collection. The code file for the sample is included in the `java_9_oop_chapter_03_01` folder, in the `example03_15.java` file.

```
double getGeneratedRectangleHeight() {
    final Rectangle rectangle = new Rectangle(37, 87);
    return rectangle.height;
}

System.out.printf("Height: %.2f\n", getGeneratedRectangleHeight());
System.gc();
```

The following screenshot shows the results of executing the previous lines in JShell. We will see the messages that indicate that the `finalize` method for the instance has been called after the call to the `getGeneratedRectangleHeight` method and the next call to force the garbage collection. When the method returns a value, rectangle becomes out of scope because its reference count goes down from one to zero.

The instanced reference by immutable variable is safe for garbage collection. Thus, when we force the garbage collection, we see the message displayed by the `finalize` method.

```
jshell> double getGeneratedRectangleHeight() {
   ...>      final Rectangle rectangle = new Rectangle(37, 87);
   ...>      return rectangle.height;
   ...> }
|  created method getGeneratedRectangleHeight()

jshell>

jshell> System.out.printf("Height: %.2f\n", getGeneratedRectangleHeight());
Initializing a new Rectangle instance
Width: 37.00, Height: 87.00
Height: 87.00
$30 ==> java.io.PrintStream@335eadca
|  created scratch variable $30 : PrintStream

jshell> System.gc();
Finalizing Rectangle
Width: 37.00
jshell> , Height:
87.00
jshell>
```

Exercises

Now that you understand an object's life cycle, it is time to spend some time in JShell creating new classes and instances.

Exercise 1

1. Create a new `Student` class with a constructor that requires two `String` arguments: `firstName` and `lastName`. Use the arguments to initialize fields with the same names as the arguments. Display a message with the values for `firstName` and `lastName` when an instance of the class is created.

2. Create an instance of the `Student` class and assign it to a variable. Check the messages printed in JShell.

3. Create an instance of the `Student` class and assign it to a variable. Check the messages printed in JShell.

Exercise 2

1. Create a function that receives two `String` arguments: `firstName` and `lastName`. Create an instance of the previously defined `Student` class with the received arguments as parameters for the creation of the instance. Use the instance properties to print a message with the first name followed by a space and the last name. You will be able to create a method and add it to the `Student` class later to perform the same task. However, we will learn more about this in the forthcoming chapters.

2. Call the previously created function with the necessary arguments. Check the message printed in JShell.

Test your knowledge

1. When Java executes the code within a constructor:
    1. We cannot access any members defined in the class.
    2. There is already a live instance of the class. We can access methods defined in the class but we cannot access its fields.
    3. There is already a live instance of the class and we can access its members.

2. Constructors are extremely useful to:
    1. Execute setup code and properly initialize a new instance.
    2. Execute cleanup code before the instance is destroyed.
    3. Declare methods that will be accessible to all the instances of the class.

3. Java 9 uses one of the following mechanisms to automatically deallocate the memory used by instances that aren't referenced anymore:
    1. Instance map reduce.
    2. Garbage compression.
    3. Garbage collection.

4. Java 9 allows us to define:
    1. A main constructor and two optional secondary constructors.
    2. Many constructors with different arguments.
    3. Only one constructor per class.

5. Any new class we create that doesn't specify a superclass will be a subclass of:
    1. `java.lang.Base`
    2. `java.lang.Object`
    3. `java.object.BaseClass`

6. Which of the following lines create an instance of the `Rectangle` class and assign its reference to the `rectangle` variable:
    1. `var rectangle = new Rectangle(50, 20);`
    2. `auto rectangle = new Rectangle(50, 20);`
    3. `Rectangle rectangle = new Rectangle(50, 20);`

7. Which of the following lines access the `width` field for the `rectangle` instance:
    1. `rectangle.field`
    2. `rectangle..field`
    3. `rectangle->field`

Summary

In this chapter, you learned about an object's life cycle. You also learned how object constructors work. We declared our first simple class to generate a blueprint for objects. We understood how types, variables, classes, constructors, instances, and garbage collection work with live examples in JShell.

Now that you have learned to start creating classes and instances, we are ready to share, protect, use, and hide data with the data encapsulation features included in Java 9, which is what we are going to discuss in the next chapter.

4

Encapsulation of Data

In this chapter, we will learn the different members of a class in Java 9 and how they are reflected in members of the instances generated from a class. We will work with instance fields, class fields, setters, getters, instance methods, and class methods. We will:

- Understand the members that compose a class in Java 9
- Declare immutable fields
- Work with setters and getters
- Understand access modifiers in Java 9
- Combine setters, getters, and a related field
- Transform values with setters and getters
- Use static fields and static methods to create values shared by all the instances of a class

Understanding members composing a class

So far, we have been working with a very simple `Rectangle` class. We created many instances of this class in JShell and we understood how the garbage collection works. Now, it is time to dive deeper into the different members that compose a class in Java 9.

The following list enumerates the most common element types that we can include in a class definition in Java 9. Each member includes its equivalent in other programming languages to make it easy to translate our experience with other object-oriented languages into Java 9. We have already worked with a few of these members:

- **Constructors**: A class might define one or more constructors. They are equivalent to initializers in other programming languages.

- **Class variables or class fields**: These variables are common to all the instances of the class, that is, their value is the same for all the instances. In Java 9, it is possible to access class variables from the class and from its instances. We don't need to create a specific instance to access a class variable. Class variables are also known as static variables because they use the `static` modifier in their declarations. Class variables are equivalent to class attributes, class properties, and type properties in other programming languages.

- **Class methods**: These methods can be invoked with the class name. In Java 9, it is possible to access class methods from the class and from its instances. We don't need to create a specific instance to access a class method. Class methods are also known as static methods because they use the `static` modifier in their declarations. Class methods are equivalent to class functions and type methods in other programming languages. Class methods operate on a class as a whole, and have access to class variables, class constants, and other class methods, but they don't have access to any instance members, such as instance fields or methods, because they operate at the class level with no instances at all. Class methods are useful when we want to include methods related to a class and we don't want to generate an instance to call them.

- **Constants**: When we declare class variables or class fields with the `final` modifier, we define constants whose value cannot be changed.

- **Fields, member variables, instance variables, or instance fields**: We worked with these in the previous examples. Each instance of the class has its own distinct copies of the instance fields, with their own values. Instance fields are equivalent to attributes and instance properties in other programming languages.

- **Methods or instance methods**: These methods require an instance to be invoked and they can access the fields for the specific instance. Instance methods are equivalent to instance functions in other programming languages.

- **Nested classes**: These classes are defined within another class. Static nested classes use the `static` modifier. Nested classes that do not use the `static` modifier are also known as **inner classes**. Nested classes are also known as nested types in other programming languages.

Declaring immutable fields

Pokemon Go is a location-based augmented-reality game in which players use the mobile device's GPS capability to locate, capture, train, and make virtual creatures fight. This game had great success and popularized location-based and augmented-reality gaming. After its great success, imagine that we have to develop a Web Service that will be consumed by a similar game that makes virtual creatures battle.

We have to move to the world of virtual creatures. We will definitely have a `VirtualCreature` base class. Each specific type of virtual creature with unique characteristics that can participate in battles will be a subclass of `VirtualCreature`.

All the virtual creatures will have a name and they will be born in a specific year. The age is going to be extremely important for their performance in battles. Thus, our base class will have the `name` and `birthYear` fields that all the subclasses will inherit.

When we design classes, we want to make sure that all the necessary data is available to the methods that will operate on this data. For this reason, we encapsulate data. However, we just want relevant information to be visible to the users of our classes that will create instances, change the values of accessible fields, and call the available methods. We want to hide or protect some data that is just needed for internal use, that is, for our methods. We don't want to make accidental changes to sensitive data.

For example, when we create a new instance of any virtual creature, we can use both its name and birth year as two parameters for the constructor. The constructor initializes the values of two properties: `name` and `birthYear`. The following lines show a sample code that declares the `VirtualCreature` class. The code file for the sample is included in the `java_9_oop_chapter_04_01` folder, in the `example04_01.java` file.

```java
class VirtualCreature {
    String name;
    int birthYear;

    VirtualCreature(String name, int birthYear) {
        this.name = name;
        this.birthYear = birthYear;
    }
}
```

The next lines create two instances that initialize the values of the two fields and then use the `System.out.printf` method to display their values in JShell. The code file for the sample is included in the `java_9_oop_chapter_04_01` folder, in the `example04_01.java` file.

```
VirtualCreature beedrill = new VirtualCreature("Beedril", 2014);
System.out.printf("%s\n", beedrill.name);
System.out.printf("%d\n", beedrill.birthYear);
VirtualCreature krabby = new VirtualCreature("Krabby", 2012);
System.out.printf("%s\n", krabby.name);
System.out.printf("%d\n", krabby.birthYear);
```

The following screenshot shows the results of the declaration of the class and the execution of the previous lines in JShell:

```
jshell> class VirtualCreature {
   ...>       String name;
   ...>       int birthYear;
   ...>
   ...>       VirtualCreature(String name, int birthYear) {
   ...>           this.name = name;
   ...>           this.birthYear = birthYear;
   ...>       }
   ...> }
|  created class VirtualCreature

jshell> VirtualCreature beedrill = new VirtualCreature("Beedril", 2014);
beedrill ==> VirtualCreature@4b9e13df
|  created variable beedrill : VirtualCreature

jshell> System.out.printf("%s\n", beedrill.name);
Beedril
$3 ==> java.io.PrintStream@d8355a8
|  created scratch variable $3 : PrintStream

jshell> System.out.printf("%d\n", beedrill.birthYear);
2014
$4 ==> java.io.PrintStream@d8355a8
|  created scratch variable $4 : PrintStream

jshell> VirtualCreature krabby = new VirtualCreature("Krabby", 2012);
krabby ==> VirtualCreature@4501b7af
|  created variable krabby : VirtualCreature

jshell> System.out.printf("%s\n", krabby.name);
Krabby
$6 ==> java.io.PrintStream@d8355a8
|  created scratch variable $6 : PrintStream

jshell> System.out.printf("%d\n", krabby.birthYear);
2012
$7 ==> java.io.PrintStream@d8355a8
|  created scratch variable $7 : PrintStream
```

We don't want a user of our `VirtualCreature` class to be able to change the name for a virtual creature after an instance is initialized because the name is not supposed to change. Well, some people change their names but this never happens with virtual creatures. There is a simple way to achieve this goal in our previously declared class. We can add the `final` keyword before the type (`String`) to define an immutable name field of type `String`. We can also add the `final` keyword before the type (`int`) when we define the `birthYear` field because the birth year will never change after we initialize a virtual creature instance.

The following lines show the new code that declares the `VirtualCreature` class with two immutable instance fields: `name` and `birthYear`. Note that the constructor code doesn't need to be changed, and it is possible to initialize the two immutable instance fields with the same code. The code file for the sample is included in the `java_9_oop_chapter_04_01` folder, in the `example04_02.java` file.

```java
class VirtualCreature {
    final String name;
    final int birthYear;

    VirtualCreature(String name, int birthYear) {
        this.name = name;
        this.birthYear = birthYear;
    }
}
```

 Immutable instance fields are also known as non-mutating instance fields.

The next lines create an instance that initializes the values of the two immutable instance fields and then use the `System.out.printf` method to display their values in JShell. The code file for the sample is included in the `java_9_oop_chapter_04_01` folder, in the `example04_02.java` file.

```java
VirtualCreature squirtle = new VirtualCreature("Squirtle", 2014);
System.out.printf("%s\n", squirtle.name);
System.out.printf("%d\n", squirtle.birthYear);
```

The next two lines of code try to assign a new value to the `name` and `birthYear` immutable instance fields. The code file for the sample is included in the `java_9_oop_chapter_04_01` folder, in the `example04_03.java` file.

```java
squirtle.name = "Tentacruel";
squirtle.birthYear = 2017;
```

The two lines will fail to do so because Java doesn't allow us to assign a value to a field declared with the final modifier that transforms it into an immutable field. The next screenshot shows the errors displayed in JShell after each line that tries to set a new value to the immutable fields:

```
jshell> class VirtualCreature {
   ...>     final String name;
   ...>     final int birthYear;
   ...>
   ...>     VirtualCreature(String name, int birthYear) {
   ...>         this.name = name;
   ...>         this.birthYear = birthYear;
   ...>     }
   ...> }
|  created class VirtualCreature

jshell> VirtualCreature squirtle = new VirtualCreature("Squirtle", 2014);
squirtle ==> VirtualCreature@4b9e13df
|  created variable squirtle : VirtualCreature

jshell> System.out.printf("%s\n", squirtle.name);
Squirtle
$3 ==> java.io.PrintStream@d8355a8
|  created scratch variable $3 : PrintStream

jshell> System.out.printf("%d\n", squirtle.birthYear);
2014
$4 ==> java.io.PrintStream@d8355a8
|  created scratch variable $4 : PrintStream

jshell> squirtle.name = "Tentacruel";
|  Error:
|  cannot assign a value to final variable name
|  squirtle.name = "Tentacruel";
|  ^-----------^

jshell> squirtle.birthYear = 2017;
|  Error:
|  cannot assign a value to final variable birthYear
|  squirtle.birthYear = 2017;
|  ^----------------^
```

When we use the final keyword to declare an instance field, we can initialize the field but it becomes immutable, that is, a constant, after its initialization.

Working with setters and getters

So far, we have been working with fields to encapsulate data in our instances. We could access the fields without any kind of restrictions as member variables for an instance. However, as it happens sometimes in real-world situations, restrictions are necessary to avoid serious problems. Sometimes, we want to restrict access or transform specific fields into read-only fields. We can combine the access restrictions to an underlying field with methods known as setters and getters.

Setters are methods that allow us to control how values are set; that is, these methods are used to change the values of related fields. **Getters** allow us to control the values that we return when we want to retrieve the value for a related field. Getters don't change the values of related fields.

 While some frameworks such as JavaBeans force you to work with setters and getters for each related field to be accessible, in other cases, setters and getters won't be necessary. In the next examples we will work with mutable objects. In the next chapter, *Chapter 5, Mutable and Immutable Classes*, we will work with both mutable and immutable objects. When working with immutable objects, getters and setters are useless.

As previously explained, we don't want a user of our `VirtualCreature` class to be able to change the birth year for a virtual creature after an instance is initialized because the virtual creature won't be born again at a different date. In fact, we want to calculate and make the age for the virtual creature available to users. Because we only take into account the birth year, we will calculate an approximated age. We keep the example simple to keep the focus on the getters and setters.

We can define a getter method called `getAge` without defining a setter method. This way, it is possible to retrieve the age for the virtual creature, but we cannot change it because there isn't a setter method. The getter method returns the result of calculating the age for the virtual creature age based on the current year and the value of the `birthYear` immutable instance field.

The following lines show the new version of the VirtualCreature class with the new getAge method. Notice that it is necessary to import java.time.Year to use the Year class that was introduced in Java 8. The code for the getAge method is highlighted in the next lines. The method calls Year.now().getValue to retrieve the year component for the current date and returns the difference between the current year and the value of the birthYear field. The code file for the sample is included in the java_9_oop_chapter_04_01 folder, in the example04_04.java file.

```java
import java.time.Year;

class VirtualCreature {
    final String name;
    final int birthYear;

    VirtualCreature(String name, int birthYear) {
        this.name = name;
        this.birthYear = birthYear;
    }

    int getAge() {
        return Year.now().getValue() - birthYear;
    }
}
```

The next lines create an instance that initializes the values of the two immutable instance fields and then use the System.out.printf method to display the value returned by the getAge method in JShell. Enter the lines after the code that creates the new version of the VirtualCreature class. The code file for the sample is included in the java_9_oop_chapter_04_01 folder, in the example04_04.java file.

```java
VirtualCreature arbok = new VirtualCreature("Arbok", 2008);
System.out.printf("%d\n", arbok.getAge());
VirtualCreature pidgey = new VirtualCreature("Pidgey", 2015);
System.out.printf("%d\n", pidgey.getAge());
```

The next screenshot shows the results of executing the previous lines in JShell:

```
jshell> import java.time.Year;

jshell>

jshell> class VirtualCreature {
   ...>      final String name;
   ...>      final int birthYear;
   ...>
   ...>      VirtualCreature(String name, int birthYear) {
   ...>          this.name = name;
   ...>          this.birthYear = birthYear;
   ...>      }
   ...>
   ...>      int getAge() {
   ...>          return Year.now().getValue() - birthYear;
   ...>      }
   ...> }
|  created class VirtualCreature

jshell>

jshell> VirtualCreature arbok = new VirtualCreature("Arbok", 2008);
arbok ==> VirtualCreature@4b9e13df
|  created variable arbok : VirtualCreature

jshell> System.out.printf("%d\n", arbok.getAge());
9
$4 ==> java.io.PrintStream@4e1d422d
|  created scratch variable $4 : PrintStream

jshell> VirtualCreature pidgey = new VirtualCreature("Pidgey", 2015);
pidgey ==> VirtualCreature@52a86356
|  created variable pidgey : VirtualCreature

jshell> System.out.printf("%d\n", pidgey.getAge());
2
$6 ==> java.io.PrintStream@4e1d422d
|  created scratch variable $6 : PrintStream
```

After a few meetings with experts in virtual creatures, we realize that some of them go to a planet to evolve and are born again from an egg after evolving. Because the evolution happens in a different planet, the birth year for the virtual creature changes to have an equivalent birth year in the Earth. Thus, it is necessary to allow the user to customize either the age or the birth year for a virtual creature. We will add a setter method with code that calculates the birth year based on the specified age and assigns this value to the birthYear field. First, we must remove the final keyword when we declare the birthYear field because we want it to become a mutable field.

There is another way of working with the evolution of a virtual creature. We can create another instance that represents the evolved virtual creature. We will use this immutable approach in the next chapter, *Chapter 5, Mutable and Immutable Classes*. In this case, we will work with a mutable object. After we understand all the possibilities, we can decide the best option based on our specific needs.

The following lines show the new version of the VirtualCreature class with the new setAge method. The code for the setAge method is highlighted in the next lines. The method receives the new age we want for the virtual creature in the age parameter. The code calls Year.now().getValue to retrieve the year component for the current date and assigns the difference between the current year and the value received in age. This way, the birthYear field will save the year in which the virtual creature was born based on the received age value. The code file for the sample is included in the java_9_oop_chapter_04_01 folder, in the example04_05.java file.

```java
import java.time.Year;

class VirtualCreature {
    final String name;
    int birthYear;

    VirtualCreature(String name, int birthYear) {
        this.name = name;
        this.birthYear = birthYear;
    }

    int getAge() {
        return Year.now().getValue() - birthYear;
    }

    void setAge(final int age) {
        birthYear = Year.now().getValue() - age;
    }
}
```

The next lines create two instances of the new version of the VirtualCreature class, call the setAge method with the desired age for the virtual creature, and then use the System.out.printf method to display the value returned by the getAge method and the birthYear field in JShell. Enter the lines after the code that creates the new version of the VirtualCreature class. The code file for the sample is included in the java_9_oop_chapter_04_01 folder, in the example04_05.java file.

```
VirtualCreature venusaur = new VirtualCreature("Venusaur", 2000);
System.out.printf("%d\n", venusaur.getAge());
VirtualCreature caterpie = new VirtualCreature("Caterpie", 2012);
System.out.printf("%d\n", caterpie.getAge());

venusaur.setAge(2);
System.out.printf("%d\n", venusaur.getAge());
System.out.printf("%d\n", venusaur.birthYear);

venusaur.setAge(14);
System.out.printf("%d\n", caterpie.getAge());
System.out.printf("%d\n", caterpie.birthYear);
```

As a result of calling the `setAge` method with a new age value, the method changes the value of the `birthYear` field. Based on the current year value, the results of running the code will be different. The next screenshot shows the results of executing the previous lines in JShell:

```
   ...>            birthYear = Year.now().getValue() - age;
   ...>     }
   ...> }
|  created class VirtualCreature

jshell> VirtualCreature venusaur = new VirtualCreature("Venusaur", 2000);
venusaur ==> VirtualCreature@4b9e13df

jshell> System.out.printf("%d\n", venusaur.getAge());
17
$4 ==> java.io.PrintStream@4e1d422d

jshell> VirtualCreature caterpie = new VirtualCreature("Caterpie", 2012);
caterpie ==> VirtualCreature@52a86356

jshell> System.out.printf("%d\n", caterpie.getAge());
5
$6 ==> java.io.PrintStream@4e1d422d

jshell> venusaur.setAge(2);

jshell> System.out.printf("%d\n", venusaur.getAge());
2
$8 ==> java.io.PrintStream@4e1d422d

jshell> System.out.printf("%d\n", venusaur.birthYear);
2015
$9 ==> java.io.PrintStream@4e1d422d

jshell> venusaur.setAge(14);

jshell> System.out.printf("%d\n", caterpie.getAge());
5
$11 ==> java.io.PrintStream@4e1d422d

jshell> System.out.printf("%d\n", caterpie.birthYear);
2012
$12 ==> java.io.PrintStream@4e1d422d
```

Both the getter and setter methods use the same code to retrieve the current year. We can add a new method that retrieves the current year and call it from both the getAge and setAge methods. In this case, it is just a line of code, but the new method provides us with an example of how we can add methods that will be consumed in our class and help other methods to do their job. Later, we will learn how to avoid these methods being called from an instance because they are intended for internal use only.

The following lines show the new version of the SuperHero class with the new getCurrentYear method. The new code for the getAge and setAge methods calls the new getCurrentYear method instead of repeating code that was intended to retrieve the current year. The code file for the sample is included in the java_9_oop_chapter_04_01 folder, in the example04_06.java file.

```java
import java.time.Year;

class VirtualCreature {
    final String name;
    int birthYear;

    VirtualCreature(String name, int birthYear) {
        this.name = name;
        this.birthYear = birthYear;
    }

    int getCurrentYear() {
        return Year.now().getValue();
    }

    int getAge() {
        return getCurrentYear() - birthYear;
    }

    void setAge(final int age) {
        birthYear = getCurrentYear() - age;
    }
}
```

The next lines create two instances of the VirtualCreature class, call the setAge method with the desired age for the virtual creature, and then use the System.out.printf method to display the value returned by the getAge method and the birthYear field in JShell. Enter the lines after the code that creates the new version of the VirtualCreature class. The code file for the sample is included in the java_9_oop_chapter_04_01 folder, in the example04_06.java file.

```
VirtualCreature persian = new VirtualCreature("Persian", 2005);
System.out.printf("%d\n", persian.getAge());
VirtualCreature arcanine = new VirtualCreature("Arcanine", 2012);
System.out.printf("%d\n", arcanine.getAge());

persian.setAge(7);
System.out.printf("%d\n", persian.getAge());
System.out.printf("%d\n", persian.birthYear);

arcanine.setAge(9);
System.out.printf("%d\n", arcanine.getAge());
System.out.printf("%d\n", arcanine.birthYear);
```

The next screenshot shows the results of executing the previous lines in JShell:

```
jshell> VirtualCreature persian = new VirtualCreature("Persian", 2005);
persian ==> VirtualCreature@4b9e13df
|  created variable persian : VirtualCreature

jshell> System.out.printf("%d\n", persian.getAge());
12
$4 ==> java.io.PrintStream@4e1d422d
|  created scratch variable $4 : PrintStream

jshell> VirtualCreature arcanine = new VirtualCreature("Arcanine", 2012);
arcanine ==> VirtualCreature@52a86356
|  created variable arcanine : VirtualCreature

jshell> System.out.printf("%d\n", arcanine.getAge());
5
$6 ==> java.io.PrintStream@4e1d422d
|  created scratch variable $6 : PrintStream

jshell> persian.setAge(7);

jshell> System.out.printf("%d\n", persian.getAge());
7
$8 ==> java.io.PrintStream@4e1d422d
|  created scratch variable $8 : PrintStream

jshell> System.out.printf("%d\n", persian.birthYear);
2010
$9 ==> java.io.PrintStream@4e1d422d
|  created scratch variable $9 : PrintStream

jshell> arcanine.setAge(9);

jshell> System.out.printf("%d\n", arcanine.getAge());
9
$11 ==> java.io.PrintStream@4e1d422d
|  created scratch variable $11 : PrintStream

jshell> System.out.printf("%d\n", arcanine.birthYear);
2008
```

Exploring access modifiers in Java 9

The previously declared `VirtualCreature` class exposes all of its members (fields and methods) without any kind of restriction because we declared them without using any access modifier. Thus, the user of our class can access any of the fields and call any of the declared methods after the user creates an instance of the class.

Java 9 allows us to control access to members of a call by using access level modifiers. Different keywords allow us to control which code has access to a specific member of a class. So far, we could access fields and methods within a class definition and outside of a class declaration.

We can use any of the following access modifiers instead of `public` to restrict access to any field:

- `protected`: Java doesn't allow users to access the member outside of the class definition. Only the code within the class or its derived classes can access the field. Any subclass of a class that declares a member with the `protected` access modifier will be able to access the member.

- `private`: Java doesn't allow users to access the field outside of the class definition. Only the code within the class can access the field. Its derived classes cannot access the field. Thus, any subclass of a class that declares a member with the `private` access modifier won't be able to access the member.

The following line shows how we can change the declaration of the `birthYear` instance field to a `protected` field. We just need to add the `protected` keyword to the field declaration.

```
protected int birthYear;
```

Whenever we use the `protected` access modifier in a field declaration, we restrict access to this field to the code written within the class definition and within subclasses. Java 9 generates a real shield for the fields marked as `protected` and there is no way to access them outside of the explained boundaries.

The following line shows how we can change the declaration of the `birthYear` protected instance field to a `private` field. We replace the `protected` access modifier with `private`.

```
private int birthYear;
```

Whenever we use the `private` access modifier in a field declaration, we restrict access to this field to the code written within the class definition and within subclasses. Java generates a real shield for the fields marked as `private` and there is no way to access them outside of the class definition. The restriction also applies to subclasses, and therefore, only the code written within the class can access attributes marked as private.

 We can apply the previously explained access modifiers for any type member, including class variables, class methods, constants, fields, methods, and nested classes.

Combining setters, getters, and fields

Sometimes, we want to have more control over the values that are set to related fields and retrieved from them, and we can take advantage of getters and setters to do so. We can combine a getter, a setter, a related field that stores a computed value, and the access protection mechanisms to prevent the user from making changes to the related field. This way, we will force the user to always use the getters and setters.

Virtual creatures love any kind of hat. The hat for a virtual creature can change over time. We have to make sure that the hat's name is in capital letters, that is, an uppercased `String`. We will define a `setHat` method that always generates an uppercased `String` from the received `String` and stores it in a private `hat` field.

We will provide a `getHat` method to retrieve the value stored in the private `hat` field. The following lines show a new version of the `VirtualCreature` class that adds a `hat` private instance field and the `getHat` and `setHat` methods. We use the previously learned access modifiers for the different members of the class. The code file for the sample is included in the `java_9_oop_chapter_04_01` folder, in the `example04_07.java` file.

```java
import java.time.Year;

public class VirtualCreature {
    public final String name;
    private int birthYear;
    private String hat = "NONE";

    VirtualCreature(String name, int birthYear, String hat) {
        this.name = name;
        this.birthYear = birthYear;
        setHat(hat);
```

```
        }

        private int getCurrentYear() {
            return Year.now().getValue();
        }

        public int getAge() {
            return getCurrentYear() - birthYear;
        }

        public void setAge(final int age) {
            birthYear = getCurrentYear() - age;
        }

        public String getHat() {
            return hat;
        }

        public void setHat(final String hat) {
            this.hat = hat.toUpperCase();
        }
    }
```

If you work with specific early versions of JDK, when you enter the previous code in JShell, you might see the following warning message:

```
|  Warning:
|  Modifier 'public'  not permitted in top-level declarations, ignored
|  public class VirtualCreature {
|    ^----^
|  created class VirtualCreature this error is corrected:
|      Modifier 'public'  not permitted in top-level declarations,
ignored
|      public class VirtualCreature {
|        ^----^
```

JShell doesn't allow us to use access modifiers in top-level declarations, such as a class declaration. However, we specify the access modifier because we want to code as if we were writing the class declaration outside of JShell. JShell simply ignores the `public` access modifier for the class and some versions of the JDK that incuded JShell made the REPL display the previously shown warning message. If you see these messages, you should upgrade the installed JDK to the newest version that doesn't display the warning messages anymore.

We declared both the `birthyear` and `hat` instance fields as `private`. We declared the `getCurrentYear` method as `protected`. When a user creates an instance of the `VirtualCreature` class, the user won't be able to access any of these `private` members. This way, the `private` members will be hidden for those who create instances of the `VirtualCreature` class.

We declared `name` as a `public` immutable instance field. We declared the following methods as `public`: `getAge`, `setAge`, `getHat`, and `setHat`. When a user creates an instance of the `VirtualCreature` class, he will be able to access all of these `public` members.

The constructor added a new argument that provides an initial value for the new `hat` field. The code in the constructor calls the `setHat` method with the received `hat` argument as a parameter to make sure that an uppercase `String` is generated from the received `String` and the resulting `String` is assigned to the `hat` field.

The next lines create two instances of the `VirtualCreature` class, use the `printf` method to display the value returned by the `getHat` method, call the `setHat` method with the desired new hat for the virtual creature, and then use the `System.out.printf` method to display the value returned by the `getHat` method again. Enter the lines after the code that creates the new version of the `VirtualCreature` class. The code file for the sample is included in the `java_9_oop_chapter_04_01` folder, in the `example04_07.java` file.

```
VirtualCreature glaceon =
    new VirtualCreature("Glaceon", 2009, "Baseball cap");
System.out.printf(glaceon.getHat());
glaceon.setHat("Hard hat")
System.out.printf(glaceon.getHat());
VirtualCreature gliscor =
    new VirtualCreature("Gliscor", 2015, "Cowboy hat");
System.out.printf(gliscor.getHat());
gliscor.setHat("Panama hat")
System.out.printf(gliscor.getHat());
```

The next screenshot shows the results of executing the previous lines in JShell:

```
jshell> VirtualCreature glaceon = new VirtualCreature("Glaceon", 2009, "Baseball cap");
glaceon ==> VirtualCreature@4b9e13df
|  created variable glaceon : VirtualCreature

jshell> System.out.printf(glaceon.getHat());
BASEBALL CAP$4 ==> java.io.PrintStream@d8355a8
|  created scratch variable $4 : PrintStream

jshell> glaceon.setHat("Hard hat")

jshell> System.out.printf(glaceon.getHat());
HARD HAT$6 ==> java.io.PrintStream@d8355a8
|  created scratch variable $6 : PrintStream

jshell> VirtualCreature gliscor = new VirtualCreature("Gliscor", 2015, "Cowboy hat");
gliscor ==> VirtualCreature@523884b2
|  created variable gliscor : VirtualCreature

jshell> System.out.printf(gliscor.getHat());
COWBOY HAT$8 ==> java.io.PrintStream@d8355a8
|  created scratch variable $8 : PrintStream

jshell> gliscor.setHat("Panama hat")

jshell> System.out.printf(gliscor.getHat());
PANAMA HAT$10 ==> java.io.PrintStream@d8355a8
|  created scratch variable $10 : PrintStream
```

> We can combine the getter and setter methods, along with access
> protection mechanisms and a related field that acts as an underlying
> field, to have absolute control over how values are set to and retrieved
> from the underlying field in mutable objects. However, we must make
> sure that the initialization must also use the setter method, as we did
> when we set the initial value received in the constructor.

The next lines will try to access a private field and a private method for the instances
of the VirtualCreature class we have created. Both lines will fail to compile
because we cannot access private members in an instance. The first line tries to access
the hat instance field and the second line tries to call the getCurrentYear instance
method. The code file for the sample is included in the java_9_oop_chapter_04_01
folder, in the example04_08.java file.

```
System.out.printf(gliscor.hat);
System.out.printf("%d", glaceon.getCurrentYear());
```

The next screenshot shows the error messages generated in JShell when we try to execute the previous lines.

```
jshell> System.out.printf(gliscor.hat);
|   Error:
|   hat has private access in VirtualCreature
|   System.out.printf(gliscor.hat);
|                       ^---------^

jshell> System.out.printf("%d", glaceon.getCurrentYear());
|   Error:
|   getCurrentYear() has private access in VirtualCreature
|   System.out.printf("%d", glaceon.getCurrentYear());
|                           ^--------------------^

jshell>
```

Transforming values with setters and getters

We can define a setter method that transforms a received value to a valid value for a related field. The getter method would just need to return the value of the related field. The user will only be able to work with the setter and getter methods and our related field will always have a valid value. This way, we can make sure that whenever we require the value, we will retrieve a valid value.

Each virtual creature has a visibility level that determines how easy it is for anybody to visualize the virtual creature's body. We will add a private `visibilityLevel` field, a `setVisibility` method, and a `getVisibility` method. We will change the constructor code to call the `setVisiblity` method to set an initial value for the `visibilityLevel` field.

We want to make sure that the visibility level is a number from 0 to 100 (inclusive). Thus, we will code the setter method to transform the values lower than 0 to 0 and values higher than 100 to 100. The `setVisibility` method saves either the transformed or the original value that is in a valid range in the related private `visibilityLevel` field.

The edited lines and the new lines are highlighted. The code file for the sample is included in the java_9_oop_chapter_04_01 folder, in the example04_09.java file.

```java
import java.time.Year;

public class VirtualCreature {
    public final String name;
    private int birthYear;
    private String hat = "NONE";
    private int visibilityLevel;

    VirtualCreature(String name,
        int birthYear,
        String hat,
        int visibilityLevel) {
        this.name = name;
        this.birthYear = birthYear;
        setHat(hat);
        setVisibilityLevel(visibilityLevel);
    }

    private int getCurrentYear() {
        return Year.now().getValue();
    }

    public int getAge() {
        return getCurrentYear() - birthYear;
    }

    public void setAge(final int age) {
        birthYear = getCurrentYear() - age;
    }

    public String getHat() {
        return hat;
    }

    public void setHat(final String hat) {
        this.hat = hat.toUpperCase();
    }
```

```
public int getVisibilityLevel() {
    return visibilityLevel;
}

public void setVisibilityLevel(final int visibilityLevel) {
    this.visibilityLevel =
        Math.min(Math.max(visibilityLevel, 0), 100);
}
}
```

The next lines create an instance of VirtualCreature that specifies 150 as the value
for the visibilityLevel argument. Then, the next line uses the System.out.
printf method to display the value returned by the getVisibilityLevel method
in JShell. Then, we call setVisibilityLevel and getVisibilityLevel three times,
to set values to visibilityLevel, and then check the values that were finally set.
Enter the lines after the code that creates the new version of the VirtualCreature
class. The code file for the sample is included in the java_9_oop_chapter_04_01
folder, in the example04_09.java file.

```
VirtualCreature lairon =
    new VirtualCreature("Lairon", 2014, "Sombrero", 150);
System.out.printf("%d", lairon.getVisibilityLevel());
lairon.setVisibilityLevel(-6);
System.out.printf("%d", lairon.getVisibilityLevel());
lairon.setVisibilityLevel(320);
System.out.printf("%d", lairon.getVisibilityLevel());
lairon.setVisibilityLevel(25);
System.out.printf("%d", lairon.getVisibilityLevel());
```

The constructor calls the setVisibilityLevel method to set the initial value for
the visibilityLevel related private field, and therefore, the method makes sure
that the value is in the valid range. The code specified 150 but the maximum value is
100, and therefore, the setVisibilityLevel assigned 100 to the visibilityLevel
related private field.

After we called the `setVisibilityLevel` with `-6` as an argument, we printed the value returned by `getVisibilityLevel` and the result was `0`. After we specified `320`, the actual printed value was `100`. Finally, after we specified `25`, the actual printed value was `25`. The next screenshot shows the results of executing the previous lines in JShell:

```
jshell> VirtualCreature lairon =
   ...>     new VirtualCreature("Lairon", 2014, "Sombrero", 150);
lairon ==> VirtualCreature@4b9e13df
|  created variable lairon : VirtualCreature

jshell> System.out.printf("%d", lairon.getVisibilityLevel());
100$4 ==> java.io.PrintStream@d8355a8
|  created scratch variable $4 : PrintStream

jshell> lairon.setVisibilityLevel(-6);

jshell> System.out.printf("%d", lairon.getVisibilityLevel());
0$6 ==> java.io.PrintStream@d8355a8
|  created scratch variable $6 : PrintStream

jshell> lairon.setVisibilityLevel(320);

jshell> System.out.printf("%d", lairon.getVisibilityLevel());
100$8 ==> java.io.PrintStream@d8355a8
|  created scratch variable $8 : PrintStream

jshell> lairon.setVisibilityLevel(25);

jshell> System.out.printf("%d", lairon.getVisibilityLevel());
25$10 ==> java.io.PrintStream@d8355a8
|  created scratch variable $10 : PrintStream

jshell>
```

Using static fields to provide class-level values

Sometimes, all the members of a class share the same attribute, and we don't need to have a specific value for each instance. For example, virtual creature types have the following profile values:

- Attack power
- Defense power
- Special attack power
- Special defense power

- Average speed
- Catch rate
- Growth rate

A first approach we might think useful for this situation is to define the following class constants to store the values that are shared by all the instances:

- ATTACK_POWER
- DEFENSE_POWER
- SPECIAL_ATTACK_POWER
- SPECIAL_DEFENSE_POWER
- AVERAGE_SPEED
- CATCH_RATE
- GROWTH_RATE

 Note the usage of uppercase and words separated by underscores (_) for class constant names. This is a naming convention in Java 9.

The following lines show a new version of the VirtualCreature class that defines the seven previously listed class constants with the public access modifier. Notice that the combination of the final and static keywords makes them class constants. The code file for the sample is included in the java_9_oop_chapter_04_01 folder, in the example04_10.java file.

```java
import java.time.Year;

public class VirtualCreature {
    public final static int ATTACK_POWER = 45;
    public final static int DEFENSE_POWER = 85;
    public final static int SPECIAL_ATTACK_POWER = 35;
    public final static int SPECIAL_DEFENSE_POWER = 95;
    public final static int AVERAGE_SPEED = 85;
    public final static int CATCH_RATE = 25;
    public final static int GROWTH_RATE = 10;

    public final String name;
    private int birthYear;
    private String hat = "NONE";
    private int visibilityLevel;
```

```
VirtualCreature(String name,
    int birthYear,
    String hat,
    int visibilityLevel) {
    this.name = name;
    this.birthYear = birthYear;
    setHat(hat);
    setVisibilityLevel(visibilityLevel);
}

private int getCurrentYear() {
    return Year.now().getValue();
}

public int getAge() {
    return getCurrentYear() - birthYear;
}

public void setAge(final int age) {
    birthYear = getCurrentYear() - age;
}

public String getHat() {
    return hat;
}

public void setHat(final String hat) {
    this.hat = hat.toUpperCase();
}

public int getVisibilityLevel() {
    return visibilityLevel;
}

public void setVisibilityLevel(final int visibilityLevel) {
    this.visibilityLevel =
        Math.min(Math.max(visibilityLevel, 0), 100);
}
}
```

The code initializes each class constant in the same line that declares them. The following lines print the value of the previously declared SPECIAL_ATTACK_POWER and SPECIAL_DEFENSE_POWER class constants. Notice that we didn't create any instance of the VirtualCreature class and that we specified the class constant name after the class name and a dot (.). The code file for the sample is included in the java_9_oop_chapter_04_01 folder, in the example04_10.java file.

```
System.out.printf("%d\n", VirtualCreature.SPECIAL_ATTACK_POWER);
System.out.printf("%d\n", VirtualCreature.SPECIAL_DEFENSE_POWER);
```

Java 9 allows us to access a class constant from an instance, and therefore, we can use either the class name or an instance to access a class constant. The following line creates an instance of the new version of the VirtualCreature class named golbat and prints the value of the GROWTH_RATE class constant, accessed from this new instance. The code file for the sample is included in the java_9_oop_chapter_04_01 folder, in the example04_10.java file.

```
VirtualCreature golbat =
    new VirtualCreature("Golbat", 2015, "Baseball cap", 75);
System.out.printf("%d\n", golbat.GROWTH_RATE);
```

The next screenshot shows the results of executing the previous lines in JShell.

```
jshell> System.out.printf("%d\n", VirtualCreature.SPECIAL_ATTACK_POWER);
35
$3 ==> java.io.PrintStream@14acaea5
|  created scratch variable $3 : PrintStream

jshell> System.out.printf("%d\n", VirtualCreature.SPECIAL_DEFENSE_POWER);
95
$4 ==> java.io.PrintStream@14acaea5
|  created scratch variable $4 : PrintStream

jshell> VirtualCreature golbat =
   ...>     new VirtualCreature("Golbat", 2015, "Baseball cap", 75);
golbat ==> VirtualCreature@59fa1d9b
|  created variable golbat : VirtualCreature

jshell> System.out.printf("%d\n", golbat.GROWTH_RATE);
10
$6 ==> java.io.PrintStream@14acaea5
|  created scratch variable $6 : PrintStream

jshell>
```

Using static methods to provide overridable class-level values

Class constants have a great limitation: we cannot provide new values to them in future subclasses of the `VirtualCreature` class that represent specific types of virtual creatures. It makes sense, because they are constants. These subclasses need to set a different value for `ATTACK_POWER` or `AVERAGE_SPEED`. Instead of working with class constants, we can create the following class methods that return the average values for each profile value. We will be able to make these methods return a different value in subclasses of the `VirtualCreature` class.

- `getAttackPower`
- `getDefensePower`
- `getSpecialAttackPower`
- `getSpecialDefensePower`
- `getAverageSpeed`
- `getCatchRate`
- `getGrowthRate`

The following lines show a new version of the `VirtualCreature` class that defines the seven previously listed class methods with the `public` access modifier. Notice that the usage of the `static` keyword in the method declarations makes them class methods. The code file for the sample is included in the `java_9_oop_chapter_04_01` folder, in the `example04_11.java` file.

```java
import java.time.Year;

public class VirtualCreature {
    public static int getAttackPower() {
        return 45;
    }

    public static int getDefensePower() {
        return 85;
    }

    public static int getSpecialAttackPower() {
        return 35;
    }

    public static int getSpecialDefensePower() {
        return 95;
```

```java
}

public static int getAverageSpeed() {
    return 85;
}

public static int getCatchRate() {
    return 25;
}

public static int getGrowthRate() {
    return 10;
}

public final String name;
private int birthYear;
private String hat = "NONE";
private int visibilityLevel;

VirtualCreature(String name,
    int birthYear,
    String hat,
    int visibilityLevel) {
    this.name = name;
    this.birthYear = birthYear;
    setHat(hat);
    setVisibilityLevel(visibilityLevel);
}

private int getCurrentYear() {
    return Year.now().getValue();
}

public int getAge() {
    return getCurrentYear() - birthYear;
}

public void setAge(final int age) {
    birthYear = getCurrentYear() - age;
}

public String getHat() {
    return hat;
}
```

```java
    public void setHat(final String hat) {
        this.hat = hat.toUpperCase();
    }

    public int getVisibilityLevel() {
        return visibilityLevel;
    }

    public void setVisibilityLevel(final int visibilityLevel) {
        this.visibilityLevel =
            Math.min(Math.max(visibilityLevel, 0), 100);
    }
}
```

The following lines print the value returned by the previously declared `getSpecialAttackPower` and `getSpecialDefensePower` class methods. Notice that we didn't create any instance of the `VirtualCreature` class and that we specified the class method name after the class name and a dot (`.`). The code file for the sample is included in the `java_9_oop_chapter_04_01` folder, in the `example04_11.java` file.

```java
System.out.printf("%d\n", VirtualCreature.getSpecialAttackPower());
System.out.printf("%d\n", VirtualCreature.getSpecialDefensePower());
```

As happened with class constants, Java 9 allows us to access a class method from an instance, and therefore, we can use either the class name or an instance to access a class method. The following line creates an instance of the new version of the `VirtualCreature` class named `vulpix` and prints the value returned by the `getGrowthRate` class method, accessed from this new instance. The code file for the sample is included in the `java_9_oop_chapter_04_01` folder, in the `example04_11.java` file.

```java
VirtualCreature vulpix =
    new VirtualCreature("Vulpix", 2012, "Fedora", 35);
System.out.printf("%d\n", vulpix.getGrowthRate())
```

The next screenshot shows the results of executing the previous lines in JShell:

```
jshell> System.out.printf("%d\n", VirtualCreature.getSpecialAttackPower());
35
$3 ==> java.io.PrintStream@14acaea5
|  created scratch variable $3 : PrintStream

jshell> System.out.printf("%d\n", VirtualCreature.getSpecialDefensePower());
95
$4 ==> java.io.PrintStream@14acaea5
|  created scratch variable $4 : PrintStream

jshell> VirtualCreature vulpix =
   ...>      new VirtualCreature("Vulpix", 2012, "Fedora", 35);
vulpix ==> VirtualCreature@59fa1d9b
|  created variable vulpix : VirtualCreature

jshell> System.out.printf("%d", vulpix.getGrowthRate())
10$6 ==> java.io.PrintStream@14acaea5
|  created scratch variable $6 : PrintStream
```

Test your knowledge

1. We use the `static` keyword followed by a method declaration to define:
    1. An instance method.
    2. A class method.
    3. A class constant.

2. We use the `final` static keywords followed by an initialized variable declaration to define a:
    1. Class constant.
    2. Class variable.
    3. Instance constant.

3. A class constant:
    1. Has its own and independent value for each instance of the class.
    2. Has the same value for all the instances of the class.
    3. Has the same value for all the instances of a class, unless it is accessed through the class name followed by a dot (.) and the constant name.

4.   An instance field:

1.   Has its own and independent value for each instance of the class.

2.   Has the same value for all the instances of the class.

3.   Has the same value for all the instances of a class, unless it is accessed through the class name followed by a dot (.) and the instance field name.

5.   In Java 9, `public`, `protected`, and `private` are:

1.   Three different classes defined in `java.lang`.

2.   Three equivalent access modifiers.

3.   Three different access modifiers.

Summary

In this chapter, you learned about the different members that can compose a class declaration in Java 9. We worked with instance fields, instance methods, class constants, and class methods. We worked with getters and setters, and we took advantage of access modifiers to hide data that we didn't want the users of our classes to be able to access.

We worked with virtual creatures. First, we declared a simple class and then we made it evolve with additional features. We tested how everything worked in JShell.

Now that you have learned about data encapsulation, you are ready to work with mutable and immutable versions of classes in Java 9, which is what we are going to discuss in the next chapter.

5
Mutable and Immutable Classes

In this chapter, we will learn about mutable and immutable classes. We will understand their differences and their advantages and disadvantages when building object-oriented code. We will:

- Create mutable classes
- Work with mutable objects in JShell
- Build immutable classes
- Work with immutable objects in JShell
- Understand the difference between mutating and non-mutating objects
- Learn the advantages of non-mutating objects when writing concurrent code
- Work with instances of the immutable `String` class

Creating mutable classes in Java 9

When we declare instance fields without the `final` keyword, we create a mutable instance field, which means that we can change their values for each new instance we create after the field is initialized. When we create an instance of a class that defines at least one mutable field, we create a mutable object, which is an object that can change its state after its initialization.

 A mutable object is also known as a mutating object.

For example, imagine that we have to develop a Web Service that renders elements in the 3D world and returns a high-resolution rendered scene. Such a task requires us to work with 3D vectors. First, we will work with a mutable 3D vector with three mutable fields: x, y, and z. The mutable 3D vector must provide the following features:

- Three mutable instance fields of type double: x, y, and z.

- A constructor that creates an instance by providing the initial values for the x, y, and z fields.

- A constructor that creates an instance with all the values initialized to 0, that is, x = 0, y = 0, and z = 0. A 3D vector with these values is known as an **origin vector**.

- A constructor that creates an instance with all the values initialized to a common value. For example, if we specify 3.0 as the common value, the constructor must generate an instance with x = 3.0, y = 3.0, and z = 3.0.

- An absolute method that sets each component of the 3D vector to its absolute value.

- A negate method that negates each component of the 3D vector in place.

- An add method that sets the value of the 3D vector to the sum of itself and the 3D vector received as an argument.

- A sub method that sets the value of the 3D vector to the difference of itself and the 3D vector received as an argument.

- An implementation of the toString method that prints the values of the three components of the 3D vector: x, y, and z.

The following lines declare the Vector3d class that represents the mutable version of a 3D vector in Java. The code file for the sample is included in the java_9_oop_ chapter_05_01 folder, in the example05_01.java file.

```java
public class Vector3d {
    public double x;
    public double y;
    public double z;

    Vector3d(double x, double y, double z) {
        this.x = x;
        this.y = y;
        this.z = z;
    }
```

```java
    Vector3d(double valueForXYZ) {
        this(valueForXYZ, valueForXYZ, valueForXYZ);
    }

    Vector3d() {
        this(0.0);
    }

    public void absolute() {
        x = Math.abs(x);
        y = Math.abs(y);
        z = Math.abs(z);
    }

    public void negate() {
        x = -x;
        y = -y;
        z = -z;
    }

    public void add(Vector3d vector) {
        x += vector.x;
        y += vector.y;
        z += vector.z;
    }

    public void sub(Vector3d vector) {
        x -= vector.x;
        y -= vector.y;
        z -= vector.z;
    }

    public String toString() {
        return String.format(
            "(x: %.2f, y: %.2f, z: %.2f)",
            x,
            y,
            z);
    }
}
```

The new `Vector3d` class declares three constructors whose lines are highlighted in the previous code listing. The first constructor receives three `double` arguments, x, y, and z, and initializes the fields with the same names and types with the values received in these arguments.

The second constructor receives a single `double` argument, `valueForXYZ`, and uses the `this` keyword to call the previously explained constructor with the received argument as the value for the three arguments.

 We can use the `this` keyword within a constructor to call other constructors with different arguments defined in our class.

The third constructor is a parameterless one and uses the `this` keyword to call the previously explained constructor with `0.0` as the value for the `valueForXYZ` argument. This way, the constructor allows us to build an origin vector.

Whenever we call the `absolute`, `negate`, `add`, or `sub` methods, we will mutate the instance, that is, we will change the state for the object. These methods change the values for the x, y, and z fields for the instance from which we call them.

Working with mutable objects in JShell

The following lines create a new `Vector3d` instance named `vector1` with `10.0`, `20.0`, and `30.0` for the initial values of x, y, and z. The second lines create a new `Vector3d` instance named `vector2` with `1.0`, `2.0`, and `3.0` for the initial values of x, y, and z. Then, the code calls the `System.out.println` method with `vector1` and then with `vector2` as an argument. Both calls to the `println` method will execute the `toString` method for each `Vector3d` instance to display the `String` representation of the mutable 3D vector. Then, the code calls the `add` method for `vector1` with `vector2` as an argument. The last line calls the `println` method again with `vector1` as an argument to print the new values of x, y and z after the object mutated with the call to the `add` method. The code file for the sample is included in the `java_9_oop_chapter_05_01` folder, in the `example05_01.java` file.

```
Vector3d vector1 = new Vector3d(10.0, 20.0, 30.0);
Vector3d vector2 = new Vector3d(1.0, 2.0, 3.0);
System.out.println(vector1);
System.out.println(vector2);
vector1.add(vector2);
System.out.println(vector1);
```

The following screenshot shows the results of the execution of the previous code in JShell:

```
jshell> Vector3d vector1 = new Vector3d(10.0, 20.0, 30.0);
vector1 ==> (x: 10.00, y: 20.00, z: 30.00)
|  created variable vector1 : Vector3d

jshell> Vector3d vector2 = new Vector3d(1.0, 2.0, 3.0);
vector2 ==> (x: 1.00, y: 2.00, z: 3.00)
|  created variable vector2 : Vector3d

jshell> System.out.println(vector1);
(x: 10.00, y: 20.00, z: 30.00)

jshell> System.out.println(vector2);
(x: 1.00, y: 2.00, z: 3.00)

jshell> vector1.add(vector2);

jshell> System.out.println(vector1);
(x: 11.00, y: 22.00, z: 33.00)

jshell>
```

The initial values for the `vector1` fields are `10.0` for x, `20.0` for y, and `30.0` for z. The `add` method changes the values of the three fields. Hence, the object state mutates as follows:

- `vector1.x` mutates from `10.0` to *10.0 + 1.0 = 11.0*
- `vector1.y` mutates from `20.0` to *20.0 + 2.0 = 22.0*
- `vector1.z` mutates from `30.0` to *30.0 + 3.0 = 33.0*

The values for the `vector1` fields after the call to the `add` method are `11.0` for x, `22.0` for y, and `33.0` for z. We can say that the method mutated the object's state. Thus, `vector1` is a mutable object and an instance of a mutable class.

The following lines use the three available constructors to create three instances of the `Vector3d` class named `vector3`, `vector4`, and `vector5`. Then, the next lines call the `System.out.println` method to print the values of x, y, and z after the objects were created. The code file for the sample is included in the `java_9_oop_chapter_05_01` folder, in the `example05_02.java` file.

```
Vector3d vector3 = new Vector3d();
Vector3d vector4 = new Vector3d(5.0);
Vector3d vector5 = new Vector3d(-15.5, -11.1, -8.8);
System.out.println(vector3);
System.out.println(vector4);
System.out.println(vector5);
```

The following screenshot shows the results of the execution of the previous code in JShell:

```
jshell> Vector3d vector3 = new Vector3d();
vector3 ==> (x: 0.00, y: 0.00, z: 0.00)
|  created variable vector3 : Vector3d

jshell> Vector3d vector4 = new Vector3d(5.0);
vector4 ==> (x: 5.00, y: 5.00, z: 5.00)
|  created variable vector4 : Vector3d

jshell> Vector3d vector5 = new Vector3d(-15.5, -11.1, -8.8);
vector5 ==> (x: -15.50, y: -11.10, z: -8.80)
|  created variable vector5 : Vector3d

jshell> System.out.println(vector3);
(x: 0.00, y: 0.00, z: 0.00)

jshell> System.out.println(vector4);
(x: 5.00, y: 5.00, z: 5.00)

jshell> System.out.println(vector5);
(x: -15.50, y: -11.10, z: -8.80)
```

The next lines call many methods for the previously created instances. The code file for the sample is included in the `java_9_oop_chapter_05_01` folder, in the `example05_02.java` file.

```
vector4.negate();
System.out.println(vector4);
vector3.add(vector4);
System.out.println(vector3);
vector4.absolute();
System.out.println(vector4);
vector5.sub(vector4);
System.out.println(vector5);
```

The initial value for the three `vector4` fields (x, y, and z) is 5.0. The call to the `vector4.negate` method changes the values of the three fields to -5.0.

The initial value for the three `vector3` fields (x, y, and z) is 0.0. The call to the `vector3.add` method changes the values of the three fields by the results of the sum of each component of `vector3` and `vector4`. Hence, the object state mutates as follows:

- `vector3.x` mutates from 0.0 to *0.0 + (-5.0) = -5.0*

- `vector3.y` mutates from 0.0 to *0.0 + (-5.0) = -5.0*

- `vector3.z` mutates from 0.0 to *0.0 + (-5.0) = -5.0*

The three fields for `vector3` fields are set to `-5.0` after the call to the `add` method. The call to the `vector4.absolute` method changes the values of the three fields from `-5.0` to `5.0`.

The initial values for the `vector5` fields are `-15.5` for x, `-11.1` for y, and `-8.8` for z. The call to the `vector5.sub` method changes the values of the three fields by the results of the subtraction of each component of `vector5` and `vector4`. Hence, the object state mutates as follows:

- `vector5.x` mutates from `-15.5` to *-15.5 - 5.0 = -20.5*

- `vector5.y` mutates from `-11.1` to *-11.1 - 5.0 = -16.1*

- `vector5.z` mutates from `-8.8` to *-8.8 - 5.0 = -13.8*

The following screenshot shows the results of the execution of the previous code in JShell:

```
jshell> vector4.negate();

jshell> System.out.println(vector4);
(x: -5.00, y: -5.00, z: -5.00)

jshell> vector3.add(vector4);

jshell> System.out.println(vector3);
(x: -5.00, y: -5.00, z: -5.00)

jshell> vector4.absolute();

jshell> System.out.println(vector4);
(x: 5.00, y: 5.00, z: 5.00)

jshell> vector5.sub(vector4);

jshell> System.out.println(vector5);
(x: -20.50, y: -16.10, z: -13.80)

jshell>
```

Building immutable classes in Java 9

So far, we have been working with mutable classes and mutating objects. Whenever we expose mutable fields, we create a class that will generate mutable instances. In certain scenarios, we might prefer an object that cannot change its state after it has been initialized. We can design classes to be immutable and to generate immutable instances that cannot change their state after they were created and initialized.

A typical scenario where immutable objects are extremely useful is when we work with concurrent code. Objects that cannot change their state solve many typical concurrency problems and avoid potential bugs that might be difficult to detect and solve. Because immutable objects cannot change their state, it is not possible to end up with an object with a corrupted or inconsistent state when many different threads modify it without the appropriate synchronization mechanisms.

[An immutable object is also known as a non-mutating object.]

We will create an immutable version of the previously coded `Vector3d` class to represent an immutable 3D vector. This way, we will notice the difference between a mutable class and its immutable version. The immutable 3D vector must provide the following features:

- Three immutable instance fields of type `double`: x, y, and z. The value for these fields cannot be changed after the instance is initialized or constructed.

- A constructor that creates an instance by providing the initial values for the x, y, and z immutable fields.

- A constructor that creates an instance with all the values set to 0, that is, x = 0, y = 0, and z = 0.

- A constructor that creates an instance with all the values initialized to a common value. For example, if we specify 3.0 as the common value, the constructor must generate an immutable instance with x = 3.0, y = 3.0, and z = 3.0.

- An `absolute` method that returns a new instance with each component of the new immutable 3D vector set to the absolute value of each component of the instance in which we call the method.

- A `negate` method that returns a new instance with each component of the new immutable 3D vector set to the negated value of each component of the instance in which we call the method.

- An `add` method that returns a new instance with each component of the new immutable 3D vector set to the sum of each component of the instance in which we call the method and each component of the immutable 3D vector received as an argument.

- A `sub` method that returns a new instance with each component of the new immutable 3D vector set to the subtraction of each component of the instance in which we call the method and each component of the immutable 3D vector received as an argument.

- An implementation of the `toString` method that prints the values of the three components of the 3D vector: x, y, and z.

The following lines declare the `ImmutableVector3d` class that represents the immutable version of a 3D vector in Java. The code file for the sample is included in the `java_9_oop_chapter_05_01` folder, in the `example05_03.java` file.

```java
public class ImmutableVector3d {
    public final double x;
    public final double y;
    public final double z;

    ImmutableVector3d(double x, double y, double z) {
        this.x = x;
        this.y = y;
        this.z = z;
    }

    ImmutableVector3d(double valueForXYZ) {
        this(valueForXYZ, valueForXYZ, valueForXYZ);
    }

    ImmutableVector3d() {
        this(0.0);
    }

    public ImmutableVector3d absolute() {
        return new ImmutableVector3d(
            Math.abs(x),
            Math.abs(y),
            Math.abs(z));
    }

    public ImmutableVector3d negate() {
        return new ImmutableVector3d(
            -x,
            -y,
            -z);
    }

    public ImmutableVector3d add(ImmutableVector3d vector) {
        return new ImmutableVector3d(
            x + vector.x,
            y + vector.y,
```

```
        z + vector.z);
    }

    public ImmutableVector3d sub(ImmutableVector3d vector) {
        return new ImmutableVector3d(
            x - vector.x,
            y - vector.y,
            z - vector.z);
    }

    public String toString() {
        return String.format(
            "(x: %.2f, y: %.2f, z: %.2f)",
            x,
            y,
            z);
    }
}
```

The new `ImmutableVector3d` class declares three immutable instance fields by using the `final` keyword: x, y, and z. The lines for the three constructors declared for this class are highlighted in the previous code listing. These constructors have the same code that we analyzed for the `Vector3d` class. The only difference is in the execution, because the constructors are initializing immutable instance fields that won't change their values after the initialization.

Whenever we call the `absolute`, `negate`, `add`, or `sub` methods, their code will return a new instance of the `ImmutableVector3d` class with the result of each operation. We will never mutate our instance; that is, we won't change the state for the object.

Working with immutable objects in JShell

The following lines create a new `ImmutableVector3d` instance named `vector10` with `100.0`, `200.0`, and `300.0` for the initial values of x, y, and z. The second lines create a new `ImmutableVector3d` instance named `vector20` with `11.0`, `12.0`, and `13.0` for the initial values of x, y, and z. Then, the code calls the `System.out.println` method with `vector10` and then with `vector20` as an argument. Both calls to the `println` method will execute the `toString` method for each `ImmutableVector3d` instance to display the `String` representation of the immutable 3D vector. Then, the code calls the `add` method for `vector10` with `vector20` as an argument and saves the returned `ImmutableVector3d` instance in `vector30`.

The last line calls the `println` method with `vector30` as an argument to print the values of x, y, and z for this instance that has the results of the addition operation between `vector10` and `vector20`. Enter the lines after the code that declares the `ImmutableVector3d` class. The code file for the sample is included in the `java_9_oop_chapter_05_01` folder, in the `example05_03.java` file.

```
ImmutableVector3d vector10 =
    new ImmutableVector3d(100.0, 200.0, 300.0);
ImmutableVector3d vector20 =
    new ImmutableVector3d(11.0, 12.0, 13.0);
System.out.println(vector10);
System.out.println(vector20);
ImmutableVector3d vector30 = vector10.add(vector20);
System.out.println(vector30);
```

The following screenshot shows the results of the execution of the previous code in JShell:

```
jshell> ImmutableVector3d vector10 =
   ...>      new ImmutableVector3d(100.0, 200.0, 300.0);
vector10 ==> (x: 100.00, y: 200.00, z: 300.00)
|  created variable vector10 : ImmutableVector3d

jshell> ImmutableVector3d vector20 =
   ...>      new ImmutableVector3d(11.0, 12.0, 13.0);
vector20 ==> (x: 11.00, y: 12.00, z: 13.00)
|  created variable vector20 : ImmutableVector3d

jshell> System.out.println(vector10);
(x: 100.00, y: 200.00, z: 300.00)

jshell> System.out.println(vector20);
(x: 11.00, y: 12.00, z: 13.00)

jshell> ImmutableVector3d vector30 = vector10.add(vector20);
vector30 ==> (x: 111.00, y: 212.00, z: 313.00)
|  created variable vector30 : ImmutableVector3d

jshell> System.out.println(vector30);
(x: 111.00, y: 212.00, z: 313.00)

jshell>
```

As a result of the `add` method, we have another immutable instance named `vector30` whose field values are 111.0 for x, 212.0 for y, and 313.0 for z. As a result of calling each method that computes an operation, we will have another immutable instance.

The following lines use the three available constructors to create three instances of the `ImmutableVector3d` class named `vector40`, `vector50`, and `vector60`. Then, the next lines call the `System.out.println` method to print the values of x, y, and z after the objects were created. The code file for the sample is included in the `java_9_oop_chapter_05_01` folder, in the `example05_03.java` file.

```
ImmutableVector3d vector40 =
    new ImmutableVector3d();
ImmutableVector3d vector50 =
    new ImmutableVector3d(-5.0);
ImmutableVector3d vector60 =
    new ImmutableVector3d(8.0, 9.0, 10.0);
System.out.println(vector40);
System.out.println(vector50);
System.out.println(vector60);
```

The following screenshot shows the results of the execution of the previous code in JShell:

```
jshell> ImmutableVector3d vector40 = new ImmutableVector3d();
vector40 ==> (x: 0.00, y: 0.00, z: 0.00)
|  created variable vector40 : ImmutableVector3d

jshell> ImmutableVector3d vector50 = new ImmutableVector3d(-5.0);
vector50 ==> (x: -5.00, y: -5.00, z: -5.00)
|  created variable vector50 : ImmutableVector3d

jshell> ImmutableVector3d vector60 = new ImmutableVector3d(8.0, 9.0, 10.0);
vector60 ==> (x: 8.00, y: 9.00, z: 10.00)
|  created variable vector60 : ImmutableVector3d

jshell> System.out.println(vector40);
(x: 0.00, y: 0.00, z: 0.00)

jshell> System.out.println(vector50);
(x: -5.00, y: -5.00, z: -5.00)

jshell> System.out.println(vector60);
(x: 8.00, y: 9.00, z: 10.00)

jshell>
```

The next lines call many methods for the previously created instances and generate new instances of the ImmutableVector3d class. The code file for the sample is included in the java_9_oop_chapter_05_01 folder, in the example05_03.java file.

```
ImmutableVector3d vector70 = vector50.negate();
System.out.println(vector70);
ImmutableVector3d vector80 = vector40.add(vector70);
System.out.println(vector80);
ImmutableVector3d vector90 = vector70.absolute();
System.out.println(vector90);
ImmutableVector3d vector100 = vector60.sub(vector90);
System.out.println(vector100);
```

The initial value for the three vector50 fields (x, y, and z) is -5.0. The call to the vector50.negate method returns a new ImmutableVector3d instance that the code saves in vector70. The new instance has 5.0 as the value for the three fields (x, y, and z).

The initial value for the three vector40 fields (x, y, and z) is 0. The call to the vector40.add method, with vector70 as an argument, returns a new ImmutableVector3d instance that the code saves in vector80. The new instance has 5.0 as the value for the three fields (x, y, and z).

The call to the vector70.absolute method returns a new ImmutableVector3d instance that the code saves in vector90. The new instance has 5.0 as the value for the three fields (x, y, and z). The absolute values for the fields were the same as the original values, but the code still generated a new instance.

The initial values for the vector60 fields are 8.0 for x, 9.0 for y, and 10.0 for z. The call to the vector60.sub method with vector90 as an argument returns a new ImmutableVector3d instance that the code saves in vector100. The values for the vector100 fields are 3.0 for x, 4.0 for y, and 5.0 for z.

The following screenshot shows the results of the execution of the previous code in JShell:

```
jshell> ImmutableVector3d vector70 = vector50.negate();
vector70 ==> (x: 5.00, y: 5.00, z: 5.00)
|  created variable vector70 : ImmutableVector3d

jshell> System.out.println(vector70);
(x: 5.00, y: 5.00, z: 5.00)

jshell> ImmutableVector3d vector80 = vector40.add(vector70);
vector80 ==> (x: 5.00, y: 5.00, z: 5.00)
|  created variable vector80 : ImmutableVector3d

jshell> System.out.println(vector80);
(x: 5.00, y: 5.00, z: 5.00)

jshell> ImmutableVector3d vector90 = vector70.absolute();
vector90 ==> (x: 5.00, y: 5.00, z: 5.00)
|  created variable vector90 : ImmutableVector3d

jshell> System.out.println(vector90);
(x: 5.00, y: 5.00, z: 5.00)

jshell> ImmutableVector3d vector100 = vector60.sub(vector90);
vector100 ==> (x: 3.00, y: 4.00, z: 5.00)
|  created variable vector100 : ImmutableVector3d

jshell> System.out.println(vector100);
(x: 3.00, y: 4.00, z: 5.00)

jshell>
```

Understanding the differences between mutating and non-mutating objects

The immutable version adds an overhead compared with the mutable version because it is necessary to create a new instance of the class as a result of calling the absolute, negate, add, or sub methods. The previously analyzed mutable class named Vector3D just changed the values for the fields, and it wasn't necessary to generate a new instance. Hence, the memory footprint for the immutable version is higher than the mutable version.

The immutable class named `ImmutableVector3d` has both a memory and performance overhead compared with the mutable version. It is more expensive to create a new instance than to change the values of a few fields. However, as previously explained, when we work with concurrent code, it makes sense to pay for the extra overhead to avoid potential issues caused by mutable objects. We just have to make sure we analyze the advantages and tradeoffs in order to decide which is the most convenient way to code our specific classes.

Now, we will write a few lines that work with the mutable version and we will generate the equivalent code for the immutable version. This way, we will be able to make a simple yet illustrative comparison of the differences between the two pieces of code.

The following lines create a new `Vector3d` instance named `mutableVector3d1` with `-30.5`, `-15.5`, and `-12.5` for the initial values of x, y, and z. Then, the code prints the `String` representation for the new instance, calls the `absolute` method, and prints the `String` representation of the mutated object. The code file for the sample is included in the `java_9_oop_chapter_05_01` folder, in the `example05_04.java` file.

```
// Mutable version
Vector3d mutableVector3d1 =
    new Vector3d(-30.5, -15.5, -12.5);
System.out.println(mutableVector3d1);
mutableVector3d1.absolute();
System.out.println(mutableVector3d1);
```

The following screenshot shows the results of the execution of the previous code in JShell:

```
jshell> Vector3d mutableVector3d1 =
   ...>     new Vector3d(-30.5, -15.5, -12.5);
mutableVector3d1 ==> (x: -30.50, y: -15.50, z: -12.50)
|  created variable mutableVector3d1 : Vector3d

jshell> System.out.println(mutableVector3d1);
(x: -30.50, y: -15.50, z: -12.50)

jshell> mutableVector3d1.absolute();

jshell> System.out.println(mutableVector3d1);
(x: 30.50, y: 15.50, z: 12.50)
```

The following lines create a new `ImmutableVector3d` instance named `immutableVector3d1` with `-30.5`, `-15.5`, and `-12.5` for the initial values of x, y, and z. Then, the code prints the `String` representation for the new instance, calls the `absolute` method that generates a new `ImmutableVector3d` instance named `immutableVector3d2`, and prints the `String` representation of the new object. The code file for the sample is included in the `java_9_oop_chapter_05_01` folder, in the `example05_04.java` file.

```
// Immutable version
ImmutableVector3d immutableVector3d1 =
    new ImmutableVector3d(-30.5, -15.5, -12.5);
System.out.println(immutableVector3d1);
ImmutableVector3d immutableVector3d2 =
    immutableVector3d1.absolute();
System.out.println(immutableVector3d2);
```

The following screenshot shows the results of the execution of the previous code in JShell:

```
jshell> ImmutableVector3d immutableVector3d1 =
   ...>      new ImmutableVector3d(-30.5, -15.5, -12.5);
immutableVector3d1 ==> (x: -30.50, y: -15.50, z: -12.50)
|  created variable immutableVector3d1 : ImmutableVector3d

jshell> System.out.println(immutableVector3d1);
(x: -30.50, y: -15.50, z: -12.50)

jshell> ImmutableVector3d immutableVector3d2 =
   ...>      immutableVector3d1.absolute();
immutableVector3d2 ==> (x: 30.50, y: 15.50, z: 12.50)
|  created variable immutableVector3d2 : ImmutableVector3d

jshell> System.out.println(immutableVector3d2);
(x: 30.50, y: 15.50, z: 12.50)

jshell>
```

The mutable version works with a single `Vector3d` instance. The constructor for the `Vector3d` class is executed only once. The original instance mutates its state when we called the `absolute` method.

The immutable version works with two `ImmutableVector3d` instances, and therefore, the memory footprint is higher than the mutable version. The constructor for the `ImmutableVector3d` class is executed twice. The first instance didn't mutate its state when we called the `absolute` method.

Learning the advantages of non-mutating objects when writing concurrent code

Now, let's imagine we are writing concurrent code that has to access the fields of the previously created instances. First, we will analyze the problems with the mutable version and then we will understand the advantage of working with the non-mutating object.

Imagine that we have two threads in which the code has a reference to the instance saved in `mutableVector3d1`. The first thread calls the `absolute` method for this mutating object. The first line of code for the `absolute` method assigns the result of `Math.abs` with the actual value of x as an argument to the x mutable field.

At this point, the method didn't finish its execution and the next line of code won't be able to access the values. However, concurrent code running in another thread that has a reference to this instance might access the values for the x, y and z fields before the `absolute` method finishes the execution. The object is in a corrupt state because the values for the fields are 30.5 for x, -15.5 for y, and -12.5 for z. These values do not represent the 3D vector that we will have when the `absolute` method finishes its execution. The fact that there are many pieces of code running concurrently and have access to the same instance without any kind of synchronization mechanism generates the issue.

Concurrent programming and threaded programming are complex topics that deserve an entire book. There are synchronization mechanisms to avoid the previously mentioned issue and make the class thread-safe. However, another solution is the usage of immutable classes that generate non-mutating objects.

If we use the immutable version, the two threads can have the reference to the same initial instance. However, when one of the threads calls the `absolute` method, the original 3D vector won't mutate, and therefore the previous problem will never happen. The other thread will continue working with its reference to the original 3D vector, with its original state. The thread that called the `absolute` method will generate a new instance that is completely independent of the original one.

Again, it is very important to understand that this topic deserves an entire book. However, it is important to understand why immutable classes might be a special requirement in specific scenarios where the instance will participate in concurrent code.

Working with instances of the immutable String class

The String class, specifically the java.lang.String class, represents character strings and is an immutable class that generates non-mutating objects. Hence, the methods provided by the String class do not mutate the object.

For example, the following lines create a new String, that is, a new instance of the java.lang.String class named welcomeMessage with an initial value of "Welcome to Virtual Creatures Land". Then, the code makes many calls to System.out.println with welcomeMessage followed by a different method as an argument. First, we call the toUpperCase method to generate a new String with all the characters converted to uppercase. Then, we call the toLowerCase method to generate a new String with all the characters converted to lowercase. Then, we call the replaceAll method to generate a new String in which the spaces were replaced by a hyphen (-). Finally, we call the System.out.println method again with welcomeMessage as an argument to check the value of the original String. The code file for the sample is included in the java_9_oop_chapter_05_01 folder, in the example05_05.java file.

```
String welcomeMessage = "Welcome to Virtual Creatures Land";
System.out.println(welcomeMessage);
System.out.println(welcomeMessage.toUpperCase());
System.out.println(welcomeMessage.toLowerCase());
System.out.println(welcomeMessage.replaceAll(" ", "-"));
System.out.println(welcomeMessage);
```

The following screenshot shows the results of the execution of the previous code in JShell:

```
jshell> String welcomeMessage = "Welcome to Virtual Creatures Land";
welcomeMessage ==> "Welcome to Virtual Creatures Land"
|  created variable welcomeMessage : String

jshell> System.out.println(welcomeMessage);
Welcome to Virtual Creatures Land

jshell> System.out.println(welcomeMessage.toUpperCase());
WELCOME TO VIRTUAL CREATURES LAND

jshell> System.out.println(welcomeMessage.toLowerCase());
welcome to virtual creatures land

jshell> System.out.println(welcomeMessage.replaceAll(" ", "-"));
Welcome-to-Virtual-Creatures-Land

jshell> System.out.println(welcomeMessage);
Welcome to Virtual Creatures Land

jshell>
```

The welcomeMessage string never changed its value. The calls to the toUpperCase, toLowerCase, and replaceAll methods generated and returned a new String instance for each of them.

No matter which method we call for a String instance, it won't mutate the object. Thus, we can say String is an immutable class.

Creating the immutable version of an existing mutable class

In the previous chapter, we created a mutable class named VirtualCreature. We provided setter methods to change the values for the hat, visibilityLevel, and birthYear fields. We were able to change the birthYear by calling the setAge method.

Virtual creatures change their age, hat, and visibility level after they evolve. When they evolve, they become a different creature, and therefore, it would make sense to generate a new instance after this evolution happens. Thus, we will create the immutable version of the VirtualCreature class and we will call it ImmutableVirtualCreature.

The following lines show the code for the new `ImmutableVirtualCreature` class. The code file for the sample is included in the `java_9_oop_chapter_05_01` folder, in the `example05_06.java` file.

```java
import java.time.Year;

public class ImmutableVirtualCreature {
    public final String name;
    public final int birthYear;
    public final String hat;
    public final int visibilityLevel;

    ImmutableVirtualCreature(final String name,
        int birthYear,
        String hat,
        int visibilityLevel) {
        this.name = name;
        this.birthYear = birthYear;
        this.hat = hat.toUpperCase();
        this.visibilityLevel =
            getValidVisibilityLevel(visibilityLevel);
    }

    private int getCurrentYear() {
        return Year.now().getValue();
    }

    private int getValidVisibilityLevel(int levelToValidate) {
        return Math.min(Math.max(levelToValidate, 0), 100);
    }

    public int getAge() {
        return getCurrentYear() - birthYear;
    }

    public ImmutableVirtualCreature evolveToAge(int age) {
        int newBirthYear = getCurrentYear() - age;
        return new ImmutableVirtualCreature(
            name,
            newBirthYear,
            hat,
            visibilityLevel);
    }
}
```

```
    public ImmutableVirtualCreature evolveToVisibilityLevel(
        final int visibilityLevel) {
        int newVisibilityLevel =
            getValidVisibilityLevel(visibilityLevel);
        return new ImmutableVirtualCreature(
            name,
            birthYear,
            hat,
            newVisibilityLevel);
    }
}
```

The `ImmutableVirtualCreature` class declares four public immutable instance fields with the `final` keyword: name, birthYear, hat, and visibilityLevel. We won't be able to change the values for any of these fields after the instance has been initialized or constructed.

The constructor generates an uppercased `String` from the `String` received in the hat argument and stores it in the public hat immutable field. We had a specific validation for the visibility level, and therefore, the constructor calls a new private method named getValidVisibilityLevel, with the value received in the visibilityLevel argument, to assign a valid value to the immutable field with the same name.

We don't have setter methods anymore because we aren't able to change the values for the immutable fields after they were initialized. The class declares the following two new public methods that return a new `ImmutableVirtualCreature` instance:

- evolveToAge: This method receives the desired age for the evolved virtual creature in the age argument. The code calculates the birth year based on the received age and the current year, and returns a new `ImmutableVirtualCreature` instance with the new initialization values.

- evolveToVisibilityLevel: This method receives the desired visibility level for the evolved virtual creature in the visibilityLevel argument. The code calls the getValidVisibilityLevel method to generate a valid visibility level based on the received value, and returns a new `ImmutableVirtualCreature` instance with the new initialization values.

The following lines create an instance of the `ImmutableVirtualCreature` class named `meowth1`. Then the code calls the `meowth1.evolveToAge` method with 3 as the value for the `age` argument and saves the new `ImmutableVirtualCreature` instance returned by this method in the `meowth2` variable. The code prints the value returned by the `meowth2.getAge` method. Finally, the code calls the `meowth2.evolveToVisibilityLevel` method with 25 as the value for the `invisibilityLevel` argument and saves the new `ImmutableVirtualCreature` instance returned by this method in the `meowth3` variable. Then, the code prints the value stored in the `meowth3.visibilityLevel` immutable field. The code file for the sample is included in the `java_9_oop_chapter_05_01` folder, in the `example05_06.java` file.

```
ImmutableVirtualCreature meowth1 =
    new ImmutableVirtualCreature(
        "Meowth", 2010, "Baseball cap", 35);
ImmutableVirtualCreature meowth2 =
    meowth1.evolveToAge(3);
System.out.printf("%d\n", meowth2.getAge());
ImmutableVirtualCreature meowth3 =
    meowth2.evolveToVisibilityLevel(25);
System.out.printf("%d\n", meowth3.visibilityLevel);
```

The following screenshot shows the results of the execution of the previous code in JShell:

```
jshell> ImmutableVirtualCreature meowth1 =
   ...>     new ImmutableVirtualCreature(
   ...>         "Meowth", 2010, "Baseball cap", 35);
meowth1 ==> ImmutableVirtualCreature@4b9e13df
|  created variable meowth1 : ImmutableVirtualCreature

jshell> ImmutableVirtualCreature meowth2 =
   ...>     meowth1.evolveToAge(3);
meowth2 ==> ImmutableVirtualCreature@31dc339b
|  created variable meowth2 : ImmutableVirtualCreature

jshell> System.out.printf("%d\n", meowth2.getAge());
3
$5 ==> java.io.PrintStream@52a86356
|  created scratch variable $5 : PrintStream

jshell> ImmutableVirtualCreature meowth3 =
   ...>     meowth2.evolveToVisibilityLevel(25);
meowth3 ==> ImmutableVirtualCreature@78c03f1f
|  created variable meowth3 : ImmutableVirtualCreature

jshell> System.out.printf("%d\n", meowth3.visibilityLevel);
25
$7 ==> java.io.PrintStream@52a86356
|  created scratch variable $7 : PrintStream

jshell>
```

Test your knowledge

1. A class that exposes mutable fields will:

    1. Generate immutable instances.

    2. Generate mutable instances.

    3. Generate mutable classes but immutable instances.

2. Which of the following keywords, used within a constructor, allows us to call other constructors with different arguments defined in our class:

    1. `self`

    2. `constructor`

    3. `this`

3. An object that cannot change its state after it has been initialized is known as:

    1. A mutable object.

    2. An immutable object.

    3. An interface object.

4. In Java 9, `java.lang.String` generates:

    1. An immutable object.

    2. A mutable object.

    3. An interface object.

5. If we call the `toUpperCase` method for a `java.lang.String`, the method will:

    1. Convert the existing `String` to uppercase characters and change its state.

    2. Return a new `String` with the contents of the original `String` converted to uppercase characters.

    3. Return a new `String` with the contents of the original `String`.

Summary

In this chapter, you learned the differences between mutable and immutable classes and the mutating and non-mutating instances that they generate. We declared mutable and immutable versions of a 3D vector class in Java 9.

Then, we took advantage of JShell to easily work with the mutating and non-mutating instances of these classes and we analyzed the difference between changing the state of an object and returning a new object whenever we have to change its state. We analyzed the advantages and disadvantages of mutable and immutable classes and we understood why the latter are useful when working with concurrent code.

Now that you have learned about mutable and immutable classes, you are ready to work with inheritance, abstraction, extension, and specialization, which are the topics we are going to discuss in the next chapter.

6
Inheritance, Abstraction, Extension, and Specialization

In this chapter, we will learn about one of the most important pillars of object-oriented programming in Java 9: inheritance. We will work with examples on how to create class hierarchies, override and overload methods, and work with the constructors defined in superclasses. We will:

- Create class hierarchies to abstract and specialize behavior
- Understand inheritance
- Create an abstract base class
- Declare classes that inherit from another class
- Overload constructors
- Override instance methods
- Overload instance methods

Creating class hierarchies to abstract and specialize behavior

In the previous chapters, we have been creating classes in Java 9 to generate blueprints for real-life objects. We declared classes and then we created instances of these classes in JShell. Now it is time to take advantage of many of the most advanced features of object-oriented programming included in Java 9 and start designing a hierarchy of classes instead of working with isolated classes. First, we will design all the classes that we need based on the requirements, and then we will use the features available in Java 9 to code the designed classes.

We worked with classes to represent virtual creatures. Now, let's imagine that we have to develop a complex Web Service that requires us to work with dozens of types of virtual animal. Many of these virtual animals will be similar to pets and domestic animals in the first stage of the project. The requirements specify that our Web Service will start working with the following four virtual animals that are going to be similar to the domestic animal species:

- **Horse (Equus ferus caballus)**. Do not confuse this with a wild horse (Equus ferus). We will have male and female horses, and female horses might be pregnant. In addition, we will have to work with the following three specific horse breeds: American Quarter Horse, Shire Horse, and Thoroughbred.

- **Cockatiel (Nymphicus hollandicus)**. This bird is also known as quarrion or weiro.

- **Maine Coon**. This is one of the largest domesticated breeds of cat (Felis silvestris catus).

- **Domestic rabbit (Oryctolagus cuniculus)**. This rabbit is also known as European rabbit.

The previous list includes the scientific name for each domestic animal species. We will definitely work with the most common name for each species and just have the scientific name as a class constant of type `String`. Hence, we won't have a complex class name, such as `VirtualEquusFerusCaballus`, but we will use `VirtualHorse` instead.

Our first requirements specify that we have to work with a limited number of breeds for the previously enumerated four domestic animal species. Additionally, in the future it will be necessary to work with other members of the listed domestic animal species, other domestic mammals, additional domestic birds, specific horse breeds, and even reptiles and birds that don't belong to the domestic animal species. Our object-oriented design must be ready to be expanded for the future requirements, as always happens in real-life projects. In fact, we will use this example to understand how object-oriented programming makes it easy to expand an existing design to consider future requirements.

We don't want to model a complete representation of the animal kingdom and its classification. We will just create the necessary classes to have a flexible model that can be easily expanded based on future requirements. The animal kingdom is extremely complex. We will keep our focus on just a few members of this huge family.

One of the main goals for the following examples is to learn that object-oriented programming doesn't sacrifice flexibility. We will start with a simple class hierarchy that we will expand as the required features complexity increases and we have more information about these new requirements. Let's remember that requirements aren't fixed and that we always must add new features, and make changes to the existing classes based on these new features.

We will create a hierarchy of classes to represent a complex classification of virtual animals and their breeds. When we extend a class, we create a subclass of this class. The following list enumerates the classes that we will create and their descriptions:

- `VirtualAnimal`: This class generalizes all the members of the animal kingdom. Horses, cats, birds, rabbits, and reptiles have one thing in common: they are animals. Hence, it makes sense to create a class that will be the baseline for the different classes of virtual animals that we may have to represent in our object-oriented design.

- `VirtualMammal`: This class generalizes all the mammalian virtual animals. Mammals are different from insects, birds, amphibians, and reptiles. We already know that we can have female horses and that they can be pregnant. We also know that we will have to model reptiles and birds, and therefore, we create a `VirtualMammal` class that extends `VirtualAnimal` and becomes a subclass of it.

- `VirtualBird`: This class generalizes all the birds. Birds are different from mammals, insects, amphibians, and reptiles. We already know that we will also have to model reptiles. A Cockatiel is a bird, and therefore, we will create a `VirtualBird` class at the same level as `VirtualMammal`.

- `VirtualDomesticMammal`: This class extends the `VirtualMammal` class. Let's do some research and we will realize that the tiger (Panthera tigris) is the largest and heaviest living species of the cat family. A tiger is a cat, but it is completely different from a Maine Coon, which is a small domestic cat. The initial requirements specified that we work with both virtual domestic and virtual wild animals, so we will create a class that generalizes all the virtual domestic mammal animals. In the future, we will have a `VirtualWildMammal` subclass that will generalize all the virtual wild mammalian animals.

- `VirtualDomesticBird`: This class extends the `VirtualBird` class. Let's do some research and we will realize that the ostrich (Struthio camelus) is the largest living bird. An ostrich is a bird, but it is completely different from a Cockatiel, which is a small domestic bird. We will work with both virtual domestic and virtual wild birds, so we will create a class that generalizes all virtual domestic birds. In the future, we will have a `VirtualWildBird` class that will generalize all virtual wild birds.

- `VirtualHorse`: This class extends the `VirtualDomesticMammal` class. We could go on specializing the `VirtualDomesticMammal` class with additional subclasses until we reach a `VirtualHorse` class. For example, we might create a `VirtualHerbivoreDomesticMammal` subclass and then make the `VirtualHorse` class inherit from it. However, the kind of Web Service we have to develop doesn't require any intermediary class between `VirtualDomesticMammal` and `VirtualHorse`. The `VirtualHorse` class generalizes the fields and methods required for a virtual horse in our application. The different subclasses of the `VirtualHorse` class will represent the diverse families of the virtual horse breed.

- `VirtualDomesticRabbit`: This class extends the `VirtualDomesticMammal` class. The `VirtualDomesticRabbit` class generalizes all the fields and methods required for a virtual domestic rabbit in our application.

- `VirtualDomesticCat`: This class extends the `VirtualDomesticMammal` class. The `VirtualDomesticCat` class generalizes all the fields and methods required for a virtual domestic cat in our application.

- `AmericanQuarterHorse`: This class extends the `VirtualHorse` class. The `AmericanQuarterHorse` class generalizes all the fields and methods required for a virtual horse that belongs to the American Quarter Horse breed.

- `ShireHorse`: This class extends the `VirtualHorse` class. The `ShireHorse` class generalizes all the fields and methods required for a virtual horse that belongs to the Shire Horse breed.

- `Thoroughbred`: This class extends the `VirtualHorse` class. The `Thoroughbred` class generalizes all the fields and methods required for a virtual horse that belongs to the Thoroughbred breed.

- `Cockatiel`: This class extends the `VirtualDomesticBird` class. The `Cockatiel` class generalizes all the fields and methods required for a virtual domestic bird that belongs to the Cockatiel family.

- `MaineCoon`: This class extends the `VirtualDomesticCat` class. The `MaineCoon` class generalizes all the fields and methods required for a virtual domestic cat that belongs to the Maine Coon breed.

The following table shows each of the classes from the previous list with its superclass, parent class, or supertype.

Subclass, child class, or subtype	Superclass, parent class, or supertype
VirtualMammal	VirtualAnimal
VirtualBird	VirtualAnimal
VirtualDomesticMammal	VirtualMammal
VirtualDomesticBird	VirtualBird
VirtualHorse	VirtualDomesticMammal
VirtualDomesticRabbit	VirtualDomesticMammal
VirtualDomesticCat	VirtualDomesticMammal
AmericanQuarterHorse	VirtualHorse
ShireHorse	VirtualHorse
Thoroughbred	VirtualHorse
Cockatiel	VirtualDomesticBird
MaineCoon	VirtualDomesticCat

The following UML diagram shows the previous classes organized in a class hierarchy. The class names that use italic text format indicate that they are abstract classes. Notice that the diagram doesn't include any members, just the class names. We will add the members later.

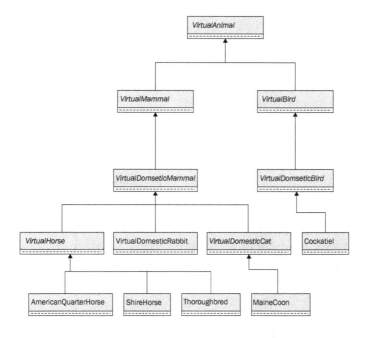

Understanding inheritance

When a class inherits from another class, it inherits all the members that compose the parent class, which is also known as the **superclass**. The class that inherits the elements is known as a **subclass** of the superclass. For example, the `VirtualBird` subclass inherits all the instance fields, class fields, instance methods, and class methods defined in the `VirtualAnimal` superclass.

> In Java 9, a subclass doesn't inherit any constructor from its superclass. However, it is possible to call the constructors defined in the superclass and we will do this in the next examples. Only the usage of the `private` access modifier in any constructor defined in a superclass can make it impossible for a subclass to call this constructor.

The `VirtualAnimal` abstract class is the baseline for our class hierarchy. We say that it is an **abstract class** because we cannot create instances of the `VirtualAnimal` class. Instead, we must create instances of the specific subclasses of `VirtualAnimal`, any subclass that isn't an abstract class. The classes that we can use to create instances of them are known as **concrete classes** or just classes in most cases. Java 9 allows us to declare classes as abstract classes when they aren't intended to generate instances.

> We cannot create instances of an abstract class by using the new keyword followed by the class name.

We require each `VirtualAnimal` to specify its age but we don't need to specify any name for them. We put names to domestic animals only. Hence, we will have to specify an age value when we create any `VirtualAnimal`, that is, any instance of any `VirtualAnimal` subclass. The class will define an `age` field and print a message whenever a virtual animal is being created.

But wait; we just explained that we are talking about an abstract class and that Java won't allow us to create an instance of an abstract class. We cannot create an instance of the `VirtualAnimal` abstract class but we will be able to create an instance of any concrete class that has `VirtualAnimal` as a superclass and this subclass can end up calling the constructor defined in the `VirtualAnimal` abstract class. It sounds a bit complicated but we will easily understand the situation after we code the classes and run the examples in JShell. We will print messages in each constructor we define to make it easy to understand what happens when we create an instance of a concrete class that has one or more superclasses, including one or more abstract superclasses. All the instances of the subclasses of `VirtualAnimal` will be instances of `VirtualAnimal` too.

The VirtualAnimal abstract class will define abstract class methods and abstract instance methods. An **abstract class method** is a class method that is declared without an implementation. An **abstract instance method**, also known as an abstract method, is an instance method that is declared without an implementation.

When we declare any of the two types of abstract methods, we only declare the arguments (if any) and then put a semicolon (;). We don't use curly braces at all. We can only declare abstract methods in an abstract class. A concrete subclass of any abstract class must provide an implementation for all the inherited abstract methods to become a class that we can use to create instances with the new keyword.

The VirtualAnimal class will declare the following seven abstract methods that fulfill requirements that are going to be common to all the members of a specific family or type. The class will just declare their required arguments without an implementation for the method. The subclasses will be responsible for fulfilling the explained requirements.

- isAbleToFly: This returns a boolean value indicating whether the virtual animal is able to fly.

- isRideable: This returns a boolean value indicating whether the virtual animal is rideable. A rideable animal is capable of being ridden over.

- isHerbivore: This returns a boolean value indicating whether the virtual animal is herbivore.

- isCarnivore: This returns a boolean value indicating whether the virtual animal is carnivore.

- getAverageNumberOfBabies: This returns the average number of babies at a time that are usually born for the virtual animal type.

- getBaby: This returns a String representation of a baby for the virtual animal type.

- getAsciiArt: This returns a String with the ASCII art (text-based visual art) that represents the virtual animal.

The `VirtualAnimal` class will define the following five methods that fulfill the requirements for each instance. These will be concrete methods that will be coded in the `VirtualAnimal` class and inherited by all its subclasses. Some of these methods call the previously explained abstract methods. We will understand how this works in detail later.

- `printAsciiArt`: This prints the `String` returned by the `getAsciiArt` method.

- `isYoungerThan`: This returns a `boolean` value indicating whether the `age` value for the `VirtualAnimal` is lower than the age for the `VirtualAnimal` instance received as an argument.

- `isOlderThan`: This returns a `boolean` value indicating whether the `age` value for the `VirtualAnimal` class is greater than the age for the `VirtualAnimal` instance received as an argument.

- `printAge`: This prints the `age` value for the virtual animal.

- `printAverageNumberOfBabies`: This prints a representation of the average number of babies at a time that are usually born for the virtual animal. This method will take into account the value returned by the `getAverageNumberOfBabies` method that is going to be implemented in the different concrete subclasses.

The `VirtualMammal` class inherits from `VirtualAnimal`. We will have to specify its age and whether it is pregnant or not when we create a new `VirtualMammal` instance. The class inherits the `age` property from the `VirtualAnimal` superclass, so it is only necessary to add a field to specify whether the virtual mammal is pregnant or not. Note that we will not specify the gender at any time in order to keep things simple. If we added gender, we would need a validation to avoid a male being pregnant. Right now, our focus is on inheritance. The class will display a message whenever a virtual mammalian animal is created; that is, whenever its constructor is executed.

Each class inherits from one class, and therefore, each new class we will define has just one superclass. In this case, we will always work with **single inheritance**. In Java, a class cannot inherit from multiple classes.

The VirtualDomesticMammal class inherits from VirtualMammal. We will have to specify its name and its favorite toy when we create a new VirtualDomesticMammal instance. We put names to any domestic mammal and they always pick a favorite toy. It is true that sometimes they just choose an object that satisfies their appetite for destruction. In many cases, the favorite toy is not exactly the toy we would like them to pick (our shoes, sneakers, flip flops, or electronic devices), but let's keep the focus on our classes. We won't be able to change the name but we can change the favorite toy. We never change the name for any domestic mammal, but we can definitely force it to change its favorite toy. The class displays a message whenever a virtual domestic mammalian animal is created.

The VirtualDomesticMammal class will declare a talk instance method that will display a message indicating the virtual domestic mammal's name concatenated with the message "says something". Each subclass must make the specific domestic mammal talk in a different way. A parrot can really talk, but we will consider a horse's nicker and a rabbit's tooth purring as if they were talking. Notice that, in this case, the talk instance method has a concrete implementation in the VirtualDomesticMammal class and it is not an abstract instance method. The subclasses will be able to provide a different implementation for this method.

The VirtualHorse class inherits from VirtualDomesticMammal and implements all the abstract methods inherited from the VirtualAnimal superclass except getBaby and getAsciiArt. These two methods will be implemented in each subclass of VirtualHorse that determines a horse breed.

We want horses to be able to neigh and nicker. Thus, we need both a neigh and a nicker method. Horses usually neigh when they are angry and they nicker when they are happy. It is a bit more complex than this, but we will keep things simple for our example.

The neigh method has to allow a virtual horse to do the following things:

- Neigh just once
- Neigh a specific number of times
- Neigh to another virtual domestic mammal that has a name just once
- Neigh to another virtual domestic mammal that has a name a specific number of times

The `nicker` method has to allow a virtual horse to do the following things:

- Nicker just once
- Nicker a specific number of times
- Nicker to another virtual domestic mammal that has a name just once
- Nicker to another virtual domestic mammal that has a name a specific number of times

In addition, a horse can neigh or nicker either happily or angrily. We can have just one `neigh` method with default values for many of the arguments or many `neigh` methods. Java 9 provides many mechanisms to solve the challenges of the different ways in which a virtual horse must be able to neigh. We will apply the same solution for both the `neigh` and `nicker` methods.

When we call the `talk` method for any virtual horse, we want it to nicker happily once. We don't want to display the message defined in the `talk` method introduced in the `VirtualDomesticMammal` class. Thus, the `VirtualHorse` class must overwrite the inherited `talk` method with its own definition.

We want to know the breed to which a virtual horse belongs. Thus, we will define a `getBreed` abstract method. Each subclass of `VirtualHorse` must return the appropriate `String` with a name when this method is called. The `VirtualHorse` class will define a method named `printBreed` that uses the `getBreed` method to retrieve the name and print the breed.

At this point, all the classes we have mentioned are abstract classes. We cannot create instances of them. The `AmericanQuarterHorse`, `ShireHorse`, and `Thoroughbred` classes inherit from the `VirtualHorse` class and implement the inherited `getBaby`, `getAsciiArt`, and `getBreed` methods. In addition, their constructors will print a message indicating that we are creating an instance of the respective class. The three classes are concrete classes and we can create instances of them.

We will work with the `VirtualBird`, `VirtualDomesticBird`, `Cockatiel`, `VirtualDomesticCat`, and `MaineCoon` classes later. First, we will create the base `VirtualAnimal` abstract class in Java 9, and then we will use simple inheritance to create the subclasses up to the `VirtualHorse` class. We will override methods and overload methods to fulfill all the requirements. We will take advantage of polymorphism, which is a very important feature in object-oriented programming that we will understand while working with the created classes in JShell. Of course, we will dive deeply into many of the topics introduced while analyzing the different classes.

The following UML diagram shows the members for all the abstract classes we will code in this chapter: `VirtualAnimal`, `VirtualMammal`, `VirtualDomesticMammal`, and `VirtualHorse`. We will code the other classes in the next chapter and we will add their members to the diagram later. We use the italic text format to indicate abstract methods. Remember that public members have a plus sign (**+**) as a prefix. One class has a protected member that uses a hash as a prefix (**#**). We will use the bold text format to indicate a method that overrides an existing method in a superclass. In this case, the `VirtualHorse` class overrides the `talk()` method.

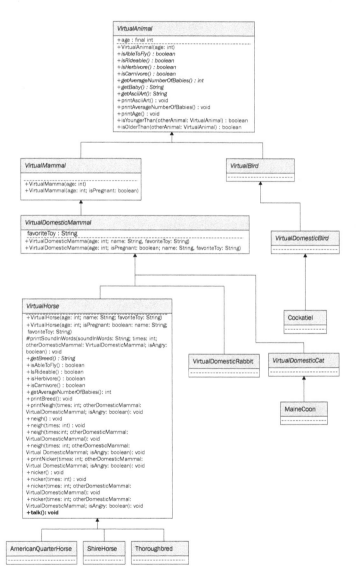

In the previous UML diagram we will notice the following conventions. We will use these conventions in all the UML diagrams that include class members.

- The constructors have the same name as the classes and do not specify any return type. They are always the first methods listed in the methods section.

- The type for a field is indicated after the field name separated by a colon (:).

- Each parameter in the parameter list for each method is separated by a semicolon (;).

- The return type of a method is indicated after the parameter list for the method, separated by a colon (:).

- We always use Java type names.

Creating an abstract base class

First, we will create the abstract class that will become our base class for the other classes. The following lines show the code for the `VirtualAnimal` abstract base class in Java 9. The `abstract` keyword before `class` indicates to Java that we are creating an abstract class. The code file for the sample is included in the `java_9_oop_chapter_06_01` folder, in the `example06_01.java` file.

```java
public abstract class VirtualAnimal {
    public final int age;

    public VirtualAnimal(int age) {
        this.age = age;
        System.out.println("VirtualAnimal created.");
    }

    public abstract boolean isAbleToFly();

    public abstract boolean isRideable();

    public abstract boolean isHerbivore();

    public abstract boolean isCarnivore();

    public abstract int getAverageNumberOfBabies();

    public abstract String getBaby();

    public abstract String getAsciiArt();
```

```
    public void printAsciiArt() {
        System.out.println(getAsciiArt());
    }

    public void printAverageNumberOfBabies() {
        System.out.println(new String(
            new char[getAverageNumberOfBabies()]).replace(
                "\0", getBaby()));
    }

    public void printAge() {
        System.out.println(
            String.format("I am %d years old", age));
    }

    public boolean isYoungerThan(VirtualAnimal otherAnimal) {
        return age < otherAnimal.age;
    }

    public boolean isOlderThan(VirtualAnimal otherAnimal) {
        return age > otherAnimal.age;
    }
}
```

The preceding class declares an immutable field of type int named age. The
constructor requires an age value to create an instance of the class and prints a
message indicating that a virtual animal is created. The class declares the following
abstract methods that include the abstract keyword before the returned type to
let Java know we just want to declare the required arguments and that we won't
provide an implementation for the methods. We have already explained the goals for
these methods that will be implemented in subclasses of VirtualAnimal.

- isAbleToFly
- isRideable
- isHerbivore
- isCarnivore
- getAverageNumberOfBabies
- getBaby
- getAsciiArt

In addition, the class declares the following five methods:

- `printAsciiArt`: This method calls `System.out.println` to print the `String` returned by the `getAsciiArt` method.

- `printAverageNumberOfBabies`: This method creates a new `char` array with a number of elements equal to the value returned by the `getAverageNumberOfBabies` method. Then, the code creates a new `String` initialized with the `char` array and calls the `replace` method to substitute each `"\0"`, with the `String` returned by the `getBaby` method. This way, we generate a `String` that concatenates `getAverageNumberOfBabies` times the `String` returned by `getBaby`. The code calls `System.out.println` to print the generated `String`.

- `printAge`: This method calls `System.out.println` to print the `String` generated with `String.format` that includes the value of the `age` immutable field.

- `isYoungerThan`: This method receives a `VirtualAnimal` instance in the `otherAnimal` argument and returns the result of applying the less than operator between the value of the `age` field for this instance and `otherAnimal.age`. This way, the method will return `true` only if the age for this instance is lower than the age for `otherAnimal`.

- `isOlderThan`: This method receives a `VirtualAnimal` instance in the `otherAnimal` argument and returns the result of applying the greater than operator between the value of the `age` field for this instance and `otherAnimal.age`. This way, the method will return `true` only if the age for this instance is greater than the age for `otherAnimal`.

If we execute the following line in JShell after declaring the `VirtualAnimal` class, Java will generate a fatal error and indicate that the `VirtualAnimal` class is abstract and that it cannot be instantiated. The code file for the sample is included in the `java_9_oop_chapter_06_01` folder, in the `example06_02.java` file.

```
VirtualAnimal virtualAnimal1 = new VirtualAnimal(5);
```

The following screenshot shows the results of the execution of the previous code in JShell:

```
    ...>        public void printAverageNumberOfBabies() {
    ...>            System.out.println(new String(
    ...>                new char[getAverageNumberOfBabies()]).replace(
    ...>                    "\0", getBaby()));
    ...>        }
    ...>
    ...>        public void printAge() {
    ...>            System.out.println(
    ...>                String.format("I am %d years old", age));
    ...>        }
    ...>
    ...>        public boolean isYoungerThan(VirtualAnimal otherAnimal) {
    ...>            return age < otherAnimal.age;
    ...>        }
    ...>
    ...>        public boolean isOlderThan(VirtualAnimal otherAnimal) {
    ...>            return age > otherAnimal.age;
    ...>        }
    ...> }
|  created class VirtualAnimal

jshell> VirtualAnimal virtualAnimal1 = new VirtualAnimal(5);
|  Error:
|  VirtualAnimal is abstract; cannot be instantiated
|  VirtualAnimal virtualAnimal1 = new VirtualAnimal(5);
|                                 ^------------------^

jshell>
```

Declaring classes that inherit from another class

Now we will create another abstract class. Specifically, we will create a subclass of the recently created `VirtualAnimal` abstract class. The following lines show the code for the `VirtualMammal` abstract class that extends the `VirtualAnimal` class. Note the `abstract class` keywords followed by the class name, `VirtualMammal`, the `extends` keyword, and `VirtualAnimal`, that is, the superclass.

The class name that follows the `extends` keyword indicates the superclass from which the new class inherits in the class definition. The code file for the sample is included in the `java_9_oop_chapter_06_01` folder, in the `example06_03.java` file.

```java
public abstract class VirtualMammal extends VirtualAnimal {
    public boolean isPregnant;

    public VirtualMammal(int age, boolean isPregnant) {
        super(age);
        this.isPregnant = isPregnant;
        System.out.println("VirtualMammal created.");
    }

    public VirtualMammal(int age) {
        this(age, false);
    }
}
```

The `VirtualMammal` abstract class inherits the members from the previously declared `VirtualAnimal` abstract class and adds a new `boolean` mutable field named `isPregnant`. The new abstract class declares two constructors. One of the constructors requires an `age` value to create an instance of the class, as it happened with the `VirtualAnimal` constructor. The other constructor requires the `age` and `isPregnant` values.

If we create an instance of this class with just one `age` argument, Java will use the first constructor. If we create an instance of this class with two arguments, an `int` value for `age` and a `boolean` value for `isPregnant`, Java will use the second constructor.

 We have overloaded the constructor and provided two different constructors. We won't use these constructors with the `new` keyword because we are declaring an abstract class. However, we will be able to call these constructors from subclasses by using the `super` keyword.

The first constructor that requires the `isPregnant` argument uses the `super` keyword to call the constructor from the base class or superclass, that is, the constructor defined in the `VirtualAnimal` class that requires the `age` argument. After the constructor defined in the superclass finishes its execution, the code sets the value for the `isPregnant` mutable field and prints a message indicating that a virtual mammal has been created.

We use the `super` keyword to reference the superclass, and we can use this keyword to call any constructor defined in the superclass. In Java 9, subclasses do not inherit the constructors from its superclasses. In other programming languages, subclasses inherit constructors or initializers, and therefore, it is very important to understand that this doesn't happen in Java 9.

The second constructor uses the `this` keyword to call the previously explained constructor with the received `age` and with `false` as the value for the `isPregnant` argument.

We will create another abstract class. Specifically, we will create a subclass of the recently created `VirtualMammal` abstract class. The following lines show the code for the `VirtualDomesticMammal` abstract class that extends the `VirtualMammal` class. Note the `abstract class` keywords followed by the class name, `VirtualDomesticMammal`, the `extends` keyword, and `VirtualMammal`, that is, the superclass. The class name that follows the `extends` keyword indicates the superclass from which the new class inherits in the class definition. The code file for the sample is included in the `java_9_oop_chapter_06_01` folder, in the `example06_04.java` file.

```java
public abstract class VirtualDomesticMammal extends VirtualMammal {
    public final String name;
    public String favoriteToy;

    public VirtualDomesticMammal(
        int age,
        boolean isPregnant,
        String name,
        String favoriteToy) {
        super(age, isPregnant);
        this.name = name;
        this.favoriteToy = favoriteToy;
        System.out.println("VirtualDomesticMammal created.");
    }

    public VirtualDomesticMammal(
        int age,
        String name,
        String favoriteToy) {
        this(age, false, name, favoriteToy);
    }

    public void talk() {
        System.out.println(
            String.format("%s: says something", name));
    }
}
```

The `VirtualDomesticMammal` abstract class inherits the members from the previously declared `VirtualMammal` abstract class. It is important to understand that the new class also inherits the members that the superclass inherited from its superclass, that is, from the `VirtualAnimal` abstract class. For example, our new class inherits the `age` immutable field declared in the `VirtualAnimal` abstract class and all the other members declared in this class.

The `VirtualDomesticMammal` class adds a new `String` immutable field called `name` and a new `String` mutable field named `favoriteToy`. The new abstract class declares two constructors. One of the constructors requires four arguments to create an instance of the class: `age`, `isPregnant`, `name`, and `favoriteToy`. The other constructor requires all the arguments except `isPregnant`.

The first constructor that requires the four arguments uses the `super` keyword to call the constructor from the base class or superclass, that is, the constructor defined in the `VirtualMammal` class that requires two arguments: `age` and `isPregnant`. After the constructor defined in the superclass finishes its execution, the code sets the value for the `name` and `favoriteToy` fields and prints a message indicating that a virtual domestic mammal has been created.

The second constructor uses the `this` keyword to call the previously explained constructor with the received arguments and with `false` as the value for the `isPregnant` argument.

Finally, the class declares a `talk` method that displays a message with the `name` value followed by a colon (`:`) and `says something`. Note that we will be able to override this method in any subclass of `VirtualDomesticMammal` because each virtual domestic mammal has a different way of talking.

Overriding and overloading methods

Java allows us to define a method with the same name many times with different arguments. This feature is known as **method overloading**. When we created the previous abstract classes, we overloaded the constructor.

For example, we can take advantage of method overloading to define multiple versions of the `neigh` and `nicker` method that we have to define in the `VirtualHorse` abstract class. However, it is very important to avoid code duplication when we overload methods.

Sometimes, we define a method in a class, and we know that a subclass might need to provide a different version of the method. A clear example is the `talk` method we defined in the `VirtualDomesticMammal` class. When a subclass provides a different implementation of a method defined in a superclass with the same name, arguments, and return type, we say that we are **overriding** a method. When we override a method, the implementation in the subclass overwrites the code provided in the superclass.

We will create another abstract class. Specifically, we will create a subclass of the recently created `VirtualDomesticMammal` abstract class. The following lines show the first code snippet for the `VirtualHorse` abstract class that extends the `VirtualDomesticMammal` class. Note the `abstract class` keywords followed by the class name, `VirtualHorse`, the `extends` keyword, and `VirtualDomesticMammal`, that is, the superclass. We will split the code for this class in many snippets to make it easier to analyze. The code file for the sample is included in the `java_9_oop_chapter_06_01` folder, in the `example06_05.java` file.

```java
public abstract class VirtualHorse extends VirtualDomesticMammal {
    public VirtualHorse(
        int age,
        boolean isPregnant,
        String name,
        String favoriteToy) {
        super(age, isPregnant, name, favoriteToy);
        System.out.println("VirtualHouse created.");
    }

    public VirtualHorse(
        int age,
        String name,
        String favoriteToy) {
        this(age, false, name, favoriteToy);
    }

    public boolean isAbleToFly() {
        return false;
    }

    public boolean isRideable() {
        return true;
    }

    public boolean isHerbivore() {
        return true;
```

```
    }

    public boolean isCarnivore() {
        return false;
    }

    public int getAverageNumberOfBabies() {
        return 1;
    }
```

The `VirtualHorse` abstract class inherits the members from the previously declared `VirtualDomesticMammal` abstract class. The new abstract class declares two constructors. One of the constructors requires four arguments to create an instance of the class: `age`, `isPregnant`, `name`, and `favoriteToy`. The other constructor requires all the arguments except `isPregnant`.

The `VirtualHorse` class implements many of the abstract methods inherited from the base class, that is, the `VirtualAnimal` superclass. When we implement a method declared as an abstract method in a superclass, we just need to use the same arguments and write the code for the method, as done in the following five methods: `isAbleToFly`, `isRideable`, `isHerbivore`, `isCarnivore`, and `getAverageNumberOfBabies`. Virtual horses cannot fly, they are rideable, they are herbivores, they aren't carnivores, and their average number of babies is one. The methods return the appropriate values for virtual horses.

The following lines show the second code snippet for the `VirtualHorse` abstract class that extends the `VirtualDomesticMammal` class. The code file for the sample is included in the `java_9_oop_chapter_06_01` folder, in the `example06_05.java` file.

```
    public abstract String getBreed();

    public void printBreed() {
        System.out.println(getBreed());
    }

    protected void printSoundInWords(
        String soundInWords,
        int times,
        VirtualDomesticMammal otherDomesticMammal,
        boolean isAngry) {
        String message = String.format("%s%s: %s%s",
            name,
            otherDomesticMammal == null ?
                "" : String.format(" to %s ",
                otherDomesticMammal.name),
```

```
        isAngry ?
            "Angry " : "",
        new String(new char[times]).replace("\0",
        soundInWords));
    System.out.println(message);
}
```

The VirtualHorse class declares an abstract instance method named getBreed that returns a String, and then declares a printBreed method that prints the value returned by the getBreed method with a call to System.out.println. The subclasses of VirtualHorse that want to become concrete classes will have to provide an implementation for the getBreed method. We won't override the printBreed instance method in the subclasses because we just need to implement the getBreed method to return the appropriate String. We will learn how to make sure that subclasses cannot override specific methods later.

The next lines declare the printSoundInWords protected method that receives four arguments: soundInWords, times, otherDomesticMammal, and isAngry. This method builds and prints a message according to the word that represents the sound (soundInWords), the specified number of times (times), the destination virtual domestic mammal (otherDomesticMammal), and whether the horse is angry or not (isAngry). The otherDomesticMammal argument can be equal to null, which means the method is not receiving the reference to any instance of the VirtualDomesticMammal class or any of its subclasses. The printed message will be different depending on whether an instance is specified or not in the otherDomesticMammal argument.

The following lines show the third and last code snippet for the VirtualHorse abstract class that extends the VirtualDomesticMammal class. The code file for the sample is included in the java_9_oop_chapter_06_01 folder, in the example06_05.java file.

```
public void printNeigh(int times,
    VirtualDomesticMammal otherDomesticMammal,
    boolean isAngry) {
    printSoundInWords("Neigh ", times, otherDomesticMammal,
    isAngry);
}

public void neigh() {
    printNeigh(1, null, false);
}

public void neigh(int times) {
    printNeigh(times, null, false);
```

```
        }

        public void neigh(int times,
            VirtualDomesticMammal otherDomesticMammal) {
            printNeigh(times, otherDomesticMammal, false);
        }

        public void neigh(int times,
            VirtualDomesticMammal otherDomesticMammal,
            boolean isAngry) {
            printNeigh(times, otherDomesticMammal, isAngry);
        }

        public void printNicker(int times,
            VirtualDomesticMammal otherDomesticMammal,
            boolean isAngry) {
            printSoundInWords("Nicker ", times, otherDomesticMammal,
            isAngry);
        }

        public void nicker() {
            printNicker(1, null, false);
        }

        public void nicker(int times) {
            printNicker(times, null, false);
        }

        public void nicker(int times,
            VirtualDomesticMammal otherDomesticMammal) {
            printNicker(times, otherDomesticMammal, false);
        }

        public void nicker(int times,
            VirtualDomesticMammal otherDomesticMammal,
            boolean isAngry) {
            printNicker(times, otherDomesticMammal, isAngry);
        }

        @Override
        public void talk() {
            nicker();
        }
    }
```

The `VirtualHorse` class overrides the `talk` method inherited from `VirtualDomesticMammal`. The code just invokes the `nicker` method without parameters because horses don't talk, they nicker. The method doesn't invoke the method with the same name for its superclass; that is, we don't use the `super` keyword to invoke the `talk` method defined in `VirtualDomesticMammal`.

> We use the `@Override` annotation before the method declaration to inform the Java 9 compiler that the method is meant to override the method with the same name declared in a superclass. It isn't mandatory to add this annotation when we override methods, but it is a good practice to include it and we will always use it when we override methods because it helps to prevent errors. For example, in case we have a typo and we write `tak()` instead of `talk()` as the method name and arguments, the usage of the `@Override` annotation makes the Java 9 compiler generate an error because the `talk` method marked with `@Override` fails to override a method with this name and arguments in one of the superclasses.

The `nicker` method is overloaded with four declarations with different arguments. The following lines show the four different declarations included within the class body:

```
public void nicker()
public void nicker(int times)
public void nicker(int times,
    VirtualDomesticMammal otherDomesticMammal)
public void nicker(int times,
    VirtualDomesticMammal otherDomesticMammal,
    boolean isAngry)
```

This way, we can call any of the defined `nicker` methods based on the provided arguments. The four methods end up invoking the `printNicker` public method with different default values for the arguments with the same names not provided in the call to `nicker`. The method calls the `printSoundInWords` public method with `"Nicker "` as the value for the `soundInWords` arguments and the other arguments set to the received arguments that have the same names. This way, the `printNicker` method builds and prints a nicker message according to the specified number of times (`times`), the optional destination virtual domestic mammal (`otherDomesticMammal`), and whether the horse is angry or not (`isAngry`).

The `VirtualHorse` class uses a similar approach for the `neigh` method. This method is also overloaded with four declarations with different arguments. The following lines show the four different declarations included within the class body. They have the same arguments we just analyzed for the `nicker` method.

```
public void neigh()
public void neigh(int times)
public void neigh(int times,
    VirtualDomesticMammal otherDomesticMammal)
public void neigh(int times,
    VirtualDomesticMammal otherDomesticMammal,
    boolean isAngry)
```

This way, we can call any of the defined `neigh` methods based on the provided arguments. The four methods end up invoking the `printNeigh` public method with different default values for the arguments with the same names not provided in the call to `nicker`. The method calls the `printSoundInWords` public method with `"Neigh "` as the value for the `soundInWords` arguments and the other arguments set to the received arguments that have the same names.

Test your knowledge

1. In Java 9, a subclass:

    1. Inherits all the constructors from its superclass.

    2. Doesn't inherit any constructor from its superclass.

    3. Inherits the constructor with the largest number of arguments from its superclass.

2. We can declare abstract methods:

    1. In any class.

    2. Only in an abstract class.

    3. Only in a concrete subclass of an abstract class.

3. A concrete subclass of any abstract class:

    1. Must provide an implementation for all the inherited abstract methods.

    2. Must provide an implementation for all the inherited constructors.

    3. Must provide an implementation for all the inherited abstract fields.

4. Which of the following lines declare an abstract class named `Dog` as a subclass of `VirtualAnimal`:

1. `public abstract class Dog subclasses VirtualAnimal`
2. `public abstract Dog subclasses VirtualAnimal`
3. `public abstract class Dog extends VirtualAnimal`

5. Which of the following annotations indicated before a method's declaration informs the Java 9 compiler that the method is meant to override the method with the same name declared in a superclass:

1. `@Overridden`
2. `@OverrideMethod`
3. `@Override`

Summary

In this chapter, you learned the difference between abstract and concrete classes. We learned how to take advantage of simple inheritance to specialize a base abstract class. We designed many classes from top to bottom using chained constructors, immutable fields, mutable fields, and instance methods.

Then we coded many of these classes in JShell, taking advantage of different features provided by Java 9. We overloaded constructors, overrode, and overloaded instance methods, and we took advantage of a special annotation to make overridden methods.

Now that you have learned about inheritance, abstraction, extension, and specialization, we are ready to finish coding the additional classes and understand how to work with typecasting and polymorphism, which are the topics we are going to discuss in the next chapter.

7
Members Inheritance and Polymorphism

In this chapter, we will learn about one of the most exciting features of object-oriented programming in Java 9: polymorphism. We will code many classes and then we will work with their instances in JShell to understand how objects can take many different forms. We will:

- Create concrete classes that inherit from abstract superclasses
- Work with instances of subclasses
- Understand polymorphism
- Control whether subclasses can or cannot override members
- Control whether classes can be subclassed
- Use methods that perform operations with instances of different subclasses

Creating concrete classes that inherit from abstract superclasses

In the previous chapter, we created an abstract base class named `VirtualAnimal` and then we coded the following three abstract subclasses: `VirtualMammal`, `VirtualDomesticMammal`, and `VirtualHorse`. Now, we will code the following three concrete classes. Each class represents a different horse breed and is a subclass of the `VirtualHorse` abstract class.

- `AmericanQuarterHorse`: This class represents a virtual horse that belongs to the American Quarter Horse breed.

- `ShireHorse`: This class represents a virtual horse that belongs to the Shire Horse breed.

- `Thoroughbred`: This class represents a virtual horse that belongs to the Thoroughbred breed.

The three concrete classes will implement the following three abstract methods they inherited from abstract superclasses:

- `String getAsciiArt()`: This abstract method is inherited from the `VirtualAnimal` abstract class.

- `String getBaby()`: This abstract method is inherited from the `VirtualAnimal` abstract class.

- `String getBreed()`: This abstract method is inherited from the `VirtualHorse` abstract class.

The following UML diagram shows the members for the three concrete classes that we will code: `AmericanQuarterHorse`, `ShireHorse`, and `Thoroughbred`. We don't use bold text format for the three methods that each of these concrete classes will declare because they aren't overriding the methods; they are implementing the abstract methods that the classes inherited.

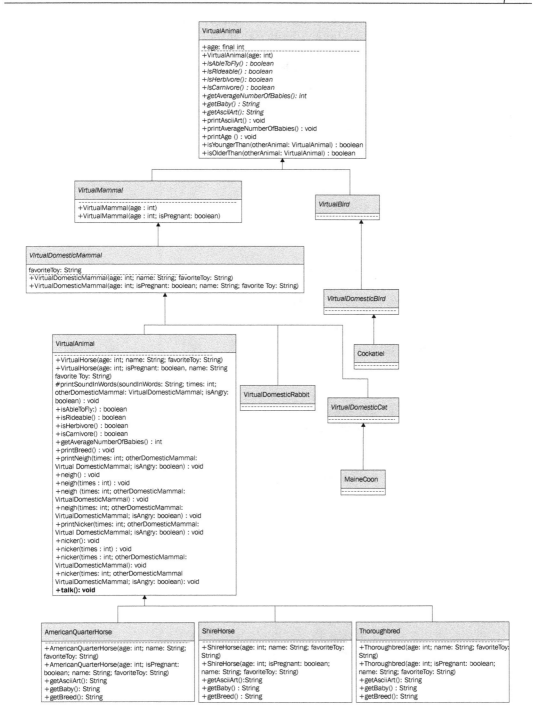

First, we will create the `AmericanQuarterHorse` concrete class. The following lines show the code for this class in Java 9. Notice that there is no `abstract` keyword before `class`, and therefore, our class must make sure that it implements all the inherited abstract methods. The code file for the sample is included in the `java_9_oop_chapter_07_01` folder, in the `example07_01.java` file.

```java
public class AmericanQuarterHorse extends VirtualHorse {
    public AmericanQuarterHorse(
        int age,
        boolean isPregnant,
        String name,
        String favoriteToy) {
        super(age, isPregnant, name, favoriteToy);
        System.out.println("AmericanQuarterHorse created.");
    }

    public AmericanQuarterHorse(
        int age, String name, String favoriteToy) {
        this(age, false, name, favoriteToy);
    }

    public String getBaby() {
        return "AQH baby ";
    }

    public String getBreed() {
        return "American Quarter Horse";
    }

    public String getAsciiArt() {
        return
            "      >>\\\\.\n" +
            "     /*  )`.\n" +
            "   // _)`^)`.   _.---. _\n" +
            "  (_,' \\  `^-)''      `.\\\\\n" +
            "      |              | \\\\\n" +
            "      \\             / |\n" +
            "     / \\  /.___.'\\  (\\ (_\n" +
            "    < ,'||     \\ |`. \\\\`-'\n" +
            "     \\\\\\ ()      )|  )/\n" +
            "     |_>|>     /_] //\n" +
            "       /_]        /_]\n";
    }
}
```

Now we will create the `ShireHorse` concrete class. The following lines show the code for this class in Java 9. The code file for the sample is included in the `java_9_oop_chapter_07_01` folder, in the `example07_01.java` file.

```java
public class ShireHorse extends VirtualHorse {
    public ShireHorse(
        int age,
        boolean isPregnant,
        String name,
        String favoriteToy) {
        super(age, isPregnant, name, favoriteToy);
        System.out.println("ShireHorse created.");
    }

    public ShireHorse(
        int age, String name, String favoriteToy) {
        this(age, false, name, favoriteToy);
    }

    public String getBaby() {
        return "ShireHorse baby ";
    }

    public String getBreed() {
        return "Shire Horse";
    }

    public String getAsciiArt() {
        return
            "                              ;;\n" +
            "                            .;;'*\\\n" +
            "             __            .;;' ' \\\n" +
            "           /'  '\\.~~.~~.~' \\ /'\\.)\n" +
            "          ,;(      )    /  |\n" +
            "         ,;' \\    /-.,,(   )\n" +
            "             ) /|    ) /|\n" +
            "             ||(_\\      ||(_\\\n" +
            "             (_\\        (_\\\n";
    }
}
```

Finally, we will create the `Thoroughbred` concrete class. The following lines show the code for this class in Java 9. The code file for the sample is included in the java_9_ oop_chapter_07_01 folder, in the example07_01.java file.

```java
public class Thoroughbred extends VirtualHorse {
    public Thoroughbred(
        int age,
        boolean isPregnant,
        String name,
        String favoriteToy) {
        super(age, isPregnant, name, favoriteToy);
        System.out.println("Thoroughbred created.");
    }

    public Thoroughbred(
        int age, String name, String favoriteToy) {
        this(age, false, name, favoriteToy);
    }

    public String getBaby() {
        return "Thoroughbred baby ";
    }

    public String getBreed() {
        return "Thoroughbred";
    }

    public String getAsciiArt() {
        return
            "                    })\\\\-=--.\n" +
            "                   // *._.-'\n" +
            "      _.-=-...-'   /\n" +
            " {{|      ,           |\n" +
            " {{\\\\     |   \\\\  /_\n" +
            " }} \\\\ ,'---'\\\\___\\\\\n" +
            " /  )/\\\\\\\\      \\\\\\\\ >\\\\\n" +
            "   //  >\\\\      >\\\\`-\n" +
            "   `-    `-       `-\n";
    }
}
```

As it happened in the other subclasses that we coded, we have more than one constructor defined for the three concrete classes. The first constructor that requires four arguments uses the super keyword to call the constructor from the base class or superclass, that is, the constructor defined in the VirtualHorse class. After the constructor defined in the superclass finishes its execution, the code prints a message indicating that an instance of each specific concrete class has been created. The constructor defined in each class prints a different message.

The second constructor uses the this keyword to call the previously explained constructor with the received arguments and with false as the value for the isPregnant argument.

Each class returns a different String in the implementation of the getBaby and getBreed methods. In addition, each class returns a different ASCII art representation for a virtual horse in the implementation of the getAsciiArt method.

Understanding polymorphism

We can use the same method, that is, a method with the same name and arguments, to cause different things to happen according to the class on which we invoke the method. In object-oriented programming, this feature is known as **polymorphism**. Polymorphism is the ability of an object to take on many forms, and we will see it in action by working with instances of the previously coded concrete classes.

The following lines create a new instance of the AmericanQuarterHorse class named american and use one of its constructors that doesn't require the isPregnant argument. The code file for the sample is included in the java_9_oop_ chapter_07_01 folder, in the example07_01.java file.

```
AmericanQuarterHorse american =
    new AmericanQuarterHorse(
        8, "American", "Equi-Spirit Ball");
american.printBreed();
```

The following lines show the messages that the different constructors displayed in JShell after we entered the previous code:

```
VirtualAnimal created.
VirtualMammal created.
VirtualDomesticMammal created.
VirtualHorse created.
AmericanQuarterHorse created.
```

The constructor defined in the AmericanQuarterHorse calls the constructor from its superclass, that is, the VirtualHorse class. Remember that each constructor calls its superclass constructor and prints a message indicating that an instance of the class is created. We don't have five different instances; we just have one instance that calls the chained constructors of five different classes to perform all the necessary initialization to create an instance of AmericanQuarterHorse.

If we execute the following lines in JShell, all of them will display true as a result, because american belongs to the VirtualAnimal, VirtualMammal, VirtualDomesticMammal, VirtualHorse, and AmericanQuarterHorse classes. The code file for the sample is included in the java_9_oop_chapter_07_01 folder, in the example07_01.java file.

```
System.out.println(american instanceof VirtualAnimal);
System.out.println(american instanceof VirtualMammal);
System.out.println(american instanceof VirtualDomesticMammal);
System.out.println(american instanceof VirtualHorse);
System.out.println(american instanceof AmericanQuarterHorse);
```

The results of the previous lines mean that the instance of the AmericanQuarterHorse class, whose reference is saved in the american variable of type AmericanQuarterHorse, can take on the form of an instance of any of the following classes:

- VirtualAnimal
- VirtualMammal
- VirtualDomesticMammal
- VirtualHorse
- AmericanQuarterHorse

The following screenshot shows the results of executing the previous lines in JShell:

```
jshell> AmericanQuarterHorse american =
   ...>     new AmericanQuarterHorse(
   ...>         8, "American", "Equi-Spirit Ball");
VirtualAnimal created.
VirtualMammal created.
VirtualDomesticMammal created.
VirtualHorse created.
AmericanQuarterHorse created.
american ==> AmericanQuarterHorse@10bdf5e5
|  created variable american : AmericanQuarterHorse

jshell> american.printBreed();
American Quarter Horse

jshell> System.out.println(american instanceof VirtualAnimal);
true

jshell> System.out.println(american instanceof VirtualMammal);
true

jshell> System.out.println(american instanceof VirtualDomesticMammal);
true

jshell> System.out.println(american instanceof VirtualHorse);
true

jshell> System.out.println(american instanceof AmericanQuarterHorse);
true

jshell>
```

We coded the `printBreed` method within the `VirtualHorse` class, and we didn't override this method in any of the subclasses. The following is the code for the `printBreed` method:

```
public void printBreed() {
    System.out.println(getBreed());
}
```

The code prints the `String` returned by the `getBreed` method, declared in the same class as an abstract method. The three concrete classes that inherit from `VirtualHorse` implemented the `getBreed` method and each of them returns a different `String`. When we called the `american.printBreed` method, JShell displayed `American Quarter Horse`.

The following lines create an instance of the ShireHorse class named zelda. Note that, in this case, we use the constructor that requires the isPregnant argument. As happened when we created an instance of the AmericanQuarterHorse class, JShell will display a message for each constructor that is executed as a result of the chained constructors we coded. The code file for the sample is included in the java_9_oop_ chapter_07_01 folder, in the example07_01.java file.

```
ShireHorse zelda =
    new ShireHorse(9, true,
        "Zelda", "Tennis Ball");
```

The next lines call the printAverageNumberOfBabies and printAsciiArt instance methods for american, the instance of AmericanQuarterHorse, and zelda, which is the instance of ShireHorse. The code file for the sample is included in the java_9_ oop_chapter_07_01 folder, in the example07_01.java file.

```
american.printAverageNumberOfBabies();
american.printAsciiArt();
zelda.printAverageNumberOfBabies();
zelda.printAsciiArt();
```

We coded the printAverageNumberOfBabies and printAsciiArt methods in the VirtualAnimal class, and we didn't override them in any of its subclasses. Hence, when we call these methods for either american or Zelda, Java will execute the code defined in the VirtualAnimal class.

The printAverageNumberOfBabies method uses the int value returned by getAverageNumberOfBabies and the String returned by the getBaby method to generate a String that represents the average number of babies for a virtual animal. The VirtualHorse class implemented the inherited getAverageNumberOfBabies abstract method with code that returns 1. The AmericanQuarterHorse and ShireHorse classes implemented the inherited getBaby abstract method with code that returns a String that represents a baby for the virtual horse breed: "AQH baby" and "ShireHorse baby". Thus, our call to the printAverageNumberOfBabies method will produce different results in each instance because they belong to a different class.

The printAsciiArt method uses the String returned by the getAsciiArt method to print the ASCII art that represents a virtual horse. The AmericanQuarterHorse and ShireHorse classes implemented the inherited getAsciiArt abstract method with code that returns a String with the ASCII art that is appropriate for each virtual horse that the class represents. Thus, our call to the printAsciiArt method will produce different results in each instance because they belong to a different class.

The following screenshot shows the results of executing the previous lines in JShell. Both instances run the same code for the two methods that were coded in the `VirtualAnimal` abstract class. However, each class provided a different implementation for the methods that end up being called to generate the result and cause the differences in the output.

```
ShireHorse created.
zelda ==> ShireHorse@31dc339b
|  created variable zelda : ShireHorse

jshell> american.printAverageNumberOfBabies();
AQH baby

jshell> american.printAsciiArt();
      >>\.
    /*  )`.
   // _)`^)`.   _.----._
  (_,' \  `^-)''      `.\
      |              | \
      \              / |
     / \  /.___.'\  (\ (_
     < ,'||      \ |`. \`-'
      \\ ()      )|  )/
      |_>|>      /_] //
        /_]        /_]


jshell> zelda.printAverageNumberOfBabies();
ShireHorse baby

jshell> zelda.printAsciiArt();
                  ;;
                 .;;'*\
           _   .;;' ' \
          /'  '\.~~.~'  \ /'\.)
       ,;(      )   /  |
       ,;' \    /-.,,(   )
          ) /|        ) /|
          ||(_\       ||(_\
          (_\         (_\


jshell>
```

The following lines create an instance of the `Thoroughbred` class named `willow`, and then call its `printAsciiArt` method. As happened before, JShell will display a message for each constructor that is executed as a result of the chained constructors we coded. The code file for the sample is included in the `java_9_oop_chapter_07_01` folder, in the `example07_01.java` file.

```
Thoroughbred willow =
    new Thoroughbred(5,
        "Willow", "Jolly Ball");
willow.printAsciiArt();
```

The following screenshot shows the results of executing the previous lines in JShell. The new instance is from a class that provides a different implementation of the `getAsciiArt` method, and therefore, we will see different ASCII art from what we saw in the previous two calls to the same method for the other instances.

```
jshell> Thoroughbred willow =
   ...>      new Thoroughbred(5,
   ...>          "Willow", "Jolly Ball");
VirtualAnimal created.
VirtualMammal created.
VirtualDomesticMammal created.
VirtualHorse created.
ShireHorse created.
willow ==> Thoroughbred@3327bd23
|  created variable willow : Thoroughbred

jshell> willow.printAsciiArt();
                })\-=--.
                // *._.-'
        _.-=-...-'  /
 {{⎽     ,         |
 {{\     |  \ /_
 }} \ ,'---'\___\
 / )/\\      \\ >\
   //  >\     >\`-
    `-   `-     `-

jshell>
```

The following lines call the `neigh` method for the instance named `willow` with a different number of arguments. This way, we take advantage of the `neigh` method that we overloaded four times with different arguments. Remember that we coded the four `neigh` methods in the `VirtualHorse` class and the `Thoroughbred` class inherits the overloaded methods from this superclass through its hierarchy tree. The code file for the sample is included in the `java_9_oop_chapter_07_01` folder, in the `example07_01.java` file.

```
willow.neigh();
willow.neigh(2);
willow.neigh(2, american);
willow.neigh(3, zelda, true);
american.nicker();
american.nicker(2);
american.nicker(2, willow);
american.nicker(3, willow, true);
```

The following screenshot shows the results of calling the `neigh` and `nicker` methods with the different arguments in JShell:

```
jshell> willow.neigh();
Willow: Neigh

jshell> willow.neigh(2);
Willow: Neigh Neigh

jshell> willow.neigh(2, american);
Willow to American : Neigh Neigh

jshell> willow.neigh(3, zelda, true);
Willow to Zelda : Angry Neigh Neigh Neigh

jshell> american.nicker();
American: Nicker

jshell> american.nicker(2);
American: Nicker Nicker

jshell> american.nicker(2, willow);
American to Willow : Nicker Nicker

jshell> american.nicker(3, willow, true);
American to Willow : Angry Nicker Nicker Nicker

jshell>
```

We called the four versions of the `neigh` method defined in the `VirtualHorse` class for the `Thoroughbred` instance named `willow`. The third and fourth lines that call the `neigh` method specify a value for the `otherDomesticMammal` argument of type `VirtualDomesticMammal`. The third line specifies `american` as the value for `otherDomesticMammal` and the fourth line specifies `zelda` as the value for the same argument. Both the `AmericanQuarterHorse` and `ShireHorse` concrete classes are subclasses of `VirtualHorse`, and `VirtualHorse` is a subclass of `VirtualDomesticMammal`. Hence, we can use `american` and `zelda` as arguments where a `VirtualDomesticMammal` instance is required.

Then, we called the four versions of the `nicker` method defined in the `VirtualHorse` class for the `AmericanQuarterHorse` instance named `american`. The third and fourth lines that call the `nicker` method specify `willow` as the value for the `otherDomesticMammal` argument of type `VirtualDomesticMammal`. The `Thoroughbred` concrete class is also a subclass of `VirtualHorse`, and `VirtualHorse` is a subclass or `VirtualDomesticMammal`. Hence, we can use `willow` as an argument where a `VirtualDomesticMammal` instance is required.

Controlling overridability of members in subclasses

We will code the `VirtualDomesticCat` abstract class and its concrete subclass: `MaineCoon`. Then, we will code the `VirtualBird` abstract class, its `VirtualDomesticBird` abstract subclass, and the `Cockatiel` concrete subclass. Finally, we will code the `VirtualDomesticRabbit` concrete class. While coding these classes, we will use Java 9 features that allow us to decide whether the subclasses can or cannot override specific members.

All the virtual domestic cats must be able to talk, and therefore, we will override the `talk` method inherited from `VirtualDomesticMammal` to print the word that represents a cat meowing: `"Meow"`. We also want to provide a method to print `"Meow"` a specific number of times. Hence, at this point, we realize that we can take advantage of the `printSoundInWords` method we declared in the `VirtualHorse` class.

We cannot access this instance method in the `VirtualDomesticCat` abstract class because it doesn't inherit from `VirtualHorse`. Thus, we will move this method from the `VirtualHorse` class to its superclass: `VirtualDomesticMammal`.

 We will use the `final` keyword before the return type for the methods that we don't want to be overridden in subclasses. When a method is marked as a final method, the subclasses cannot override the method and the Java 9 compiler shows an error if they try to do so.

Not all the birds are able to fly in real-life. However, all our virtual birds are able to fly, and therefore, we will implement the inherited `isAbleToFly` abstract method as a final method that returns `true`. This way, we make sure that all the classes that inherit from the `VirtualBird` abstract class will always run this code for the `isAbleToFly` method and that they won't be able to override it.

The following UML diagram shows the members for the new abstract and concrete classes that we will code. In addition, the diagram shows the `printSoundInWords` method moved from the `VirtualHorse` abstract class to the `VirtualDomesticMammal` abstract class.

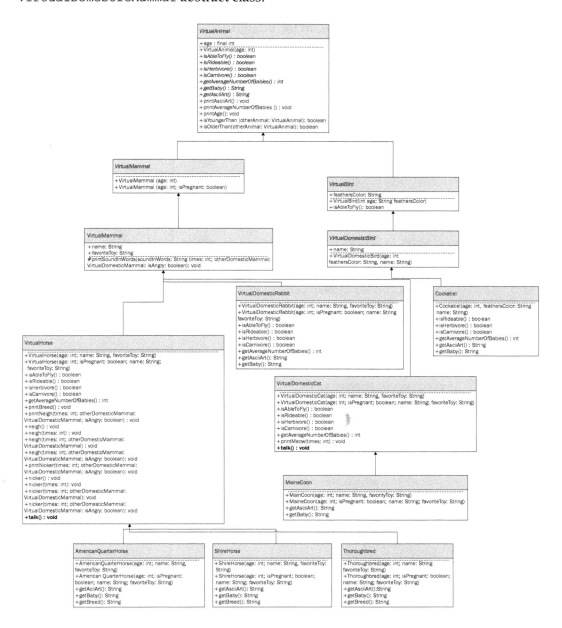

First, we will create a new version of the `VirtualDomesticMammal` abstract class. We will add the `printSoundInWords` method that we have in the `VirtualHorse` abstract class and we will use the `final` keyword to indicate that we don't want to allow subclasses to override this method. The following lines show the new code for the `VirtualDomesticMammal` class. The code file for the sample is included in the `java_9_oop_chapter_07_01` folder, in the `example07_02.java` file.

```
public abstract class VirtualDomesticMammal extends VirtualMammal {
    public final String name;
    public String favoriteToy;

    public VirtualDomesticMammal(
        int age,
        boolean isPregnant,
        String name,
        String favoriteToy) {
        super(age, isPregnant);
        this.name = name;
        this.favoriteToy = favoriteToy;
        System.out.println("VirtualDomesticMammal created.");
    }

    public VirtualDomesticMammal(
        int age, String name, String favoriteToy) {
        this(age, false, name, favoriteToy);
    }

    protected final void printSoundInWords(
        String soundInWords,
        int times,
        VirtualDomesticMammal otherDomesticMammal,
        boolean isAngry) {
        String message = String.format("%s%s: %s%s",
            name,
            otherDomesticMammal == null ?
                "" : String.format(" to %s ",
                otherDomesticMammal.name),
            isAngry ?
                "Angry " : "",
            new String(new char[times]).replace("\0",
            soundInWords));
        System.out.println(message);
    }
```

```
public void talk() {
    System.out.println(
        String.format("%s: says something", name));
    }
}
```

After we enter the previous lines, JShell will display the following messages:

```
|    update replaced class VirtualHorse which cannot be referenced until
this error is corrected:
|       printSoundInWords(java.lang.String,int,VirtualDomesticMammal,boole
an) in VirtualHorse cannot override printSoundInWords(java.lang.String,in
t,VirtualDomesticMammal,boolean) in VirtualDomesticMammal
|        overridden method is final
|         protected void printSoundInWords(String soundInWords, int
times,
|              ^----------------------------------------------------------
--...
|    update replaced class AmericanQuarterHorse which cannot be
referenced until class VirtualHorse is declared
|    update replaced class ShireHorse which cannot be referenced until
class VirtualHorse is declared
|    update replaced class Thoroughbred which cannot be referenced until
class VirtualHorse is declared
|    update replaced variable american which cannot be referenced until
class AmericanQuarterHorse is declared
|    update replaced variable zelda which cannot be referenced until
class ShireHorse is declared
|    update replaced variable willow which cannot be referenced until
class Thoroughbred is declared
|    update overwrote class VirtualDomesticMammal
```

JShell indicates us that the `VirtualHorse` class and its subclasses cannot be referenced until we correct an error for this class. The class declares the `printSoundInWords` method and overrides the recently added method with the same name and arguments in the `VirtualDomesticMammal` class. We used the `final` keyword in the new declaration to make sure that any subclass cannot override it, and therefore, the Java compiler generates the error message that JShell displays.

Now, we will create a new version of the VirtualHorse abstract class. The following lines show the new version that removes the printSoundInWords method and uses the final keyword to make sure that many methods cannot be overridden by any of the subclasses. The declarations that use the final keyword to avoid the methods to be overridden are highlighted in the next lines. The code file for the sample is included in the java_9_oop_chapter_07_01 folder, in the example07_02.java file.

```java
public abstract class VirtualHorse extends VirtualDomesticMammal {
    public VirtualHorse(
        int age,
        boolean isPregnant,
        String name,
        String favoriteToy) {
        super(age, isPregnant, name, favoriteToy);
        System.out.println("VirtualHorse created.");
    }

    public VirtualHorse(
        int age, String name, String favoriteToy) {
        this(age, false, name, favoriteToy);
    }

    public final boolean isAbleToFly() {
        return false;
    }

    public final boolean isRideable() {
        return true;
    }

    public final boolean isHerbivore() {
        return true;
    }

    public final boolean isCarnivore() {
        return false;
    }

    public int getAverageNumberOfBabies() {
        return 1;
    }

    public abstract String getBreed();
```

```
public final void printBreed() {
    System.out.println(getBreed());
}

public final void printNeigh(
    int times,
    VirtualDomesticMammal otherDomesticMammal,
    boolean isAngry) {
    printSoundInWords("Neigh ", times, otherDomesticMammal,
    isAngry);
}

public final void neigh() {
    printNeigh(1, null, false);
}

public final void neigh(int times) {
    printNeigh(times, null, false);
}

public final void neigh(int times,
    VirtualDomesticMammal otherDomesticMammal) {
    printNeigh(times, otherDomesticMammal, false);
}

public final void neigh(int times,
    VirtualDomesticMammal otherDomesticMammal,
    boolean isAngry) {
    printNeigh(times, otherDomesticMammal, isAngry);
}

public final void printNicker(int times,
    VirtualDomesticMammal otherDomesticMammal,
    boolean isAngry) {
    printSoundInWords("Nicker ", times, otherDomesticMammal,
    isAngry);
}

public final void nicker() {
    printNicker(1, null, false);
}

public final void nicker(int times) {
    printNicker(times, null, false);
```

```
        }

        public final void nicker(int times,
            VirtualDomesticMammal otherDomesticMammal) {
            printNicker(times, otherDomesticMammal, false);
        }

        public final void nicker(int times,
            VirtualDomesticMammal otherDomesticMammal,
            boolean isAngry) {
            printNicker(times, otherDomesticMammal, isAngry);
        }

        @Override
        public final void talk() {
            nicker();
        }
    }
```

After we enter the previous lines, JShell will display the following messages:

```
|   update replaced class AmericanQuarterHorse
|   update replaced class ShireHorse
|   update replaced class Thoroughbred
|   update replaced variable american, reset to null
|   update replaced variable zelda, reset to null
|   update replaced variable willow, reset to null
|   update overwrote class VirtualHorse
```

We replaced the definition for the VirtualHorse class and the subclasses were also updated. It is important to know that the variables we declared in JShell that held references to instances of subclasses of VirtualHorse were set to null.

Controlling subclassing of classes

The final keyword has one additional usage. We can use final as a modifier before the class keyword in the class declaration to indicate Java that we want to generate a **final class**, that is, a class that cannot be extended or subclassed. Java 9 won't allow us to create a subclass for a final class.

Now, we will create the `VirtualDomesticCat` abstract class and then we will declare a concrete subclass named `MaineCoon` as a final class. This way, we will make sure that nobody will be able to create a subclass of `MaineCoon`. The following lines show the code for the `VirtualDomesticCat` abstract class. The code file for the sample is included in the `java_9_oop_chapter_07_01` folder, in the `example07_02.java` file.

```java
public abstract class VirtualDomesticCat extends VirtualDomesticMammal
{
    public VirtualDomesticCat(
        int age,
        boolean isPregnant,
        String name,
        String favoriteToy) {
        super(age, isPregnant, name, favoriteToy);
        System.out.println("VirtualDomesticCat created.");
    }

    public VirtualDomesticCat(
        int age, String name, String favoriteToy) {
        this(age, false, name, favoriteToy);
    }

    public final boolean isAbleToFly() {
        return false;
    }

    public final boolean isRideable() {
        return false;
    }

    public final boolean isHerbivore() {
        return false;
    }

    public final boolean isCarnivore() {
        return true;
    }

    public int getAverageNumberOfBabies() {
        return 5;
    }

    public final void printMeow(int times) {
        printSoundInWords("Meow ", times, null, false);
```

```
        }

        @Override
        public final void talk() {
            printMeow(1);
        }
    }
```

The `VirtualDomesticCat` abstract class implements many of the abstract methods inherited from the `VirtualDomesticMammal` superclass as final methods, and overrides the `talk` method with a final method. Thus, we won't be able to create a subclass of `VirtualDomesticCat` that overrides the `isAbleToFly` method to return `true`. We won't have virtual cats that will be able to fly.

The following lines show the code for the `MaineCoon` concrete class that inherits from `VirtualDomesticCat`. We declare `MaineCoon` as a final class and it overrides the inherited `getAverageNumberOfBabies` method to return 6. In addition, the final class implements the following inherited abstract methods: `getBaby` and `getAsciiArt`. The code file for the sample is included in the `java_9_oop_chapter_07_01` folder, in the `example07_02.java` file.

```java
public final class MaineCoon extends VirtualDomesticCat {
    public MaineCoon(
        int age,
        boolean isPregnant,
        String name,
        String favoriteToy) {
        super(age, isPregnant, name, favoriteToy);
        System.out.println("MaineCoon created.");
    }

    public MaineCoon(
        int age, String name, String favoriteToy) {
        this(age, false, name, favoriteToy);
    }

    public String getBaby() {
        return "Maine Coon baby ";
    }

    @Override
    public int getAverageNumberOfBabies() {
        return 6;
    }

    public String getAsciiArt() {
        return
```

```
"    ^_^\n" +
"   (*.*)\n" +
"    |-|\n" +
"   /   \\\n";
    }
}
```

 We didn't mark any method as `final` because all the methods in a final class are implicitly final.

However, when we run Java code outside of JShell, the final class will be created and we won't be able to subclass it.

Now, we will create the `VirtualBird` abstract class that inherits from `VirtualAnimal`. The following lines show the code for the `VirtualBird` abstract class. The code file for the sample is included in the `java_9_oop_chapter_07_01` folder, in the `example07_02.java` file.

```java
public abstract class VirtualBird extends VirtualAnimal {
    public String feathersColor;

    public VirtualBird(int age, String feathersColor) {
        super(age);
        this.feathersColor = feathersColor;
        System.out.println("VirtualBird created.");
    }

    public final boolean isAbleToFly() {
        // Not all birds are able to fly in real-life
        // However, all our virtual birds are able to fly
        return true;
    }

}
```

The `VirtualBird` abstract class inherits the members from the previously declared `VirtualAnimal` abstract class and adds a new `String` mutable field named `feathersColor`. The new abstract class declares a constructor that requires initial values for `age` and `feathersColor` to create an instance of the class. The constructor uses the `super` keyword to call the constructor from the base class or superclass, that is, the constructor defined in the `VirtualAnimal` class that requires the `age` argument. After the constructor defined in the superclass finishes its execution, the code sets the value for the `feathersColor` mutable field and prints a message indicating that a virtual bird has been created.

The `VirtualBird` abstract class implements the inherited `isAbleToFly` method as a final method that returns `true`. We want to make sure that all the virtual birds in our application domain are able to fly.

Now, we will create the `VirtualDomesticBird` abstract class that inherits from `VirtualBird`. The following lines show the code for the `VirtualDomesticBird` abstract class. The code file for the sample is included in the `java_9_oop_chapter_07_01` folder, in the `example07_02.java` file.

```java
public abstract class VirtualDomesticBird extends VirtualBird {
    public final String name;

    public VirtualDomesticBird(int age,
        String feathersColor,
        String name) {
        super(age, feathersColor);
        this.name = name;
        System.out.println("VirtualDomesticBird created.");
    }
}
```

The `VirtualDomesticBird` abstract class inherits the members from the previously declared `VirtualBird` abstract class and adds a new `String` immutable field called `name`. The new abstract class declares a constructor that requires initial values for `age`, `feathersColor`, and `name` to create an instance of the class. The constructor uses the `super` keyword to call the constructor from the superclass, that is, the constructor defined in the `VirtualBird` class that requires the `age` and `feathersColor` arguments. After the constructor defined in the superclass finishes its execution, the code sets the value for the `name` immutable field and prints a message indicating that a virtual domestic bird has been created.

The following lines show the code for the `Cockatiel` concrete class that inherits from `VirtualDomesticBird`. We declare `Cockatiel` as a final class and it implements the following inherited abstract methods: `isRideable`, `isHerbivore`, `isCarnivore`, `getAverageNumberOfBabies`, `getBaby`, and `getAsciiArt`. As previously explained, all the methods in a final class are implicitly final. The code file for the sample is included in the `java_9_oop_chapter_07_01` folder, in the `example07_02.java` file.

```java
public final class Cockatiel extends VirtualDomesticBird {
    public Cockatiel(int age,
        String feathersColor, String name) {
        super(age, feathersColor, name);
        System.out.println("Cockatiel created.");
    }

    public boolean isRideable() {
        return true;
    }

    public boolean isHerbivore() {
        return true;
    }

    public boolean isCarnivore() {
        return true;
    }

    public int getAverageNumberOfBabies() {
        return 4;
    }

    public String getBaby() {
        return "Cockatiel baby ";
    }

    public String getAsciiArt() {
        return
            "      ///\n" +
            "     .////.\n" +
            "     //   //\n" +
            "     \\\\  (*)\\\\\n" +
            "     (/    \\\\\n" +
            "      /\\\\    \\\\\n" +
            "      ///     \\\\\\\\\n" +
            "      ///|    |\n" +
            "      ////|    |\n" +
            "     //////   /\n" +
            "     ////  \\\\  \\\\\n" +
            "     \\\\\\\\    ^    ^\n" +
            "      \\\\\n" +
            "       \\\\";
    }
}
```

The following lines show the code for the `VirtualDomesticRabbit` concrete class that inherits from `VirtualDomesticMammal`. We declare `VirtualDomesticRabbit` as a final class because we don't want additional subclasses. We will just have one type of virtual domestic rabbit in our application domain. The final class implements the following inherited abstract methods: `isAbleToFly`, `isRideable`, `isHerbivore`, `isCarnivore`, `getAverageNumberOfBabies`, `getBaby`, and `getAsciiArt`. The code file for the sample is included in the `java_9_oop_chapter_07_01` folder, in the `example07_02.java` file.

```java
public final class VirtualDomesticRabbit extends VirtualDomesticMammal
{
    public VirtualDomesticRabbit(
        int age,
        boolean isPregnant,
        String name,
        String favoriteToy) {
        super(age, isPregnant, name, favoriteToy);
        System.out.println("VirtualDomesticRabbit created.");
    }

    public VirtualDomesticRabbit(
        int age, String name, String favoriteToy) {
        this(age, false, name, favoriteToy);
    }

    public final boolean isAbleToFly() {
        return false;
    }

    public final boolean isRideable() {
        return false;
    }

    public final boolean isHerbivore() {
        return true;
    }

    public final boolean isCarnivore() {
        return false;
    }

    public int getAverageNumberOfBabies() {
        return 6;
    }
```

```
public String getBaby() {
    return "Rabbit baby ";
}

public String getAsciiArt() {
    return
        "   /\\ /\\\n" +
        "   \\ V /\n" +
        "   | **)\n" +
        "   /  /\n" +
        "   /  \\\_\\\_\n" +
        "*(__\\\_\\\\n";
}
}
```

 JShell ignores the final modifier, and therefore, a class declared with the final modifier will allow subclasses in JShell.

Creating methods that work with instances of different subclasses

After we declare all the new classes, we will create the following two methods that receive a VirtualAnimal instance as an argument, that is, a VirtualAnimal instance or an instance of any subclass of VirtualAnimal. Each method calls a different instance method defined in the VirtualAnimal class: printAverageNumberOfBabies and printAsciiArg. The code file for the sample is included in the java_9_oop_chapter_07_01 folder, in the example07_02.java file.

```
void printBabies(VirtualAnimal animal) {
    animal.printAverageNumberOfBabies();
}

void printAsciiArt(VirtualAnimal animal) {
    animal.printAsciiArt();
}
```

Then the following lines create instances of the next classes: `Cockatiel`, `VirtualDomesticRabbit`, and `MaineCoon`. The code file for the sample is included in the `java_9_oop_chapter_07_01` folder, in the `example07_02.java` file.

```
Cockatiel tweety =
    new Cockatiel(3, "White", "Tweety");
VirtualDomesticRabbit bunny =
    new VirtualDomesticRabbit(2, "Bunny", "Sneakers");
MaineCoon garfield =
    new MaineCoon(3, "Garfield", "Lassagna");
```

The following screenshot shows the results of executing the previous lines in JShell. We will see the messages that the different constructors displayed in JShell after we enter the code to create each instance. These messages will allow us to easily understand all the chained constructors that were called when Java created each instance.

```
jshell> Cockatiel tweety =
   ...>     new Cockatiel(3, "White", "Tweety");
VirtualAnimal created.
VirtualBird created.
VirtualDomesticBird created.
Cockatiel created.
tweety ==> Cockatiel@76707e36
|  created variable tweety : Cockatiel

jshell> VirtualDomesticRabbit bunny =
   ...>     new VirtualDomesticRabbit(2, "Bunny", "Sneakers");
VirtualAnimal created.
VirtualMammal created.
VirtualDomesticMammal created.
VirtualDomesticRabbit created.
bunny ==> VirtualDomesticRabbit@1f554b06
|  created variable bunny : VirtualDomesticRabbit

jshell> MaineCoon garfield =
   ...>     new MaineCoon(3, "Garfield", "Lassagna");
VirtualAnimal created.
VirtualMammal created.
VirtualDomesticMammal created.
VirtualDomesticCat created.
MaineCoon created.
garfield ==> MaineCoon@1c3a4799
|  created variable garfield : MaineCoon

jshell>
```

Then the following lines call the `printBabies` and `printAsciiArt` methods with the previously created instances as arguments. The code file for the sample is included in the `java_9_oop_chapter_07_01` folder, in the `example07_02.java` file.

```
System.out.println(tweety.name);
printBabies(tweety);
printAsciiArt(tweety);

System.out.println(bunny.name);
printBabies(bunny);
printAsciiArt(bunny);

System.out.println(garfield.name);
printBabies(garfield);
printAsciiArt(garfield);
```

The three instances become a `VirtualAnimal` argument for the different methods, that is, they take the form of a `VirtualAnimal` instance. However, the values used for the fields and the methods aren't those declared in the `VirtualAnimal` class. The call to the `printAverageNumberOfBabies` and `printAsciiArt` instance methods take into account all the members declared in the subclasses because each instance is an instance of a subclass of `VirtualAnimal`:

The `printBabies` and `printAsciiArt` methods that receive a `VirtualAnimal` instance as an argument can only access the members defined in the `VirtualAnimal` class for the instances that they receive as arguments because the argument type is `VirtualAnimal`. We can unwrap the `Cockatiel`, `VirtualDomesticRabbit`, and `MaineCoon` instances that are received in the `animal` argument if necessary. However, we will work with these scenarios later as we cover more advanced topics.

The following screenshot shows the results of executing the previous lines for the `Cockatiel` instance named `tweety` in JShell.

```
jshell> printf(tweety.name);
Tweety
jshell> printBabies(tweety);
Cockatiel baby Cockatiel baby Cockatiel baby Cockatiel baby

jshell> printAsciiArt(tweety);
    ///
    .////.
    //   //
    \ (*)\
    (/     \
     /\     \
    ///      \\
   ///|      |
   ////|      |
  //////     /
 ////  \   \
  \\    ^    ^
   \
    \
```

The following screenshot shows the results of executing the previous lines for the `VirtualDomesticRabbit` instance named `bunny` in JShell.

```
jshell> printf(bunny.name);
Bunny
jshell> printBabies(bunny);
Rabbit baby Rabbit baby Rabbit baby Rabbit baby Rabbit baby Rabbit baby

jshell> printAsciiArt(bunny);
  /\ /\
  \ V /
  | **)
  / /
 /  \_\_
*(__\_\
```

The following screenshot shows the results of executing the previous lines for the MaineCoon instance named garfield in JShell.

```
jshell> printf(garfield.name);
Garfield
jshell> printBabies(garfield);
Maine Coon baby Maine Coon baby Maine Coon baby Maine Coon baby Maine Coon baby Maine Coon baby

jshell> printAsciiArt(garfield);
  ^ ^
 (*.*)
  |-|
 /   \


jshell>
```

Now we will create another method that receives a VirtualDomesticMammal instance as an argument, that is, a VirtualDomesticMammal instance or an instance of any subclass of VirtualDomesticMammal. The following function calls the talk instance method defined in the VirtualDomesticMammal class. The code file for the sample is included in the java_9_oop_chapter_07_01 folder, in the example07_02. java file.

```
void makeItTalk(VirtualDomesticMammal domestic) {
    domestic.talk();
}
```

Then, the following two lines call the makeItTalk method with the VirtualDomesticRabbit and MaineCoon instances as arguments: bunny and garfield. The code file for the sample is included in the java_9_oop_ chapter_07_01 folder, in the example07_02.java file.

```
makeItTalk(bunny);
makeItTalk(garfield);
```

The call to the same method for a `VirtualDomesticMammal` instance received as an argument produces different results. The `VirtualDomesticRabbit` didn't override the inherited `talk` method while the `MaineCoon` class inherited the `talk` method overridden in the `VirtualDomesticCat` abstract class to make domestic cat meow. The following screenshot shows the results of the two method calls in JShell:

```
jshell> void makeItTalk(VirtualDomesticMammal domestic) {
   ...>     domestic.talk();
   ...> }
|  created method makeItTalk(VirtualDomesticMammal)

jshell> makeItTalk(bunny);
Bunny: says something

jshell> makeItTalk(garfield);
Garfield: Meow

jshell>
```

The `VirtualAnimal` abstract class declared two instance methods that allow us to determine whether a virtual animal is younger or older than an other virtual animal: `isYoungerThan` and `isOlderThan`. These two methods receive a `VirtualAnimal` argument and return the results of applying an operator between the `age` value for the instance and the `age` value of the received instance.

The following lines call the `printAge` method for the three instances: `tweety`, `bunny`, and `garfield`. This method was declared in the `VirtualAnimal` class. Then, the next lines call the `isOlderThan` and `isYoungerThan` methods with these instances as arguments to display the results of comparing the age of the different instances. The code file for the sample is included in the `java_9_oop_chapter_07_01` folder, in the `example07_02.java` file.

```
tweety.printAge();
bunny.printAge();
garfield.printAge();
tweety.isOlderThan(bunny);
garfield.isYoungerThan(tweety);
bunny.isYoungerThan(garfield);
```

The following screenshot shows the results of executing the previous lines in JShell:

```
jshell> tweety.printAge();
I am 3 years old

jshell> bunny.printAge();
I am 2 years old

jshell> garfield.printAge();
I am 3 years old

jshell> tweety.isOlderThan(bunny);
$58 ==> true
|   created scratch variable $58 : boolean

jshell> garfield.isYoungerThan(tweety);
$59 ==> false
|   created scratch variable $59 : boolean

jshell> bunny.isYoungerThan(garfield);
$60 ==> true
|   created scratch variable $60 : boolean

jshell>
```

Test your knowledge

1. Which of the following lines declares an instance method that cannot be overridden in any subclass:

    1. `public void talk(): final {`
    2. `public final void talk() {`
    3. `public notOverrideable void talk() {`

2. We have an abstract superclass named `Shape`. The `Circle` class is a subclass of `Shape` and is a concrete class. If we create an instance of `Circle` named `circle`, this instance will also be:

    1. An instance of `Shape`.
    2. A subclass of `Circle`.
    3. An abstract superclass of `Circle`.

3. In UML diagrams, class names that use italic text format indicate that they are:

   1. Concrete classes.

   2. Classes that override at least one member inherited from its superclass.

   3. Abstract classes.

4. Which of the following lines declares a class that cannot be subclassed:

   1. `public final class Dog extends VirtualAnimal {`

   2. `public final class Dog subclasses VirtualAnimal {`

   3. `public final Dog subclasses VirtualAnimal {`

5. Which of the following lines declares a concrete class named `Circle` that can be subclassed and whose superclass is the `Shape` abstract class:

   1. `public final class Shape extends Circle {`

   2. `public class Shape extends Circle {`

   3. `public concrete class Shape extends Circle {`

Summary

In this chapter, we created many abstract and concrete classes. We learned to control whether subclasses can or cannot override members, and whether classes can be subclassed.

We worked with instances of many subclasses and we understood that objects can take many forms. We worked with many instances and their methods in JShell to understand how the classes and the methods that we coded are executed. We used methods that performed operations with instances of different classes that had a common superclass.

Now that you have learned about members inheritance and polymorphism, we are ready to use contract programming with interfaces in Java 9, which is the topic we are going to discuss in the next chapter.

8
Contract Programming with Interfaces

In this chapter, we will work with complex scenarios in which we will have to use instances that belong to more than one blueprint. We will take advantage of the interfaces to work with contract programming. We will:

- Learn about interfaces in Java 9
- Understand how interfaces work in combination with classes
- Declare interfaces in Java 9
- Declare classes that implement interfaces
- Take advantage of the multiple inheritance of interfaces
- Combine class inheritance with interfaces

Understanding how interfaces work in combination with classes

Let's imagine we have to develop a Web Service in which we have to work with two different types of character: comic and game characters.

A comic character must be drawable in a comic strip. A comic character must be able to provide a nickname and perform the following tasks:

- Draw a speech balloon, also known as speech bubble, with a message
- Draw a thought balloon, also known as thought bubble, with a message
- Draw a speech balloon with a message and another comic character, drawable in a comic strip, as a destination

A game character must be drawable in a game scene. A game character must be able to provide a full name and its current score. In addition, a game character must be able to perform the following tasks:

- Set its desired location to a specific 2D position indicated by the x and y coordinates
- Provide the value for its x coordinate
- Provide the value for its y coordinate
- Draw itself at its current position
- Check whether it intersects with another game character, drawable in a game scene

We have to be able to work with objects that can be both a comic character and a game character; that is, they are both drawable in a comic strip and drawable in a game scene. However, we will also work with objects that will just be either a comic or game character; that is, they are drawable in a comic strip or drawable in a game scene.

We don't want to code a generic way of performing the previously described tasks. We want to make sure that many classes are capable of performing these tasks with a common interface. Each object that declares itself as drawable in a comic strip must define the tasks related to speech and thought balloons. Each object that declares itself as drawable in a game scene must define how to set its desired 2D position, draw itself, and check whether it intersects with another game character, drawable in a game scene.

SpiderDog is a comic character, drawable in a comic strip, that has a specific way of drawing speech and thought balloons. **WonderCat** is both a comic and game character, drawable in a comic strip and also in a game scene. Thus, WonderCat must define all the tasks required by both character types.

WonderCat is a very versatile character, and it can use different costumes to participate in either games or comics with different names. WonderCat can also be hideable, powerable, or fightable:

- A hideable character is capable of being hidden. It can provide a specific number of eyes and must be able to show and hide itself.
- A powerable character is capable of being powered. It can provide a spell power score value and use this spell power to make a hideable character disappear.
- A fightable character is able to fight. It has a sword and can provide both the sword power and weight values. In addition, a fightable character can unsheathe his sword with or without a hideable character as a target.

Let's imagine that Java 9 provides support for multiple inheritance. We need base blueprints to represent a comic character and a game character. Then, each class that represents any of these types of character can provide its implementation of the methods. In this case, comic and game characters are very different, and they don't perform similar tasks that might lead to confusion and problems for multiple inheritance. Thus, we can use multiple inheritance to create a WonderCat class that implements both comic and game character blueprints. In some cases, multiple inheritance is not convenient because similar blueprints might have methods with the same names, and it can be extremely confusing to use multiple inheritance.

In addition, we can use multiple inheritance to combine the WonderCat class with Hideable, Powerable, and Fightable. This way, we will have a Hideable + WonderCat, a Powerable + WonderCat, and a Fightable + WonderCat. We would be able to use any of them, Hideable + WonderCat, Powerable + WonderCat, or Fightable + WonderCat, as either a comic or game character.

Our goals are simple, but we face a little problem: Java 9 doesn't support the multiple inheritance of classes. Instead, we can use multiple inheritance with interfaces or combine interfaces with classes. So, we will use interfaces and classes to fulfill our previous requirements.

In the previous chapters, we have been working with abstract classes and concrete classes. When we coded the abstract classes, we declared constructors, instance fields, instance methods, and abstract methods. The abstract classes had concrete instance methods mixed with abstract methods.

In this case, we don't need to provide implementation for any method; we just have to make sure that we provide the appropriate methods with specific names and arguments. You can think of an **interface** as a group of related abstract methods that a class must implement to be considered a member of the type identified with the interface name. Java 9 doesn't allow us to specify requirements for constructors or instance fields in interfaces. It is also important to take into account that an interface is not a class.

[In other programming languages, interfaces are known as protocols.]

For example, we can create a Hideable interface that specifies the following parameterless methods with empty bodies:

- getNumberOfEyes()
- appear()
- disappear()

Once we define an interface, we create a new type. Hence, we can use the interface name to specify the required type for an argument. This way, instead of using classes as types, we will use interfaces as types, and we can use an instance of any class that implements the specific interface as an argument. For example, if we use `Hideable` as the required type for an argument, we can pass an instance of any class that implements the `Hideable` interface as an argument.

> We can declare interfaces that inherit from more than one interface; that is, interfaces support multiple inheritance.

However, you must take into account some limitations for interfaces compared with abstract classes. Interfaces cannot specify requirements for constructors or instance fields because interfaces have to do with methods and signature. Interfaces can declare requirements for the following members:

- Class constants
- Static methods
- Instance methods
- Default methods
- Nested types

> Java 8 added the possibility to add default methods to interfaces. They allow us to declare methods that actually provide an implementation. Java 9 keeps this feature alive.

Declaring interfaces

It is time to code the necessary interfaces in Java 9. We will code the following five interfaces:

- `DrawableInComic`
- `DrawableInGame`
- `Hideable`
- `Powerable`
- `Fightable`

Some programming languages, such as C#, use I as a prefix for interfaces. Java 9 doesn't use this naming convention for interface names. Thus, if you see an interface named `IDrawableInComic`, it was probably coded by someone who has C# experience and transferred the naming convention to the Java land.

The following UML diagram shows the five interfaces that we will code with their required methods included in the diagram. Notice that we include the **<<interface>>** text before the class name in each diagram that declares an interface.

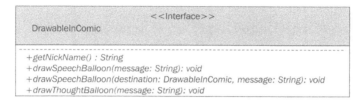

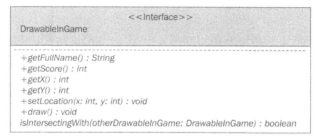

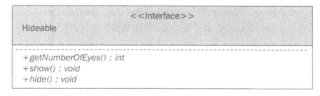

The following lines show the code for the DrawableInComic interface. The public modifier, followed by the interface keyword and the interface name, DrawableInComic, composes the interface declaration. As it happens with class declarations, the interface body is enclosed in curly brackets ({}). The code file for the sample is included in the java_9_oop_chapter_08_01 folder, in the example08_01.java file.

```java
public interface DrawableInComic {
    String getNickName();
    void drawSpeechBalloon(String message);
    void drawSpeechBalloon(DrawableInComic destination, String
    message);
    void drawThoughtBalloon(String message);
}
```

 The members declared in an interface have an implicit public modifier, and therefore, there is no need to specify public for each method declaration.

The DrawableInComic interface declared a getNickName method requirement, a drawSpeechBalloon method requirement overloaded twice, and a drawThoughtBalloon method requirement. The interface includes only the method declaration because the classes that implement the DrawableInComic interface will be responsible for providing the implementation of the getNickName method, the drawThoughtBalloon methods and the two overloads of the drawSpeechBalloon method. Note that there is no method body, as happened when we declared abstract methods for abstract classes. There is no need to use the abstract keyword to declare the methods because they are implicitly abstract.

The following lines show the code for the DrawableInGame interface. The code file for the sample is included in the java_9_oop_chapter_08_01 folder, in the example08_01.java file.

```java
public interface DrawableInGame {
    String getFullName();
    int getScore();
    int getX();
    int getY();
    void setLocation(int x, int y);
    void draw();
    boolean isIntersectingWith(DrawableInGame
    otherDrawableInGame);
}
```

The `DrawableInGame` interface declaration includes seven method requirements: `getFullName`, `getScore`, `getX`, `getY`, `setLocation`, `draw`, and `isIntersectingWith`.

The following lines show the code for the `Hideable` interface. The code file for the sample is included in the `java_9_oop_chapter_08_01` folder, in the `example08_01.java` file.

```java
public interface Hideable {
    int getNumberOfEyes();
    void show();
    void hide();
}
```

The `Hideable` interface declaration includes three method requirements: `getNumberOfEyes`, `show`, and `hide`.

The following lines show the code for the `Powerable` interface. The code file for the sample is included in the `java_9_oop_chapter_08_01` folder, in the `example08_01.java` file.

```java
public interface Powerable {
    int getSpellPower();
    void useSpellToHide(Hideable hideable);
}
```

The `Powerable` interface declaration includes two method requirements: `getSpellPower` and `useSpellToHide`. As it happened in other method requirement declarations included in the previously declared interface, we use an interface name as the type of an argument within a method declaration. In this case, the `hideable` argument for the `useSpellToHide` method declaration is `Hideable`. Hence, we will be able to call the method with any class that implements the `Hideable` interface.

The following lines show the code for the `Fightable` interface. The code file for the sample is included in the `java_9_oop_chapter_08_01` folder, in the `example08_01.java` file.

```java
public interface Fightable {
    int getSwordPower();
    int getSwordWeight();
    void unsheathSword();
    void unsheathSword(Hideable hideable);
}
```

The `Fightable` interface declaration includes four method requirements: `getSwordPower`, `getSwordWeight`, and the two overloads of the `unsheathSword` method.

Declaring classes that implement interfaces

Now, we will declare a concrete class that specifies that it implements the DrawableInComic interface in its declaration in JShell. Instead of specifying a superclass, the class declaration includes the name of the previously declared DrawableInComic interface after the class name (SiperDog) and the implements keyword. We can read the class declaration as "the SpiderDog class implements the DrawableInComic interface." The code file for the sample is included in the java_9_oop_chapter_08_01 folder, in the example08_02.java file.

```
public class SpiderDog implements DrawableInComic {
}
```

The Java compiler will generate an error because the SpiderDog class is declared as a concrete class and doesn't override all the abstract methods declared in the DrawableInComic interface. JShell displays us the following error, indicating that the first method declaration in the interface isn't overridden:

```
jshell> public class SpiderDog implements DrawableInComic {
   ...> }
|  Error:
|  SpiderDog is not abstract and does not override abstract method
drawThoughtBalloon(java.lang.String) in DrawableInComic
```

Now, we will replace the previous declaration of the empty SuperDog class with a class that tries to implement the DrawableInComic interface, but it still doesn't achieve its goal. The following lines show the new code for the SuperDog class. The code file for the sample is included in the java_9_oop_chapter_08_01 folder, in the example08_03.java file.

```
public class SpiderDog implements DrawableInComic {
    protected final String nickName;

    public SpiderDog(String nickName) {
        this.nickName = nickName;
    }

    protected void speak(String message) {
        System.out.println(
            String.format("%s -> %s",
                nickName,
                message));
```

```
        }

        protected void think(String message) {
            System.out.println(
                String.format("%s -> ***%s***",
                    nickName,
                    message));
        }

        @Override
        String getNickName() {
            return nickName;
        }

        @Override
        void drawSpeechBalloon(String message) {
            speak(message);
        }

        @Override
        void drawSpeechBalloon(DrawableInComic destination,
            String message) {
            speak(String.format("message: %s, %s",
                destination.getNickName(),
                message));
        }

        @Override
        void drawThoughtBalloon(String message) {
            think(message);
        }
    }
}
```

The Java compiler will generate many errors because the SpiderDog concrete class doesn't implement the DrawableInComic interface. JShell displays us the following error messages, indicating that the interface required many methods to be declared as public methods.

```
|  Error:
|  drawThoughtBalloon(java.lang.String) in SpiderDog cannot implement
drawThoughtBalloon(java.lang.String) in DrawableInComic
|     attempting to assign weaker access privileges; was public
|     @Override
|     ^---------...
```

```
|   Error:

|   drawSpeechBalloon(DrawableInComic,java.lang.String) in SpiderDog
cannot implement drawSpeechBalloon(DrawableInComic,java.lang.String) in
DrawableInComic

|     attempting to assign weaker access privileges; was public

|       @Override

|       ^--------...

|   Error:

|   drawSpeechBalloon(java.lang.String) in SpiderDog cannot implement
drawSpeechBalloon(java.lang.String) in DrawableInComic

|     attempting to assign weaker access privileges; was public

|       @Override

|       ^--------...

|   Error:

|   getNickName() in SpiderDog cannot implement getNickName() in
DrawableInComic

|     attempting to assign weaker access privileges; was public

|       @Override

|       ^--------...
```

The public `DrawableInComic` interface specified methods that are implicitly public.
Thus, when we declare a class that doesn't declare the required members as `public`,
the Java compiler generates errors and indicates that we cannot attempt to assign a
weaker access privilege than the one required by the interface.

Whenever we declare a class that specifies that it implements an interface,
it must fulfill all the requirements specified in the interface. If it doesn't,
the Java compiler will generate errors indicating which requirements
aren't fulfilled, as it happened in the previous example. When we work
with interfaces, the Java compiler makes sure that the requirements
specified in them are honored in any class that implements them.

Finally, we will replace the previous declaration of the `SpiderDog` class with a class
that really implements the `DrawableInComic` interface. The following lines show
the new code for the `SpiderDog` class. The code file for the sample is included in the
`java_9_oop_chapter_08_01` folder, in the `example08_04.java` file.

```java
public class SpiderDog implements DrawableInComic {
    protected final String nickName;

    public SpiderDog(String nickName) {
```

```java
            this.nickName = nickName;
    }

    protected void speak(String message) {
        System.out.println(
            String.format("%s -> %s",
                nickName,
                message));
    }

    protected void think(String message) {
        System.out.println(
            String.format("%s -> ***%s***",
                nickName,
                message));
    }

    @Override
    public String getNickName() {
        return nickName;
    }

    @Override
    public void drawSpeechBalloon(String message) {
        speak(message);
    }

    @Override
    public void drawSpeechBalloon(DrawableInComic destination,
        String message) {
        speak(String.format("message: %s, %s",
            destination.getNickName(),
            message));
    }

    @Override
    public void drawThoughtBalloon(String message) {
        think(message);
    }
}
```

The `SpiderDog` class declares a constructor that assigns the value of the required `nickName` argument to the `nickName` immutable protected field. The class implements the `getNickName` method that just returns the `nickName` immutable protected field. The class declares the code for the two versions of the `drawSpeechBalloon` method. Both methods call the protected `speak` method that prints a message with a specific format that includes the `nickName` value as a prefix. In addition, the class declares the code for the `drawThoughtBalloon` method that invokes the protected `think` method that also prints a message including the `nickName` value as a prefix.

The `SpiderDog` class implements the methods declared in the `DrawableInComic` interface. The class also declares a constructor, a `protected` immutable field, and two `protected` methods.

 As long as we implement all the members declared in the interface or interfaces listed in the class declaration after the `implements` keyword, we can add any desired additional member to the class.

Now, we will declare another class that implements the same interface that the `SpiderDog` class implemented, that is, the `DrawableInComic` interface. The following lines show the code for the `WonderCat` class. The code file for the sample is included in the `java_9_oop_chapter_08_01` folder, in the `example08_04.java` file.

```java
public class WonderCat implements DrawableInComic {
    protected final String nickName;
    protected final int age;

    public WonderCat(String nickName, int age) {
        this.nickName = nickName;
        this.age = age;
    }

    public int getAge() {
        return age;
    }

    @Override
    public String getNickName() {
        return nickName;
    }

    @Override
```

```java
    public void drawSpeechBalloon(String message) {
        String meow =
            (age > 2) ? "Meow" : "Meeoow Meeoow";
        System.out.println(
            String.format("%s -> %s",
                nickName,
                meow));
    }


    @Override
    public void drawSpeechBalloon(DrawableInComic destination,
        String message) {
        System.out.println(
            String.format("%s ==> %s --> %s",
                destination.getNickName(),
                nickName,
                message));
    }


    @Override
    public void drawThoughtBalloon(String message) {
        System.out.println(
            String.format("%s thinks: '%s'",
                nickName,
                message));
    }
}
}
```

The `WonderCat` class declares a constructor that assigns the value of the required `nickName` and `age` arguments to the `nickName` and `age` immutable fields. The class declares the code for the two versions of the `drawSpeechBalloon` method. The version that requires only a `message` argument uses the value of the `age` property to generate a different message when the `age` value is greater than 2. In addition, the class declares the code for the `drawThoughtBalloon` and `getNickName` methods.

The `WonderCat` class implements the methods declared in the `DrawableInComic` interface. However, the class also declares an additional immutable field, `age`, and a `getAge` method that aren't required by the interface.

 Interfaces in Java 9 allow us to make sure that the classes that implement them define all the members specified in the interface. If they don't, the code won't compile.

Taking advantage of the multiple inheritance of interfaces

Java 9 doesn't allow us to declare a class with multiple superclasses or base classes, so there is no support for multiple inheritance of classes. A subclass can inherit from just one class. However, a class can implement one or more interfaces. In addition, we can declare classes that inherit from a superclass and implement one or more interfaces. Hence, we can combine class-based inheritance with the implementation of interfaces.

We want the WonderCat class to implement both the DrawableInComic and DrawableInGame interfaces. We want to be able to use any WonderCat instance as both a comic character and a game character. In order to do so, we must change the class declaration and add the DrawableInGame interface to the list of interfaces that the class implements and declare all the methods included in this added interface within the class.

The following lines show the new class declaration that specifies that the WonderCat class implements both the DrawableInComic and the DrawableInGame interfaces. The class body remains without changes, and therefore, we don't repeat the code. The code file for the sample is included in the java_9_oop_chapter_08_01 folder, in the example08_05.java file.

```
public class WonderCat implements
    DrawableInComic, DrawableInGame {
```

After we change the class declaration, the Java compiler will generate many errors because the new version of the WonderCat concrete class doesn't implement the DrawableInGame interface. JShell displays us the following error message.

```
| Error:
|  WonderCat is not abstract and does not override abstract method isInte
rsectingWith(DrawableInGame) in DrawableInGame
|  public class WonderCat implements
|  ^--------------------------------...
```

The following lines show the new version of the WonderCat class that really implements both the DrawableInComic and the DrawableInGame interfaces. The changes are highlighted in the next code snippet. The code file for the sample is included in the java_9_oop_chapter_08_01 folder, in the example08_06.java file.

```
public class WonderCat implements
    DrawableInComic, DrawableInGame {
    protected final String nickName;
```

```java
protected final int age;
protected int score;
protected final String fullName;
protected int x;
protected int y;

public WonderCat(String nickName,
    int age,
    String fullName,
    int score,
    int x,
    int y) {
    this.nickName = nickName;
    this.age = age;
    this.fullName = fullName;
    this.score = score;
    this.x = x;
    this.y = y;
}

public int getAge() {
    return age;
}

@Override
public String getNickName() {
    return nickName;
}

@Override
public void drawSpeechBalloon(String message) {
    String meow =
        (age > 2) ? "Meow" : "Meeoow Meeoow";
    System.out.println(
        String.format("%s -> %s",
            nickName,
            meow));
}

@Override
public void drawSpeechBalloon(DrawableInComic destination,
    String message) {
    System.out.println(
        String.format("%s ==> %s --> %s",
```

```
                destination.getNickName(),
                nickName,
                message));
    }

    @Override
    public void drawThoughtBalloon(String message) {
        System.out.println(
            String.format("%s thinks: '%s'",
                nickName,
                message));
    }

    @Override
    public String getFullName() {
        return fullName;
    }

    @Override
    public int getScore() {
        return score;
    }

    @Override
    public int getX() {
        return x;
    }

    @Override
    public int getY() {
        return y;
    }

    @Override
    public void setLocation(int x, int y) {
        this.x = x;
        this.y = y;
        System.out.println(
            String.format("Moving WonderCat %s to x:%d, y:%d",
                fullName,
                this.x,
                this.y));
    }
```

```
@Override
public void draw() {
    System.out.println(
        String.format("Drawing WonderCat %s at x:%d, y:%d",
            fullName,
            x,
            y));
}

@Override
public boolean isIntersectingWith(
    DrawableInGame otherDrawableInGame) {
    return ((x == otherDrawableInGame.getX()) &&
        (y == otherDrawableInGame.getY())));
}
}
}
```

The new constructor assigns the value of the additional required `fullName`, `score`, x, and y arguments to the fields with the same names. Hence, we will need to specify these additional arguments whenever we want to create an instance of the `AngryCat` class. In addition, the class added the implementation of all the methods specified in the `DrawableInGame` interface.

Combining class inheritance and interfaces

We can combine class inheritance with the implementation of interfaces. The following lines show the code for a new `HideableWonderCat` class that inherits from the `WonderCat` class and implements the `Hideable` interface. Note that the class declaration includes the superclass (`WonderCat`) after the `extends` keyword and the implemented interface (`Hideable`) after the `implements` keyword. The code file for the sample is included in the `java_9_oop_chapter_08_01` folder, in the `example08_07.java` file.

```
public class HideableWonderCat extends WonderCat implements Hideable {
    protected final int numberOfEyes;

    public HideableWonderCat(String nickName, int age,
        String fullName, int score,
        int x, int y, int numberOfEyes) {
        super(nickName, age, fullName, score, x, y);
        this.numberOfEyes = numberOfEyes;
    }
```

```
    @Override
    public int getNumberOfEyes() {
        return numberOfEyes;
    }

    @Override
    public void show() {
        System.out.println(
            String.format(
                "My name is %s and you can see my %d eyes.",
                getFullName(),
                numberOfEyes));
    }

    @Override
    public void hide() {
        System.out.println(
            String.format(
                "%s is hidden.",
                getFullName()));
    }
}
```

As a result of the previous code, we have a new class named `HideableWonderCat` that implements the following three interfaces:

- `DrawableInComic`: This interface is implemented by the `WonderCat` superclass and inherited by `HideableWonderCat`

- `DrawableInGame`: This interface is implemented by the `WonderCat` superclass and inherited by `HideableWonderCat`

- `Hideable`: This interface is implemented by `HideableWonderCat`

The constructor defined in the `HideableWonderCat` class adds a `numberOfEyes` argument to the argument list defined in the constructor declared in the `WonderCat` superclass. In this case, the constructor calls the constructor defined in the superclass by using the `super` keyword and then initializes the `numberOfEyes` immutable field with the value received in the `numberOfEyes` argument. The class implements the `getNumberOfEyes`, `show`, and `hide` methods required by the `Hideable` interface.

The following lines show the code for a new PowerableWonderCat class that inherits from the WonderCat class and implements the Powerable interface. Note that the class declaration includes the superclass (WonderCat) after the extends keyword and the implemented interface (Powerable) after the implements keyword. The code file for the sample is included in the java_9_oop_chapter_08_01 folder, in the example08_07.java file.

```
public class PowerableWonderCat extends WonderCat implements Powerable
{
    protected final int spellPower;

    public PowerableWonderCat(String nickName,
        int age,
        String fullName,
        int score,
        int x,
        int y,
        int spellPower) {
        super(nickName, age, fullName, score, x, y);
        this.spellPower = spellPower;
    }

    @Override
    public int getSpellPower() {
        return spellPower;
    }

    @Override
    public void useSpellToHide(Hideable hideable) {
        System.out.println(
            String.format(
                "%s uses his %d spell power to hide the Hideable with
%d eyes.",
                getFullName(),
                spellPower,
                hideable.getNumberOfEyes()));
    }
}
```

As it happened with the HideableWonderCat class, the new PowerableWonderCat class implements three interfaces. Two of these interfaces are implemented by the WonderCat superclass and inherited by HideableWonderCat: DrawableInComic and DrawableInGame. The HideableWonderCat class adds the implementation of the Powerable interface.

The constructor defined in the PowerableWonderCat class adds a spellPower argument to the argument list defined in the constructor declared in the WonderCat superclass. In this case, the constructor calls the constructor defined in the superclass by using the super keyword and then initializes the spellPower immutable field with the value received in the spellPower argument. The class implements the getSpellPower and useSpellToHide methods required by the Powerable interface.

The hide method receives a Hideable as an argument. Hence, any instance of HideableWonderCat would qualify as an argument for this method, that is, any instance of any class that conforms to the Hideable instance.

The following lines show the code for a new FightableWonderCat class that inherits from the WonderCat class and implements the Fightable interface. Note that the class declaration includes the superclass (WonderCat) after the extends keyword and the implemented interface (Fightable) after the implements keyword. The code file for the sample is included in the java_9_oop_chapter_08_01 folder, in the example08_07.java file.

```
public class FightableWonderCat extends WonderCat implements Fightable
{
    protected final int swordPower;
    protected final int swordWeight;

    public FightableWonderCat(String nickName,
        int age,
        String fullName,
        int score,
        int x,
        int y,
        int swordPower,
        int swordWeight) {
        super(nickName, age, fullName, score, x, y);
        this.swordPower = swordPower;
        this.swordWeight = swordWeight;
    }

    private void printSwordInformation() {
        System.out.println(
            String.format(
                "%s unsheaths his sword.",
                getFullName()));
```

```
        System.out.println(
            String.format(
                "Sword power: %d. Sword weight: %d.",
                swordPower,
                swordWeight));
    }

    @Override
    public int getSwordPower() {
        return swordPower;
    }

    @Override
    public int getSwordWeight() {
        return swordWeight;
    }

    @Override
    public void unsheathSword() {
        printSwordInformation();
    }

    @Override
    public void unsheathSword(Hideable hideable) {
        printSwordInformation();
        System.out.println(
            String.format("The sword targets a Hideable with %d
eyes.",
                hideable.getNumberOfEyes()));
    }
}
```

As it happened with the two previously coded classes that are inherited from
the WonderCat class and implemented interfaces, the new FightableWonderCat
class implements three interfaces. Two of these interfaces are implemented by the
WonderCat superclass and inherited by FightableWonderCat: DrawableInComic
and DrawableInGame. The FightableWonderCat class adds the implementation of
the Fightable interface.

The constructor defined in the FightableWonderCat class adds the swordPower and swordWeight arguments to the parameters list defined in the constructor declared in the WonderCat superclass. In this case, the constructor calls the constructor defined in the superclass by using the super keyword and then initializes the swordPower and swordWeight immutable fields with the value received in the swordPower and swordWeight arguments.

The class implements getSpellPower, getSwordWeight, and the two versions of the unsheathSword method required by the Fightable interface. The two versions of the unsheathSword method call the protected printSwordInformation method and the overloaded version that receives a Hideable instance as an argument prints an additional message with the number of eyes of the Hideable instance that the sword has as a target.

The following table summarizes the interfaces that each of the classes we created implements:

Class name	Implements the following interfaces
SpiderDog	DrawableInComic
WonderCat	DrawableInComic and DrawableInGame
HideableWonderCat	DrawableInComic, DrawableInGame, and Hideable
PowerableWonderCat	DrawableInComic, DrawableInGame, and Powerable
FightableWonderCat	DrawableInComic, DrawableInGame, and Fightable

The following simplified UML diagram shows the hierarchy tree for the classes and their relationship with interfaces. The diagram doesn't include any members for the interfaces and classes to make it simpler to understand the relationships. The dashed lines that end with an arrow indicate that the class implements the interface indicated by the arrow.

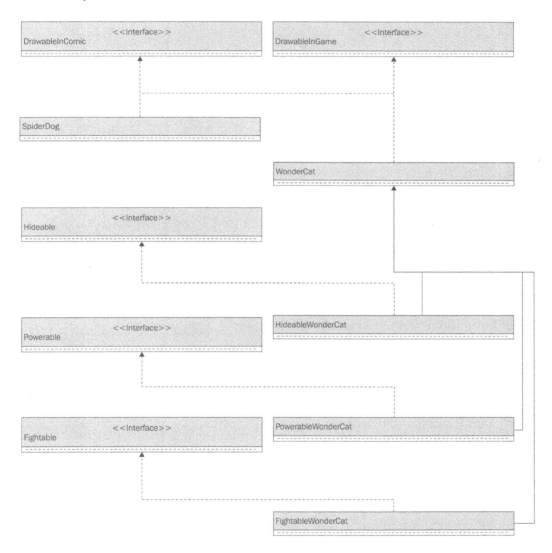

The following UML diagram shows the interfaces and the classes with all their members. Notice that we don't repeat the members declared in the interfaces that the classes implement to make the diagram simpler and to avoid repeating information. We can use the diagram to understand all the things that we will analyze with the next code samples based on the usage of these classes and the previously defined interfaces:

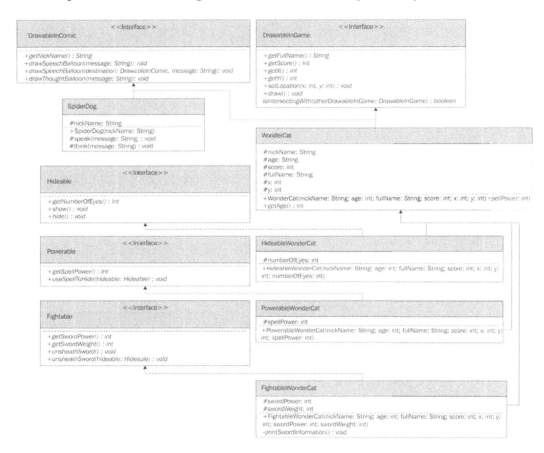

The following lines create one instance of each of the previously created classes. The code file for the sample is included in the `java_9_oop_chapter_08_01` folder, in the `example08_08.java` file.

```
SpiderDog spiderDog1 =
    new SpiderDog("Buddy");
WonderCat wonderCat1 =
    new WonderCat("Daisy", 1, "Mrs. Daisy", 100, 15, 15);
```

```
HideableWonderCat hideableWonderCat1 =
    new HideableWonderCat("Molly", 5, "Mrs. Molly", 450, 20, 10, 3);
PowerableWonderCat powerableWonderCat1 =
    new PowerableWonderCat("Princess", 5, "Mrs. Princess", 320, 20,
        10, 7);
FightableWonderCat fightableWonderCat1 =
    new FightableWonderCat("Abby", 3, "Mrs. Abby", 1200, 40, 10, 7,
        5);
```

The following table summarizes the instance name and its class name for the instances we have created with the previous code snippet:

Instance name	Class name
spiderDog1	SpiderDog
wonderCat1	WonderCat
hideableWonderCat1	HideableWonderCat
powerableWonderCat1	PowerableWonderCat
fightableWonderCat1	FightableWonderCat

Now, we will evaluate many expressions that use the instanceof keyword to determine whether the instances are an instance of the specified class or of a class that implements a specific interface. Note that all the expressions are evaluated to true because the type specified at the right-hand side after the instanceof keyword for each instance is its main class, its superclass, or an interface that the main class implements.

For example, powerableWonderCat1 is an instance of PowerableWonderCat. In addition, powerableWonderCat1 belongs to WonderCat because WonderCat is the superclass of the PowerableWonderCat class. It is also true that powerableWonderCat1 implements three interfaces: DrawableInComic, DrawableInGame, and Powerable. The superclass of PowerableWonderCat, WonderCat, implements the following two interfaces: DrawableInComic and DrawableInGame. Hence, PowerableWonderCat inherits the implementation of the interfaces. Finally, the PowerableWonderCat class not only inherits from WonderCat, but also implements the Powerable interface.

In *Chapter 3, Classes and Instances*, we learned that the `instanceof` keyword allows us to test whether an object is of the specified type. This type can be either a class or an interface. If we execute the following lines with many expressions in JShell, all of them will print `true` as a result of their evaluation. The code file for the sample is included in the `java_9_oop_chapter_08_01` folder, in the `example08_08.java` file.

```
spiderDog1 instanceof SpiderDog
spiderDog1 instanceof DrawableInComic

wonderCat1 instanceof WonderCat
wonderCat1 instanceof DrawableInComic
wonderCat1 instanceof DrawableInGame

hideableWonderCat1 instanceof WonderCat
hideableWonderCat1 instanceof HideableWonderCat
hideableWonderCat1 instanceof DrawableInComic
hideableWonderCat1 instanceof DrawableInGame
hideableWonderCat1 instanceof Hideable

powerableWonderCat1 instanceof WonderCat
powerableWonderCat1 instanceof PowerableWonderCat
powerableWonderCat1 instanceof DrawableInComic
powerableWonderCat1 instanceof DrawableInGame
powerableWonderCat1 instanceof Powerable

fightableWonderCat1 instanceof WonderCat
fightableWonderCat1 instanceof FightableWonderCat
fightableWonderCat1 instanceof DrawableInComic
fightableWonderCat1 instanceof DrawableInGame
fightableWonderCat1 instanceof Fightable
```

The following two screenshots show the results of evaluating the previous expressions in JShell:

```
jshell> spiderDog1 instanceof SpiderDog
$17 ==> true
|  created scratch variable $17 : boolean

jshell> spiderDog1 instanceof DrawableInComic
$18 ==> true
|  created scratch variable $18 : boolean

jshell> wonderCat1 instanceof WonderCat
$19 ==> true
|  created scratch variable $19 : boolean

jshell> wonderCat1 instanceof DrawableInComic
$20 ==> true
|  created scratch variable $20 : boolean

jshell> wonderCat1 instanceof DrawableInGame
$21 ==> true
|  created scratch variable $21 : boolean

jshell> hideableWonderCat1 instanceof WonderCat
$22 ==> true
|  created scratch variable $22 : boolean

jshell> hideableWonderCat1 instanceof HideableWonderCat
$23 ==> true
|  created scratch variable $23 : boolean

jshell> hideableWonderCat1 instanceof DrawableInComic
$24 ==> true
|  created scratch variable $24 : boolean

jshell> hideableWonderCat1 instanceof DrawableInGame
$25 ==> true
|  created scratch variable $25 : boolean

jshell> hideableWonderCat1 instanceof Hideable
$26 ==> true
|  created scratch variable $26 : boolean
```

```
jshell> powerableWonderCat1 instanceof WonderCat
$27 ==> true
|  created scratch variable $27 : boolean

jshell> powerableWonderCat1 instanceof PowerableWonderCat
$28 ==> true
|  created scratch variable $28 : boolean

jshell> powerableWonderCat1 instanceof DrawableInComic
$29 ==> true
|  created scratch variable $29 : boolean

jshell> powerableWonderCat1 instanceof DrawableInGame
$30 ==> true
|  created scratch variable $30 : boolean

jshell> powerableWonderCat1 instanceof Powerable
$31 ==> true
|  created scratch variable $31 : boolean

jshell> fightableWonderCat1 instanceof WonderCat
$32 ==> true
|  created scratch variable $32 : boolean

jshell> fightableWonderCat1 instanceof FightableWonderCat
$33 ==> true
|  created scratch variable $33 : boolean

jshell> fightableWonderCat1 instanceof DrawableInComic
$34 ==> true
|  created scratch variable $34 : boolean

jshell> fightableWonderCat1 instanceof DrawableInGame
$35 ==> true
|  created scratch variable $35 : boolean

jshell> fightableWonderCat1 instanceof Fightable
$36 ==> true
|  created scratch variable $36 : boolean
```

Test your knowledge

1. A class can implement:

    1. Only one interface.

    2. One or more interfaces.

    3. A maximum of two interfaces.

2. When a class implements an interface:

    1. It can also inherit from a superclass.

    2. It cannot inherit from a superclass.

    3. It can inherit only from an abstract superclass but not from concrete superclasses.

3. An interface:

    1. Can inherit from a superclass.

    2. Cannot inherit from either a superclass or another interface.

    3. Can inherit from another interface.

4. Which of the following lines declares a class named `WonderDog` that implements the `Hideable` interface:

    1. `public class WonderDog extends Hideable {`

    2. `public class WonderDog implements Hideable {`

    3. `public class WonderDog: Hideable {`

5. An interface is:

    1. A method.

    2. A type.

    3. An abstract class.

Summary

In this chapter, you learned about the declaration and combination of multiple blueprints to generate a single instance. We declared interfaces that specified the required methods. Then, we created many classes that implemented single and multiple interfaces.

We combined class inheritance with the implementation of interfaces. We realized that a single class can implement multiple interfaces. We executed code in JShell to understand that a single instance belongs to class types and to interface types.

Now that you have learned about interfaces and the basics for contract programming, we are ready to work with advanced contract programming scenarios, which is the topic we are going to discuss in the next chapter.

9
Advanced Contract Programming with Interfaces

In this chapter, we will dive deeper into contract programming with interfaces. We will have a better understanding of how interfaces work as types. We will:

- Work with methods receiving interfaces as arguments
- Downcast with interfaces and classes
- Understand boxing and unboxing
- Treat instances of an interface type as a different subclass
- Take advantage of default methods in interfaces in Java 9

Working with methods receiving interfaces as arguments

In the previous chapter, we created the following five interfaces: `DrawableInComic`, `DrawableInGame`, `Hideable`, `Powerable`, and `Fightable`. Then, we created the following classes that implemented different interfaces, and, many of them, also inherited from superclasses: `SpiderDog`, `WonderCat`, `HideableWonderCat`, `PowerableWonderCat`, and `FightableWonderCat`.

Run the following command in JShell to check all the types we have created:

```
/types
```

The following screenshot shows the results of executing the previous command in JShell. JShell enumerates the five interfaces and the five classes we have created in the session.

```
jshell> /types
|    interface DrawableInComic
|    interface DrawableInGame
|    interface Hideable
|    interface Powerable
|    interface Fightable
|    class SpiderDog
|    class WonderCat
|    class HideableWonderCat
|    class PowerableWonderCat
|    class FightableWonderCat

jshell>
```

When we work with interfaces, we use them to specify the argument types instead of using class names. Multiple classes might implement a single interface, and therefore, instances of different classes might qualify as an argument of a specific interface.

Now we will create additional instances of the previously mentioned classes and we will call methods that specified their required arguments with interface names instead of class names. We will understand what happens under the hood when we use interfaces as types for arguments in methods.

In the following code, the first two lines create two instances of the SpiderDog class named teddy and winston. Then, the code calls the two versions of the drawSpeechBalloon method for teddy. The second call to this method passes winston as the DrawableInComic argument because winston is an instance of SpiderDog, which is a class that implements the DrawableInComic instance. The code file for the sample is included in the java_9_oop_chapter_09_01 folder, in the example09_01.java file.

```
SpiderDog teddy = new SpiderDog("Teddy");
SpiderDog winston = new SpiderDog("Winston");
teddy.drawSpeechBalloon(
    String.format("Hello, my name is %s", teddy.getNickName()));
teddy.drawSpeechBalloon(winston, "How do you do?");
winston.drawThoughtBalloon("Who are you? I think.");
```

The following code creates an instance of the WonderCat class named oliver. The value specified for the nickName argument in the constructor is "Oliver". The next line calls the drawSpeechBalloon method for the new instance to introduce Oliver in the comic strip, and then teddy calls the drawSpeechBalloon method and passes oliver as the DrawableInComic argument because oliver is an instance of WonderCat, which is a class that implements the DrawableInComic instance. Hence, we can also use instances of WonderCat whenever we need a DrawableInComic argument. The code file for the sample is included in the java_9_oop_chapter_09_01 folder, in the example09_01.java file.

```
WonderCat oliver =
    new WonderCat("Oliver", 10, "Mr. Oliver", 0, 15, 25);
oliver.drawSpeechBalloon(
    String.format("Hello, my name is %s", oliver.getNickName()));
teddy.drawSpeechBalloon(oliver,
    String.format("Hello %s", oliver.getNickName()));
```

The following code creates an instance of the HideableWonderCat class named misterHideable. The value specified for the nickName argument in the constructor is "Mr. Hideable". The next line checks whether the call to the isIntersectingWith method with oliver as a parameter returns true. The method requires a DrawableInComic argument, and therefore, we can use oliver. The method will return true because the x and y fields of both instances have the same value. The line within the if block calls the setLocation method for misterHideable. Then, the code calls the show method. The code file for the sample is included in the java_9_oop_chapter_09_01 folder, in the example09_01.java file.

```
HideableWonderCat misterHideable =
    new HideableWonderCat("Mr. Hideable", 310,
        "Mr. John Hideable", 67000, 15, 25, 3);
if (misterHideable.isIntersectingWith(oliver)) {
    misterHideable.setLocation(
        oliver.getX() + 30, oliver.getY() + 30);
}
misterHideable.show();
```

The following code creates an instance of the `PowerableWonderCat` class named `merlin`. The value specified for the `nickName` argument in the constructor is `"Merlin"`. The next lines call the `setLocation` and `draw` methods. Then, the code calls the `useSpellToHide` method with `misterHideable` as the `Hideable` argument. The method requires a `Hideable` argument, and therefore, we can use `misterHideable`, which is the previously created instance of `HideableWonderCat` that implements the `Hideable` interface. Then, a call to the `show` method for `misterHideable` makes the `Hideable` with three eyes appear again. The code file for the sample is included in the `java_9_oop_chapter_09_01` folder, in the `example09_01.java` file.

```
PowerableWonderCat merlin =
    new PowerableWonderCat("Merlin", 35,
        "Mr. Merlin", 78000, 30, 40, 200);
merlin.setLocation(
    merlin.getX() + 5, merlin.getY() + 5);
merlin.draw();
merlin.useSpellToHide(misterHideable);
misterHideable.show();
```

The following code creates an instance of the `FightableWonderCat` class named `spartan`. The value specified for the `nickName` argument in the constructor is `"Spartan"`. The next lines call the `setLocation` and `draw` methods. Then, the code calls the `unsheathSword` method with `misterHideable` as a parameter. The method requires a `Hideable` argument, and therefore, we can use `misterHideable`, the previously created instance of `HideableWonderCat` that implements the `Hideable` interface. The code file for the sample is included in the `java_9_oop_chapter_09_01` folder, in the `example09_01.java` file.

```
FightableWonderCat spartan =
    new FightableWonderCat("Spartan", 28,
        "Sir Spartan", 1000000, 60, 60, 100, 50);
spartan.setLocation(
    spartan.getX() + 30, spartan.getY() + 10);
spartan.draw();
spartan.unsheathSword(misterHideable);
```

Finally, the code calls the `drawThoughtBalloon` and `drawSpeechBalloon` methods for `misterHideable`. We can call these methods because `misterHideable` is an instance of `HideableWonderCat`, and this class inherits the implementation of the `DrawableInComic` interface from its superclass: `WonderCat`.

The call to the `drawSpeechBalloon` method passes `spartan` as the `DrawableInComic` argument because `spartan` is an instance of `FightableWonderCat`, which is a class that also inherits the implementation of the `DrawableInComic` interface from its superclass: `WonderCat`. Hence, we can also use instances of `FightableWonderCat` whenever we need a `DrawableInComic` argument, as done in the next lines. The code file for the sample is included in the `java_9_oop_chapter_09_01` folder, in the `example09_01.java` file.

```
misterHideable.drawThoughtBalloon(
    "I guess I must be friendly...");
misterHideable.drawSpeechBalloon(
    spartan, "Pleased to meet you, Sir!");
```

After we execute all the previously explained code snippets in JShell, we will see the following text output:

```
Teddy -> Hello, my name is Teddy
Teddy -> message: Winston, How do you do?
Winston -> ***Who are you? I think.***
Oliver -> Meow
Teddy -> message: Oliver, Hello Oliver
Moving WonderCat Mr. John Hideable to x:45, y:55
My name is Mr. John Hideable and you can see my 3 eyes.
Moving WonderCat Mr. Merlin to x:35, y:45
Drawing WonderCat Mr. Merlin at x:35, y:45
Mr. Merlin uses his 200 spell power to hide the Hideable with 3 eyes.
My name is Mr. John Hideable and you can see my 3 eyes.
Moving WonderCat Sir Spartan to x:90, y:70
Drawing WonderCat Sir Spartan at x:90, y:70
Sir Spartan unsheaths his sword.
Sword power: 100. Sword weight: 50.
The sword targets a Hideable with 3 eyes.
Mr. Hideable thinks: 'I guess I must be friendly...'
Spartan ==> Mr. Hideable --> Pleased to meet you, Sir!
```

Downcasting with interfaces and classes

The `DrawableInComic` interface defines one of the method requirements for the `drawSpeechBalloon` method with `destination` as an argument of the `DrawableInComic` type, which is the same type that the interface defines. The following is the first line in our sample code that called this method:

```
teddy.drawSpeechBalloon(winston, "How do you do?");
```

We called the method implemented in the `SpiderDog` class because `teddy` is an instance of `SpiderDog`. We passed a `SpiderDog` instance, `winston`, to the `destination` argument. The method works with the `destination` argument as an instance that implements the `DrawableInComic` interface. Hence, whenever we reference the `destination` variable, we will only be able to see what the `DrawableInComic` type defines.

We can easily understand what happens under the hood when Java downcasts a type from its original type to a target type, such as an interface to which the class conforms. In this case, `SpiderDog` is downcasted to `DrawableInComic`. If we enter the following code in JShell and press the *Tab* key, JShell will enumerate the members for the `SpiderDog` instance named `winston`:

```
winston.
```

JShell will display the following members:

```
drawSpeechBalloon(    drawThoughtBalloon(    equals(
getClass()            getNickName()          hashCode()
nickName              notify()               notifyAll()
speak(                think(                 toString()
wait(
```

Whenever we ask JShell to list the members, it will include the following members inherited from `java.lang.Object`:

```
equals(      getClass()    hashCode()    notify()    notifyAll()
toString()   wait(
```

Delete the previously entered code (`winston.`). If we enter the following code in JShell and press the *Tab* key, the `DrawableInComic` interface type enclosed in parentheses as a prefix for the `winston` variable forces the downcast to the `DrawableInComic` interface type. Hence, JShell will only enumerate the members for the `SpiderDog` instance named `winston` that are required members in the `DrawableInComic` interface:

```
((DrawableInComic) winston).
```

JShell will display the following members:

```
drawSpeechBalloon(      drawThoughtBalloon(     equals(
getClass()              getNickName()           hashCode()
notify()                notifyAll()             toString()
wait(
```

Let's take a look at the difference between the results when we entered `winston`. and pressed the *Tab* key, and the latest results. The displayed members in the last list don't include the two methods that are defined in the `SpiderDog` class but aren't required in the `DrawableInComic` interface: `speak` and `think`. Hence, when Java downcasts `winston` to `DrawableInComic`, we can only work with the members required by the `DrawableInComic` interface.

 If we work with any IDE that supports auto-completion features, we will notice that same difference in the enumeration of the members when we use the auto-completion features instead of pressing the *Tab* key in JShell.

Now we will analyze another case in which we downcast an instance to one of the interfaces that it implements. The `DrawableInGame` interface defines a method requirement for the `isIntersectingWith` method with `otherDrawableInGame` as an argument of the `DrawableInGame` type, which is the same type that the interface defines. The following is the first line in our sample code that called this method:

```
if (misterHideable.isIntersectingWith(oliver)) {
```

We called the method defined within the `WonderCat` class because `misterHideable` is an instance of `HideableWonderCat` that inherits the implementation of the `isIntersectingWith` method from the `WonderCat` class. We passed a `WonderCat` instance, `oliver`, to the `otherDrawableInGame` argument. The method works with the `otherDrawableInGame` argument as an instance that implements the `DrawableInGame` instance. Hence, whenever we reference the `otherDrawableInGame` variable, we will only be able to see what the `DrawableInGame` type defines. In this case, `WonderCat` is downcasted to `DrawableInGame`.

If we enter the following code in JShell and press the *Tab* key, JShell will enumerate the members for the `WonderCat` instance named `oliver`:

```
oliver.
```

JShell will display the following members for `oliver`:

age	draw()	drawSpeechBalloon(
drawThoughtBalloon(	equals(	fullName
getAge()	getClass()	getFullName()
getNickName()	getScore()	getX()
getY()	hashCode()	isIntersectingWith(
nickName	notify()	notifyAll()
score	setLocation(	toString()
wait(	x	y

Delete the previously entered code (`oliver.`). If we enter the following code in JShell and press the *Tab* key, the `DrawableInGame` interface type enclosed in parentheses as a prefix for the `oliver` variable forces the downcast to the `DrawableInGame` interface type. Hence, JShell will only enumerate the members for the `WonderCat` instance named `oliver` that are required members in the `DrawableInGame` instance:

```
((DrawableInComic) oliver).
```

JShell will display the following members:

draw()	equals(	getClass()
getFullName()	getScore()	getX()
getY()	hashCode()	isIntersectingWith(
notify()	notifyAll()	setLocation(
toString()	wait(	

Let's take a look at the difference between the results when we entered `oliver.` and pressed the *Tab* key, and the latest results. When Java downcasts `oliver` to `DrawableInGame`, we can only work with the members required by the `DrawableInGame` interface.

We can use a similar syntax to force a cast of the previous expression to the original type, that is, to the `WonderCat` type. If we enter the following code in JShell and press the *Tab* key, JShell will enumerate all the members for the `WonderCat` instance named `oliver`, again:

```
((WonderCat) ((DrawableInGame) oliver)).
```

JShell will display the following members, that is, all the members that JShell enumerated when we entered `oliver.` without any kind of casting and pressed the *Tab* key:

`age`	`draw()`	`drawSpeechBalloon(`
`drawThoughtBalloon(`	`equals(`	`fullName`
`getAge()`	`getClass()`	`getFullName()`
`getNickName()`	`getScore()`	`getX()`
`getY()`	`hashCode()`	`isIntersectingWith(`
`nickName`	`notify()`	`notifyAll()`
`score`	`setLocation(`	`toString()`
`wait(`	`x`	`y`

Treating instances of an interface type as a different subclass

In *Chapter 7, Members Inheritance and Polymorphism*, we worked with polymorphism. The next example doesn't represent a best practice because polymorphism is the way to make it work. However, we will write some code that doesn't represent a best practice just to understand a bit more about typecasting.

The following lines create a method called `doSomethingWithWonderCat` in JShell. We will use this method to understand how we can treat an instance received with an interface type as a different subclass. The code file for the sample is included in the `java_9_oop_chapter_09_01` folder, in the `example09_02.java` file.

```
// The following code is just for educational purposes
// and it doesn't represent a best practice
// We should always take advantage of polymorphism instead
public void doSomethingWithWonderCat(WonderCat wonderCat) {
    if (wonderCat instanceof HideableWonderCat) {
        HideableWonderCat hideableCat = (HideableWonderCat)
            wonderCat;
        hideableCat.show();
    } else if (wonderCat instanceof FightableWonderCat) {
        FightableWonderCat fightableCat = (FightableWonderCat)
            wonderCat;
        fightableCat.unsheathSword();
```

```
        } else if (wonderCat instanceof PowerableWonderCat) {
            PowerableWonderCat powerableCat = (PowerableWonderCat)
                wonderCat;
            System.out.println(
                String.format("Spell power: %d",
                    powerableCat.getSpellPower()));
        } else {
            System.out.println("This WonderCat isn't cool.");
        }
    }
}
```

The doSomethingWithWonderCat method receives a WonderCat instance in the wonderCat argument. The method evaluates many expressions that use the instanceof keyword to determine whether the instance received in the wonderCat argument is an instance of HideableWonderCat, FightableWonderCat, or PowerableWonder.

In case wonderCat is an instance of HideableWonderCat or of any potential subclass of HideableWonderCat, the code declares a HideableWonderCat local variable named hideableCat to save the reference of wonderCat casted to HideableWonderCat. Then, the code calls the hideableCat.show method.

In case wonderCat is not an instance of HideableWonderCat, the code evaluates the next expression. In case wonderCat is an instance of FightableWonderCat or of any potential subclass of FightableWonderCat, the code declares a FightableWonderCat local variable named fightableCat to save the reference of wonderCat casted to FightableWonderCat. Then, the code calls the fightableCat.unsheathSword method.

In case wonderCat is not an instance of FightableWonderCat, the code evaluates the next expression. In case wonderCat is an instance of PowerableWonderCat or of any potential subclass of PowerableWonderCat, the code declares a PowerableWonderCat local variable named powerableCat to save the reference of wonderCat casted to PowerableWonderCat. Then, the code uses the results returned by the powerableCat.getSpellPower() method to print the spell power value.

Finally, if the last expression evaluates to false, it means that the wonderCat instance just belongs to WonderCat, and the code prints a message indicating that WonderCat isn't cool.

 In case we have to do something similar to the code shown in this method, we must take advantage of polymorphism instead of using the instanceof keyword to run code based on the class to whom an instance belongs. Remember that we are using the example to learn a bit more about typecasting.

Now we will make many calls to the recently coded doSomethingWithWonderCat method in JShell. We will call this method with instances of WonderCat and its subclasses that we created before we declared this method. We will call the doSomethingWithWonderCat method with the following values for the wonderCat argument:

- misterHideable: An instance of the HideableWonderCat class
- spartan: An instance of the FightableWonderCat class
- merlin: An instance of the PowerableWonderCat class
- oliver: An instance of the WonderCat class

The following four lines call the doSomethingWithWonderCat method in JShell with the previously enumerated arguments. The code file for the sample is included in the java_9_oop_chapter_09_01 folder, in the example09_02.java file.

```
doSomethingWithWonderCat(misterHideable);
doSomethingWithWonderCat(spartan);
doSomethingWithWonderCat(merlin);
doSomethingWithWonderCat(oliver);
```

The following screenshot shows the output generated in JShell for the previous lines. Each call triggers a different type cast and calls a method of the typecasted instance:

```
jshell> doSomethingWithWonderCat(misterHideable);
My name is Mr. John Hideable and you can see my 3 eyes.

jshell> doSomethingWithWonderCat(spartan);
Sir Spartan unsheaths his sword.
Sword power: 100. Sword weight: 50.

jshell> doSomethingWithWonderCat(merlin);
Spell power: 200

jshell> doSomethingWithWonderCat(oliver);
This WonderCat isn't cool.

jshell>
```

Taking advantage of default methods in interfaces in Java 9

Both the SpiderDog and WonderCat classes implement the DrawableInComic interface. All the classes that inherit from the WonderCat class, inherit the implementation of the DrawableInComic interface. Imagine that we have to add a new method requirement to the DrawableInComic interface and that we will create new classes that implement this new version of the interface. We will add a new drawScreamBalloon method that draws a scream balloon, also known as scream bubble, with a message.

We will add the implementation of the new method in the SpiderDog class. However, imagine that we cannot make changes to the code in one of the classes that implement the DrawableInComic interface: WonderCat. We have a big problem because as soon as we change the code for the DrawableInComic interface, the Java compiler will generate a compile error for the WonderCat class and we won't be able to compile this class and its subclasses.

In this scenario, the default methods for interfaces introduced in Java 8 and also available in Java 9 are extremely useful. We can declare a default implementation for the drawScreamBalloon method and include it in the new version of the DrawableInComic interface. This way, the WonderCat class and its subclasses will be able to use the default implementation for the method provided in the interface and they will comply with the requirements specified in the interface.

The following UML diagram shows the new version of the DrawableInComic interface with the default method named drawScreamBalloon and the new version of the SpiderDog class that overrides the default method. Notice that the drawScreamBalloon method is the only one that doesn't use italic text because it is not an abstract method.

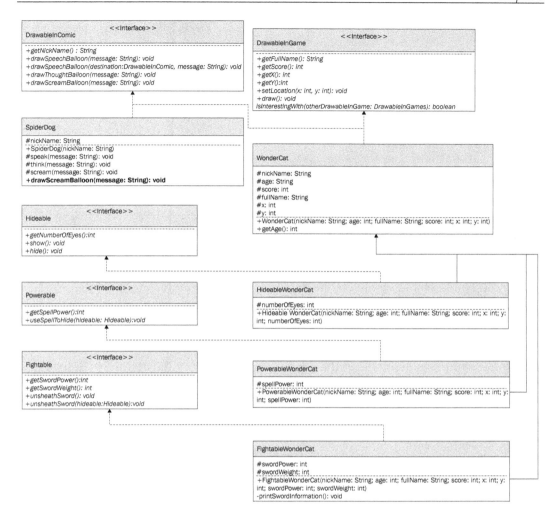

The following lines show the code that declares the new version of the `DrawableInComic` interface that includes a method requirement for the `drawScreamBalloon` method with a default implementation. Notice the `default` keyword before the method's return type to indicate that we are declaring a default method. The default implementation calls the `drawSpeechBalloon` method that each class that implements the interface will declare. This way, by default, the classes that implement this interface will draw a speech balloon when they receive the request to draw a scream balloon.

The code file for the sample is included in the `java_9_oop_chapter_09_01` folder, in the `example09_03.java` file.

```java
public interface DrawableInComic {
    String getNickName();
    void drawSpeechBalloon(String message);
    void drawSpeechBalloon(DrawableInComic destination, String
        message);
    void drawThoughtBalloon(String message);
    default void drawScreamBalloon(String message) {
        drawSpeechBalloon(message);
    }
}
```

 After we create the new version of the interface, JShell will reset all the variables that hold references of instances of classes that implement the `DrawableInComic` interface to null. Hence, we won't be able to use the instances we have been creating to test the changes in the interface.

The following lines show the code for the new version of the `SpiderDog` class with the new `drawScreamBalloon` method. The new lines are highlighted. The code file for the sample is included in the `java_9_oop_chapter_09_01` folder, in the `example09_03.java` file.

```java
public class SpiderDog implements DrawableInComic {
    protected final String nickName;

    public SpiderDog(String nickName) {
        this.nickName = nickName;
    }

    protected void speak(String message) {
        System.out.println(
            String.format("%s -> %s",
                nickName,
                message));
    }

    protected void think(String message) {
        System.out.println(
            String.format("%s -> ***%s***",
                nickName,
                message));
```

```
    }

    protected void scream(String message) {
        System.out.println(
            String.format("%s screams +++ %s +++",
                nickName,
                message));
    }

    @Override
    public String getNickName() {
        return nickName;
    }

    @Override
    public void drawSpeechBalloon(String message) {
        speak(message);
    }

    @Override
    public void drawSpeechBalloon(DrawableInComic destination,
        String message) {
        speak(String.format("message: %s, %s",
            destination.getNickName(),
            message));
    }

    @Override
    public void drawThoughtBalloon(String message) {
        think(message);
    }

    @Override
    public void drawScreamBalloon(String message) {
        scream(message);
    }
}
```

The SpiderDog class overrides the default implementation of the drawScreamBalloon
method with a new version that calls the protected scream method that prints
the received message with a specific format that includes the nickName value as
a prefix. This way, this class won't use the default implementation declared in the
DrawableInComic interface and will use its own implementation instead.

In the following code, the first lines create an instance of the new version of the SpiderDog class named rocky, and an instance of the new version of the FightableWonderCat class named maggie. Then, the code calls the drawScreamBalloon method with a message for the two created instances: rocky and maggie. The code file for the sample is included in the java_9_oop_ chapter_09_01 folder, in the example09_03.java file.

```
SpiderDog rocky = new SpiderDog("Rocky");
FightableWonderCat maggie =
    new FightableWonderCat("Maggie", 2,
        "Mrs. Maggie", 5000000, 10, 10, 80, 30);
rocky.drawScreamBalloon("I am Rocky!");
maggie.drawScreamBalloon("I am Mrs. Maggie!");
```

When we call rocky.drawScreamBalloon, Java executes the overridden implementation for this method declared in the SpiderDog class. When we call maggie.drawScreamBalloon, Java executes the default method declared in the DrawableInComic interface because neither the WonderCat nor the FightableWonderCat classes override the default implementation for this method. Don't forget that FightableWonderCat is a subclass of WonderCat. The following screenshot shows the results of executing the previous lines in JShell:

```
|    update replaced variable spiderDog1, reset to null
|    update replaced variable teddy, reset to null
|    update replaced variable winston, reset to null
|    update overwrote class SpiderDog

jshell> SpiderDog rocky = new SpiderDog("Rocky");
rocky ==> SpiderDog@2f943d71
|  created variable rocky : SpiderDog

jshell> FightableWonderCat maggie =
   ...>     new FightableWonderCat("Maggie", 2,
   ...>         "Mrs. Maggie", 5000000, 10, 10, 80, 30);
maggie ==> FightableWonderCat@4b553d26
|  created variable maggie : FightableWonderCat

jshell> rocky.drawScreamBalloon("I am Rocky!");
Rocky screams +++ I am Rocky! +++

jshell> maggie.drawScreamBalloon("I am Mrs. Maggie!");
Maggie -> Meeoow Meeoow

jshell>
```

Test your knowledge

1. A default method allows us to declare:

    1. A default constructor for an interface that Java will use when the class that implements the interface doesn't declare a constructor.

    2. A method that will be called before any method is executed for the instance of a class that implements the interface.

    3. A default implementation for a method in an interface that Java will use when a class that implements the interface doesn't provide its own implementation of this method.

2. Consider that we have an existing interface that many classes implement and all the classes compile without errors. If we add a default method to this interface:

    1. The classes that implement the interface won't compile until they provide an implementation for the new method requirement.

    2. The classes that implement the interface won't compile until they provide an implementation for the new constructor requirement.

    3. The classes that implement the interface will compile.

3. Which of the following keywords allow us to determine whether an instance is an instance of a class that implements a specific interface:

    1. `instanceof`

    2. `isinterfaceimplementedby`

    3. `implementsinterface`

4. Which of the following code snippets forces the downcast of the `winston` variable to the `DrawableInComic` interface:

    1. `(winston as DrawableInComic)`

    2. `((DrawableInComic) < winston)`

    3. `((DrawableInComic) winston)`

5. Which of the following code snippets forces the downcast of the `misterHideable` variable to the `HideableWonderCat` class:

    1. `(misterHideable as HideableWonderCat)`

    2. `((HideableWonderCat) < misterHideable)`

    3. `((HideableWonderCat) misterHideable)`

Summary

In this chapter, you learned what happens under the hood when a method receives an argument of an interface type. We worked with methods that received arguments of interface types and we downcasted with interfaces and classes. We understood how we could treat an object as an instance of different compatible types and what happens when we do this. JShell allowed us to easily understand what happens when we use typecasting.

We took advantage of default methods in interfaces. We could add a new method to an interface and provide a default implementation to avoid breaking existing code that we couldn't edit.

Now that you have learned advanced scenarios in which we worked with interfaces, we are ready to maximize code reuse with generics in Java 9, which is the topic we are going to discuss in the next chapter.

10

Maximization of Code Reuse with Generics

In this chapter, we will learn about parametric polymorphism and how Java 9 implements this object-oriented concept by allowing us to write generic code. We will start creating classes that use one constrained generic type. We will:

- Understand parametric polymorphism
- Learn the differences between parametric polymorphism and duck typing
- Understand Java 9 generics and generic code
- Declare an interface to be used as a type constraint
- Declare a class that conforms to multiple interfaces
- Declare subclasses that inherit the implementation of interfaces
- Create exception classes
- Declare a class that works with a constrained generic type
- Use a generic class for multiple compatible types

Understanding parametric polymorphism, Java 9 generics, and generic code

Imagine that we have develop a Web Service that has to work with the representation of the organization of a party of specific wild animals. We definitely don't want to mix lions with hyenas because the party would end up with the hyenas intimidating a lonely lion. We want a well-organized party, and we don't want intruders such as dragons or cats in a party where only lions should attend.

We want to describe the procedures to start, welcome members, organize the party and say goodbye to the different members of the party. Then, we want to replicate these procedures with swans in a party of swans. Thus, we want to reuse our procedures for a party of lions and a party of swans. In the future, we will need to use the same procedures for parties of other wild and domestic animals, such as foxes, alligators, cats, tigers, and dogs. Obviously, we wouldn't like to become intruders in a party of alligators. Neither would we like to participate in the party of tigers.

In the previous chapters, *Chapter 8, Contract Programming with Interfaces*, and *Chapter 9, Advanced Contract Programming with Interfaces*, we learned to work with interfaces in Java 9. We can declare an interface to specify the requirements for an animal that can participate in a party and then take advantage of Java 9 features to write generic code that works with any class that implements the interface.

> **Parametric polymorphism** allows us to write generic and reusable code that can work with values without depending on the type while keeping the full static-type safety.

We can take advantage of parametric polymorphism in Java 9 through generics, also known as generic programming. After we declare an interface that indicates the requirements for an animal that can participate in a party, we can create a class that works with any instance that implements this interface. This way, we can reuse the code that generates a party of lions and create a party of swans, hyenas, or any other animal. Specifically, we can reuse code that generates a party of any instance of a class that implements the interface that specifies the requirements for an animal that can participate in a party.

We require animals to be sociable in order to participate in a party, and therefore, we can create an interface named `Sociable` to specify the requirements for an animal that can participate in a party. However, take into account that many wild animals we will use as an example are not very sociable.

> Many modern strongly typed programming languages allow us to work with parametric polymorphism through generics. If you have worked with C# or Swift, you will find that the syntax in Java 9 is very similar to the syntax used in these programming languages. C# also works with interfaces, but Swift uses protocols instead of interfaces.

Other programming languages, such as Python, JavaScript, and Ruby, work with a different philosophy known as **duck typing**, where the presence of certain fields and methods make an object suitable to its usage as a specific sociable animal. With duck typing, if we require sociable animals to have the getName and danceAlone methods, we can consider any object as a sociable animal as long as it provides the required methods. Thus, with duck typing, any instance of any type that provides the required methods can be used as a sociable animal.

Let's move to a real-life situation to understand the duck typing philosophy. Imagine that we see a bird and this bird quacks, swims, and walks like a duck. We can definitely call this bird a duck because it satisfies all the conditions required for this bird to be a duck. Similar examples related to a bird and a duck generate the duck typing name. We don't need additional information to work with the bird as a duck. Python, JavaScript, and Ruby are examples of languages where duck typing is extremely popular.

It is possible to work with duck typing in Java 9, but it is not the natural way of doing things in this programming language. It would require many complex workarounds to implement duck typing in Java 9. Thus, we will focus on learning to write generic code with parametric polymorphism through generics.

Declaring an interface to be used as a type constraint

First, we will create a Sociable interface to specify the requirements that a type must meet in order to be considered a potential member of a party, that is, a sociable animal in our application domain. Then, we will create a SociableAnimal abstract base class that implements this interface, and then, we will specialize this class in three concrete subclasses: SocialLion, SocialParrot, and SocialSwan. Then, we will create a Party class that will be able to work with instances of any class that implements the Sociable interface through generics. We will create two new classes that will represent specific exceptions. We will work with a party of sociable lions, one of sociable parrots, and another of sociable swans.

The following UML diagram shows the interface, the abstract class that implements it, and the concrete subclasses that we will create, including all the fields and methds:

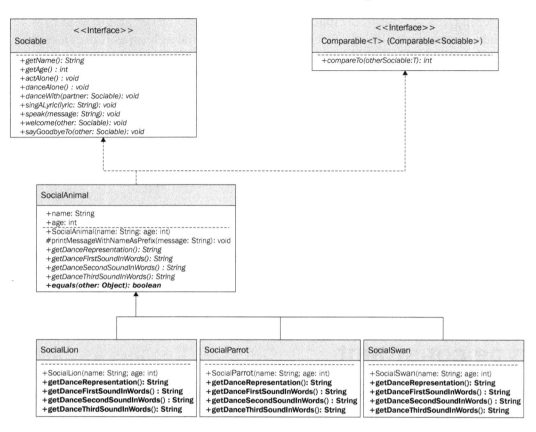

The following lines show the code for the Sociable interface. The code file for the sample is included in the `java_9_oop_chapter_10_01` folder, in the `example10_01.java` file.

```java
public interface Sociable {
    String getName();
    int getAge();
    void actAlone();
    void danceAlone();
    void danceWith(Sociable partner);
    void singALyric(String lyric);
```

```
        void speak(String message);
        void welcome(Sociable other);
        void sayGoodbyeTo(Sociable other);
}
```

The interface declares the following nine method requirements:

- getName: This method must return a String with the name for Sociable.

- getAge: This method must return an int with the age for Sociable.

- actAlone: This method must make Sociable act alone.

- danceAlone: This method must make Sociable dance alone.

- danceWith: This method must make Sociable dance with another Sociable received in the partner argument.

- singALyric: This method must make Sociable sing the lyric received as an argument.

- speak: This method makes Sociable say a message.

- welcome: This method makes Sociable say a welcome message to another Sociable received in the other argument.

- sayGoodbyeTo: This method makes Sociable say goodbye to another Sociable received in the other argument.

We didn't include any default method in the interface declaration, and therefore, the classes that implement the Sociable interface are responsible for implementing the previously enumerated nine methods.

Declaring a class that conforms to multiple interfaces

Now, we will declare an abstract class named SocialAnimal that implements both the previously defined Sociable interface and the Comparable<Sociable> interface. The latter makes it possible to compare two objects of the Sociable type. In order to implement the Comparable<Sociable> interface, we must implement the compareTo method that receives a Sociable instance and will return the results of comparing their age values. In addition, the class will override the equals method inherited from the java.lang.Object class. We will explain the code for this complex method later, when we review the code for the class. We can read the class declaration as "the SocialAnimal class implements both the Sociable and the Comparable of Sociable interfaces."

The `SocialAnimal` abstract class has too many lines of code, and therefore, we will use three code snippets instead of just one. The following lines show the first code snippet for the `SocialAnimal` abstract class. The code file for the sample is included in the `java_9_oop_chapter_10_01` folder, in the `example10_01.java` file.

```java
public abstract class SocialAnimal implements Sociable,
Comparable<Sociable> {
    public final String name;
    public final int age;

    public SocialAnimal(String name, int age) {
        this.name = name;
        this.age = age;
    }

    protected void printMessageWithNameAsPrefix(String message) {
        System.out.println(
            String.format("%s %s",
                getName(),
                message));
    }

    public abstract String getDanceRepresentation();

    public abstract String getFirstSoundInWords();

    public abstract String getSecondSoundInWords();

    public abstract String getThirdSoundInWords();

    @Override
    public String getName() {
        return name;
    }

    @Override
    public int getAge() {
        return age;
    }
```

The first code snippet for the `SocialAnimal` class declares a constructor that assigns the value of the required `name` and `age` arguments to the immutable `name` and `age` protected fields. Then the class declares a protected `printMessageWithNameAsPrefix` method that receives a message and prints the name for the `SocialAnimal` followed by a space and this message. Many methods will call this method to easily add the name as a prefix for many messages.

The class declares the following four abstract methods that must return a String. Each concrete subclass must provide an implementation for these methods and return the appropriate String values according to the sociable animal:

- getDanceRepresentation
- getFirstSoundInWords
- getSecondSoundInWords
- getThirdSoundInWords

The methods we will declare in the next code snippets will call the previously enumerated abstract methods. The class implements the getName and getAge methods that return the values for the name and age protected fields. The Sociable interface required these methods.

The following lines show the second code snippet for the SocialAnimal abstract class. The code file for the sample is included in the java_9_oop_chapter_10_01 folder, in the example10_01.java file.

```java
@Override
public void actAlone() {
    printMessageWithNameAsPrefix("to be or not to be");
}

@Override
public void danceAlone() {
    printMessageWithNameAsPrefix(
        String.format("dances alone %s",
            getDanceRepresentation()));
}

@Override
public void danceWith(Sociable partner) {
    printMessageWithNameAsPrefix(
        String.format("dances with %s %s",
            partner.getName(),
            getDanceRepresentation()));
}

@Override
public void singALyric(String lyric) {
    printMessageWithNameAsPrefix(
        String.format("sings %s %s %s %s",
            lyric,
            getFirstSoundInWords(),
```

```java
            getSecondSoundInWords(),
            getThirdSoundInWords()));
}

@Override
public void speak(String message) {
    printMessageWithNameAsPrefix(
        String.format("says: %s %s",
            message,
            getDanceRepresentation()));
}

@Override
public void welcome(Sociable other) {
    printMessageWithNameAsPrefix(
        String.format("welcomes %s",
            other.getName()));
}

@Override
public void sayGoodbyeTo(Sociable other) {
    printMessageWithNameAsPrefix(
        String.format("says goodbye to %s%s%s%s",
            other.getName(),
            getFirstSoundInWords(),
            getSecondSoundInWords(),
            getThirdSoundInWords()));
}
```

The second code snippet for the SocialAnimal class implements the other methods required by the Sociable interface:

- actAlone: This method prints the name followed by "to be or not to be".

- danceAlone: This method uses the String retrieved with a call to the getDanceRepresentation method to print the name followed by a message indicating that the social animal is dancing.

- danceWith: This method uses the String retrieved with a call to the getDanceRepresentation method to print the name followed by a message indicating that the social animal is dancing with the partner specified in the partner argument of the Sociable type. The message prints the name for the partner.

- `singALyric`: This method uses the strings retrieved with calls to `getFirstSoundInWords`, `getSecondSoundInWords`, and `getThirdSoundInWords` and the lyric received as an argument to print the name followed by a message indicating that the social animal sings the lyric.

- `speak`: This method uses the `String` retrieved with a call to `getDanceRepresentation` and the message received as an argument to print the name followed by the words that the animal says followed by its dance representation characters.

- `welcome`: This method prints a message to say welcome to another `Sociable` received in the other argument. The message includes the name for the destination.

- `sayGoodbyeTo`: This method uses the strings retrieved with calls to `getFirstSoundInWords`, `getSecondSoundInWords`, and `getThirdSoundInWords` and to build and print a message to say goodbye to another `Sociable` received in the other argument. The message includes the name for the destination.

The third code snippet for the `SocialAnimal` class overrides the `compareTo` method to implement the `Comparable<Sociable>` interface. In addition, this last code snippet for the `SocialAnimal` class overrides the `equals` method. The code file for the sample is included in the `java_9_oop_chapter_10_01` folder, in the `example10_01.java` file.

```
@Override
public boolean equals(Object other) {
    // Is other this object?
    if (this == other) {
        return true;
    }
    // Is other null?
    if (other == null) {
        return false;
    }
    // Does other have the same type?
    if (!getClass().equals(other.getClass())) {
        return false;
    }
    SocialAnimal otherSocialAnimal = (SocialAnimal) other;
    // Make sure both the name and age are equal
    return Objects.equals(getName(),
    otherSocialAnimal.getName())
    && Objects.equals(getAge(), otherSocialAnimal.getAge());
}
```

```
        @Override
        public int compareTo(final Sociable otherSociable) {
            return Integer.compare(getAge(),
                    otherSociable.getAge());
        }
    }
```

The third code snippet for the `SocialAnimal` class overrides the `equals` method inherited from `java.lang.Object` that receives the instance that we must compare with the actual instance in the `other` argument. Unluckily, we must use the `Object` type for the other argument in order to override the inherited method, and therefore, the code for the method has to use typecasting to cast the received instance to the `SocialAnimal` type.

First, the code checks whether the received `Object` is a reference to the actual instance. In this case, the code returns `true` and nothing else has to be checked.

Then, the code checks whether the value for `other` is equal to `null`. In case the method received `null`, the code returns `false` because the actual instance is not `null`.

Then, the code checks whether the `String` returned by the `getClass` method for the actual instance matches the `String` returned by the same method for the received instance. If these values do not match, it means that the received `Object` is an instance of a different type, and therefore, it is different and the code returns `false`.

At this point, we know that the actual instance has the same type as the received instance. Thus, it is safe to typecast the other argument to `SocialAnimal` and save the casted reference in the `otherSocialAnimal` local variable of the `SocialAnimal` type.

Finally, the code returns the results of evaluating whether the calls to `Object.equals` for `getName` and `getAge` for the current instance and `otherSocialAnimal` are both `true`.

It is a good practice to follow the previously explained steps when we override the `equals` method inherited from `java.lang.Object`. In case you have experience with C#, it is important to understand that Java 9 doesn't provide an equivalent to the `IEquatable<T>` interface. In addition, take into account that Java doesn't support user-defined operator overloading, a feature that is included in other object-oriented programming languages such as C++, C#, and Swift.

The `SocialAnimal` abstract class also implements the `compareTo` method required by the `Comparable<Sociable>` interface. In this case, the code is very simple because the method receives a `Sociable` instance in the `otherSociable` argument and returns the results of calling the `Integer.compare` method, that is, the `compare` class method for the `java.lang.Integer` class. The code calls this method with the `int` values returned by `getAge` for the current instance and `otherSociable` as the two arguments. The `Integer.compare` method returns the following:

- `0` if the first argument is equal to the second one.
- Less than `0` if the first argument is lower than the second one.
- Greater than `0` if the first argument is greater than the second one.

All the concrete subclasses that inherit from `SocialAnimal` will be able to use the `equals` and `compareTo` methods implemented in the `SocialAnimal` abstract class.

Declaring subclasses that inherit the implementation of interfaces

We have the `SocialAnimal` abstract class that implements both the `Sociable` and `Comparable<Sociable>` interfaces. We cannot create instances of this abstract class. Now, we will create a concrete subclass of `SocialAnimal` named `SocialLion`. The class declares a constructor that ends up calling the constructor defined in the superclass. The class implements the four abstract methods declared in its superclass to return the appropriate values for a lion that will participate in a party. The code file for the sample is included in the `java_9_oop_chapter_10_01` folder, in the `example10_01.java` file.

```java
public class SocialLion extends SocialAnimal {
    public SocialLion(String name, int age) {
        super(name, age);
    }

    @Override
    public String getDanceRepresentation() {
        return "*-* ^\\/^ (-)";
    }

    @Override
    public String getFirstSoundInWords() {
        return "Roar";
    }
```

```
    @Override
    public String getSecondSoundInWords() {
        return "Rrooaarr";
    }

    @Override
    public String getThirdSoundInWords() {
        return "Rrrrrrroooooaaarrrr";
    }
}
```

We will create another concrete subclass of SocialAnimal named SocialParrot. This new subclass also implements the abstract methods defined in the SocialAnimal superclass but, in this case, returns the appropriate values for a parrot. The code file for the sample is included in the java_9_oop_chapter_10_01 folder, in the example10_01.java file.

```
public class SocialParrot extends SocialAnimal {
    public SocialParrot(String name, int age) {
        super(name, age);
    }

    @Override
    public String getDanceRepresentation() {
        return "/|\\ -=- % % +=+";
    }

    @Override
    public String getFirstSoundInWords() {
        return "Yeah";
    }

    @Override
    public String getSecondSoundInWords() {
        return "Yeeaah";
    }

    @Override
    public String getThirdSoundInWords() {
        return "Yeeeaaaah";
    }
}
```

Finally, we will create another concrete subclass of `SocialAnimal` named `SocialSwan`. This new subclass also implements the abstract methods defined in the `SocialAnimal` superclass but, in this case, returns the appropriate values for a swan. The code file for the sample is included in the `java_9_oop_chapter_10_01` folder, in the `example10_01.java` file.

```java
public class SocialSwan extends SocialAnimal {
    public SocialSwan(String name, int age) {
        super(name, age);
    }

    @Override
    public String getDanceRepresentation() {
        return "^- ^- ^- -^ -^ -^";
    }

    @Override
    public String getFirstSoundInWords() {
        return "OO-OO-OO";
    }

    @Override
    public String getSecondSoundInWords() {
        return "WHO-HO WHO-HO";
    }

    @Override
    public String getThirdSoundInWords() {
        return "WHO-WHO WHO-WHO";
    }
}
```

We have three concrete classes that inherit the implementation of two interfaces from its abstract superclass: `SociableAnimal`. The following three concrete classes implement both the `Sociable` and `Comparable<Sociable>` interfaces, and they can use the inherited overridden `equals` method to compare their instances:

- `SocialLion`
- `SocialParrot`
- `SocialSwan`

Creating exception classes

We will create two exception classes because we need to throw exception types that aren't represented by any of the types included in the Java 9 platform. Specifically, we will create two subclasses of the java.lang.Exception class.

The following lines declare the InsufficientMembersException class that inherits from Exception. We will throw this exception when a party has an insufficient number of members to perform an operation that requires more members to be executed. The class defines an immutable numberOfMembers private field of the int type that is initialized with the value received in the constructor. In addition, the class declares a getNumberOfMembers method that returns the value for this field. The code file for the sample is included in the java_9_oop_chapter_10_01 folder, in the example10_01.java file.

```java
public class InsufficientMembersException extends Exception {
    private final int numberOfMembers;

    public InsufficientMembersException(int numberOfMembers) {
        this.numberOfMembers = numberOfMembers;
    }

    public int getNumberOfMembers() {
        return numberOfMembers;
    }
}
```

The following lines declare the CannotRemovePartyLeaderException class that inherits from Exception. We will throw this exception when a method tries to remove the current party leader from the party's member list. In this case, we just declare an empty class that inherits from Exception because we don't need additional features, we just want the new type. The code file for the sample is included in the java_9_oop_chapter_10_01 folder, in the example10_01.java file.

```java
public class CannotRemovePartyLeaderException extends Exception {
}
```

Declaring a class that works with a constrained generic type

The following lines declare a `Party` class that takes advantage of generics to work with many types. We import `java.util.concurrent.ThreadLocalRandom` because it is an extremely useful class to easily generate a pseudo-random number within a range. The class name, `Party`, is followed by a less than sign (`<`), a `T` that identifies the generic type parameter, the `extends` keyword, and an interface name that the `T` generic type parameter must implement, `Sociable`, an ampersand (`&`), and another interface name that the `T` generic type must also implement, `Comparable<Sociable>`. The greater than sign (`>`) ends the type constraint declaration that is included within angle brackets (`<>`). Thus, the `T` generic type parameter has to be a type that must implement both the `Sociable` and `Comparable<Sociable>` interfaces. The following code highlights the lines that use the `T` generic type parameter. The code file for the sample is included in the `java_9_oop_chapter_10_01` folder, in the `example10_01.java` file.

```java
import java.util.concurrent.ThreadLocalRandom;

public class Party<T extends Sociable & Comparable<Sociable>> {
    protected final List<T> members;
    protected T partyLeader;

    public Party(T partyLeader) {
        this.partyLeader = partyLeader;
        members = new ArrayList<>();
        members.add(partyLeader);
    }

    public T getPartyLeader() {
        return partyLeader;
    }
    public void addMember(T newMember) {
        members.add(newMember);
        partyLeader.welcome(newMember);
    }

    public T removeMember(T memberToRemove) throws
    CannotRemovePartyLeaderException {
        if (memberToRemove.equals(partyLeader)) {
            throw new CannotRemovePartyLeaderException();
        }
        int memberIndex = members.indexOf(memberToRemove);
```

```
            if (memberIndex >= 0) {
                members.remove(memberToRemove);
                memberToRemove.sayGoodbyeTo(partyLeader);
                return memberToRemove;
            } else {
                return null;
            }
        }

        public void makeMembersAct() {
            for (T member : members) {
                member.actAlone();
            }
        }

        public void makeMembersDance() {
            for (T member : members) {
                member.danceAlone();
            }
        }

        public void makeMembersSingALyric(String lyric) {
            for (T member : members) {
                member.singALyric(lyric);
            }
        }

        public void declareNewPartyLeader() throws
        InsufficientMembersException {
            if (members.size() == 1) {
                throw new
                InsufficientMembersException(members.size());
            }
            T newPartyLeader = partyLeader;
            while (newPartyLeader.equals(partyLeader)) {
                int pseudoRandomIndex =
                    ThreadLocalRandom.current().nextInt(
                        0,
                        members.size());
                newPartyLeader = members.get(pseudoRandomIndex);
            }
            partyLeader.speak(
                String.format("%s is our new party leader.",
                    newPartyLeader.getName()));
```

```
newPartyLeader.danceWith(partyLeader);
if (newPartyLeader.compareTo(partyLeader) < 0) {
    // The new party leader is younger
    newPartyLeader.danceAlone();
}
partyLeader = newPartyLeader;
    }
}
```

Now we will analyze many code snippets to understand how the code included in the `Party<T>` class works. The following line starts the class body, declares a protected `List<T>`, that is, a `List` of elements whose type is `T` or implements the `T` interface. `List` uses generics to specify the type of the elements that will be accepted and added to the list.

```
protected final List<T> members;
```

The following line declares a protected `partyLeader` field whose type is `T`:

```
protected T partyLeader;
```

The following lines declare a constructor that receives a `partyLeader` argument whose type is `T`. The argument specifies the first party leader and also the first member of the party, that is, the first element added to the `membersList<T>`. The code that creates a new `ArrayList<T>` takes advantage of type inference that was introduced with Java 7, improved in Java 8, and persists in Java 9. We specify `new ArrayList<>()` instead of `new ArrayList<T>()` because Java 9 can use the empty set of type parameters (`<>`) to infer the type arguments from the context. The `members` protected field has a `List<T>` type, and therefore, Java's type inference can determine that `T` is the type and that `ArrayList<>()` means `ArrayList<T>()`. The last line adds the `partyLeader` to the `members` list.

```
public Party(T partyLeader) {
    this.partyLeader = partyLeader;
    members = new ArrayList<>();
    members.add(partyLeader);
}
```

When we invoke the constructor of a generic class with an empty set of type parameters, the pair of angle brackets (`<>`) is known as the **diamond**, and the notation is named **diamond notation**.

The following lines declare the `getPartyLeader` method that specifies `T` as the return type. The method returns `partyLeader`.

```
public T getPartyLeader() {
    return partyLeader;
}
```

The following lines declare the `addMember` method that receives a `newMember` argument whose type is `T`. The code adds the new member received as an argument to the `members` list and calls the `partyLeader.sayWelcomeTo` method with `newMember` as an argument to make the party leader welcome the new member:

```
public void addMember(T newMember) {
    members.add(newMember);
    partyLeader.welcome(newMember);
}
```

The following lines declare the `removeMember` method that receives a `memberToRemove` argument whose type is `T`, returns `T`, and can throw a `CannotRemovePartyLeaderException` exception. The `throws` keyword after the method arguments followed by the exception name indicates that the method can throw the specified exception. The code checks whether the member to be removed matches the party leader with the help of the `equals` method. The method throws a `CannotRemovePartyLeaderException` exception in case the member is the party leader. The code retrieves the index for `memberToRemove` in the list and calls the `members.remove` method with `memberToRemove` as an argument in case it was a member of the list. Then, the code calls the `sayGoodbyeTo` method for the successfully removed member with `partyLeader` as an argument. This way, the member that leaves the party says goodbye to the party leader. In case the member is removed, the method returns the removed member. Otherwise, the method returns `null`.

```
public T removeMember(T memberToRemove) throws
CannotRemovePartyLeaderException {
    if (memberToRemove.equals(partyLeader)) {
        throw new CannotRemovePartyLeaderException();
    }
    int memberIndex = members.indexOf(memberToRemove);
    if (memberIndex >= 0) {
        members.remove(memberToRemove);
        memberToRemove.sayGoodbyeTo(partyLeader);
        return memberToRemove;
    } else {
        return null;
    }
}
```

The following lines declare the `makeMembersAct` method that calls the `actAlone` method for each member of the `members` list:

```java
public void makeMembersAct() {
    for (T member : members) {
        member.actAlone();
    }
}
```

> In the forthcoming chapters, we will learn other ways of coding the same method that performs an action for each member of a list because we will mix object-oriented programming with functional programming in Java 9.

The following lines declare the `makeMembersDance` method that calls the `danceAlone` method for each member of the `members` list:

```java
public void makeMembersDance() {
    for (T member : members) {
        member.danceAlone();
    }
}
```

The following lines declare the `makeMembersSingALyric` method that receives a `lyricString` and calls the `singALyric` method with the received `lyric` as an argument for each member of the `members` list:

```java
public void makeMembersSingALyric(String lyric) {
    for (T member : members) {
        member.singALyric(lyric);
    }
}
```

> Notice that methods are not marked as final, and therefore, we will be able to override these methods in a future subclass.

Finally, the following lines declare the declareNewPartyLeader method that can throw an InsufficientMembersException. As it happened with the removeMember method, the throws keyword after the method arguments followed by InsufficientMembersException indicates that the method can throw an InsufficientMembersException exception. In case we have just one member in the members list, the code throws an InsufficientMembersException exception and uses the value returned from members.size() to create the instance of the class that inherits from Exception. Remember that this exception class uses this value to initialize a field and the code that calls this method will be able to retrieve the number of members that is insufficient. If we have at least two members, the code generates a new pseudo-random party leader that is different from the existing one. The code uses ThreadLocalRandom.current().nextInt to generate a pseudo-random int number within a range. The code calls the speak method for the actual leader to make it explain to the other party members that they have a new party leader. The code calls the danceWith method for the new leader with the previous party leader as an argument. If the result of calling the newPartyLeader.compareTo method with the previous party leader as an argument returns less than 0, it means that the new party leader is younger than the previous one and the code calls the newPartyLeader.danceAlone method. Finally, the code sets the new value to the partyLeader field.

```
public void declareNewPartyLeader() throws
InsufficientMembersException {
    if (members.size() == 1) {
        throw new InsufficientMembersException(members.size());
    }
    T newPartyLeader = partyLeader;
    while (newPartyLeader.equals(partyLeader)) {
        int pseudoRandomIndex =
            ThreadLocalRandom.current().nextInt(
                0,
                members.size());
        newPartyLeader = members.get(pseudoRandomIndex);
    }
    partyLeader.speak(
        String.format("%s is our new party leader.",
            newPartyLeader.getName()));
    newPartyLeader.danceWith(partyLeader);
    if (newPartyLeader.compareTo(partyLeader) < 0) {
        // The new party leader is younger
        newPartyLeader.danceAlone();
    }
    partyLeader = newPartyLeader;
}
```

Using a generic class for multiple compatible types

We can create instances of the `Party<T>` class by replacing the `T` generic type parameter with any type name that adapts to the type constraints specified in the declaration of the `Party<T>` class. So far, we have three concrete classes that implement both the `Sociable` and `Comparable<Sociable>` interfaces: `SocialLion`, `SocialParrot`, and `SocialSwan`. Hence, we can use `SocialLion` to create an instance of `Party<SocialLion>`, that is, a `Party` of `SocialLion`. We take advantage of type inference and we use the previously explained diamond notation. This way, we will create a party of lions, and `Simba` is the party leader. The code file for the sample is included in the `java_9_oop_chapter_10_01` folder, in the `example10_01.java` file.

```
SocialLion simba = new SocialLion("Simba", 10);
SocialLion mufasa = new SocialLion("Mufasa", 5);
SocialLion scar = new SocialLion("Scar", 9);
SocialLion nala = new SocialLion("Nala", 7);
Party<SocialLion> lionsParty = new Party<>(simba);
```

The `lionsParty` instance will only accept a `SocialLion` instance for all the arguments in which the class definition uses the generic type parameter named `T`. The following lines add the previously created three instances of `SocialLion` to the lions' party by calling the `addMember` method for each instance. The code file for the sample is included in the `java_9_oop_chapter_10_01` folder, in the `example10_01.java` file.

```
lionsParty.addMember(mufasa);
lionsParty.addMember(scar);
lionsParty.addMember(nala);
```

The following lines call the `makeMembersAct` method to make all the lions act, call the `makeMembersDance` method to make all the lions dance, use the `removeMember` method to remove a member that isn't the party leader, use the `declareNewPartyLeader` method to declare a new leader, and finally call the `makeMembersSingALyric` method to make all the lions sing. We will add the `try` keyword before the calls to `removeMember` and `declareNewPartyLeader` because these methods can throw exceptions. In this case, we don't check the result returned by `removeMember`. The code file for the sample is included in the `java_9_oop_chapter_10_01` folder, in the `example10_01.java` file.

```
lionsParty.makeMembersAct();
lionsParty.makeMembersDance();
try {
```

```
        lionsParty.removeMember(nala);
    } catch (CannotRemovePartyLeaderException e) {
        System.out.println(
            "We cannot remove the party leader.");
    }
    try {
        lionsParty.declareNewPartyLeader();
    } catch (InsufficientMembersException e) {
        System.out.println(
            String.format("We just have %s member",
                e.getNumberOfMembers()));
    }
    lionsParty.makeMembersSingALyric("Welcome to the jungle");
```

The following lines show the output after we run the preceding code snippets in JShell. However, we must take into account that there is a pseudo-random selection of the new party leader, and therefore, the results will vary in each execution:

```
Simba welcomes Mufasa
Simba welcomes Scar
Simba welcomes Nala
Simba to be or not to be
Mufasa to be or not to be
Scar to be or not to be
Nala to be or not to be
Simba dances alone *-* ^\/^ (-)
Mufasa dances alone *-* ^\/^ (-)
Scar dances alone *-* ^\/^ (-)
Nala dances alone *-* ^\/^ (-)
Nala says goodbye to Simba RoarRrooaarrRrrrrrrrooooooaaarrrr
Simba says: Scar is our new party leader. *-* ^\/^ (-)
Scar dances with Simba *-* ^\/^ (-)
Scar dances alone *-* ^\/^ (-)
Simba sings Welcome to the jungle Roar Rrooaarr Rrrrrrrrooooooaaarrrr
Mufasa sings Welcome to the jungle Roar Rrooaarr Rrrrrrrrooooooaaarrrr
Scar sings Welcome to the jungle Roar Rrooaarr Rrrrrrrrooooooaaarrrr
```

We can use `SocialParrot` to create an instance of `Party<SocialParrot>`, that is, a `Party` of `SocialParrot`. We use the previously explained diamond notation. This way, we will create a party of parrots, and `Rio` is the party leader. The code file for the sample is included in the `java_9_oop_chapter_10_01` folder, in the `example10_01.java` file.

```
SocialParrot rio = new SocialParrot("Rio", 3);
SocialParrot thor = new SocialParrot("Thor", 6);
SocialParrot rambo = new SocialParrot("Rambo", 4);
SocialParrot woody = new SocialParrot("Woody", 5);
Party<SocialParrot> parrotsParty = new Party<>(rio);
```

The `parrotsParty` instance will only accept a `SocialParrot` instance for all the arguments in which the class definition uses the generic type parameter named `T`. The following lines add the previously created three instances of `SocialParrot` to the parrots' party by calling the `addMember` method for each instance. The code file for the sample is included in the `java_9_oop_chapter_10_01` folder, in the `example10_01.java` file.

```
parrotsParty.addMember(thor);
parrotsParty.addMember(rambo);
parrotsParty.addMember(woody);
```

The following lines call the `makeMembersDance` method to make all the parrots dance, use the `removeMember` method to remove a member that isn't the party leader, use the `declareNewPartyLeader` method to declare a new leader, and finally call the `makeMembersSingALyric` method to make all the parrots sing. The code file for the sample is included in the `java_9_oop_chapter_10_01` folder, in the `example10_01.java` file.

```
parrotsParty.makeMembersDance();
try {
    parrotsParty.removeMember(rambo);
} catch (CannotRemovePartyLeaderException e) {
    System.out.println(
        "We cannot remove the party leader.");
}
try {
    parrotsParty.declareNewPartyLeader();
} catch (InsufficientMembersException e) {
    System.out.println(
        String.format("We just have %s member",
            e.getNumberOfMembers()));
}
parrotsParty.makeMembersSingALyric("Fly like a bird");
```

The following lines show the output after we run the preceding code snippets in JShell. Again, we must take into account that there is a pseudo-random selection of the new party leader, and therefore, the results will vary in each execution:

```
Rio welcomes Thor
Rio welcomes Rambo
Rio welcomes Woody
Rio dances alone /|\ -=- % % +=+
Thor dances alone /|\ -=- % % +=+
Rambo dances alone /|\ -=- % % +=+
Woody dances alone /|\ -=- % % +=+
Rambo says goodbye to Rio YeahYeeaahYeeeaaaah
Rio says: Woody is our new party leader. /|\ -=- % % +=+
Woody dances with Rio /|\ -=- % % +=+
Rio sings Fly like a bird Yeah Yeeaah Yeeeaaaah
Thor sings Fly like a bird Yeah Yeeaah Yeeeaaaah
Woody sings Fly like a bird Yeah Yeeaah Yeeeaaaah
```

The following lines will fail to compile because we use incompatible types. First, we try to add a SocialParrot instance, rio, to the Party<SocialLion>, lionsParty. Then, we try to add a SocialLion instance, simba, to the Party<SocialParrot>, parrotsParty. Both lines will fail to compile and JShell will display a message indicating that the types are incompatible and they cannot be converted to the necessary type required by each party. The code file for the sample is included in the java_9_oop_chapter_10_01 folder, in the example10_02.java file.

```java
// The following lines won't compile
// and will generate errors in JShell
lionsParty.addMember(rio);
parrotsParty.addMember(simba);
```

The following screenshot shows the errors displayed in JShell when we try to execute the previous lines:

```
jshell> lionsParty.addMember(rio);
|   Error:
|   incompatible types: SocialParrot cannot be converted to SocialLion
|   lionsParty.addMember(rio);
|                        ^-^

jshell> parrotsParty.addMember(simba);
|   Error:
|   incompatible types: SocialLion cannot be converted to SocialParrot
|   parrotsParty.addMember(simba);
|                          ^---^

jshell>
```

We can use SocialSwan to create an instance of Party<SocialSwan>, that is, a Party of SocialSwan. This way, we will create a party of swans, and Kevin is the party leader. The code file for the sample is included in the java_9_oop_chapter_10_01 folder, in the example10_03.java file.

```
SocialSwan kevin = new SocialSwan("Kevin", 3);
SocialSwan brandon = new SocialSwan("Brandon", 5);
SocialSwan nicholas = new SocialSwan("Nicholas", 6);
Party<SocialSwan> swansParty = new Party<>(kevin);
```

The swansParty instance will only accept a SocialSwan instance for all the arguments in which the class definition uses the generic type parameter named T. The following lines add the previously created two instances of SocialSwan to the swans' party by calling the addMember method for each instance. The code file for the sample is included in the java_9_oop_chapter_10_01 folder, in the example10_03.java file.

```
swansParty.addMember(brandon);
swansParty.addMember(nicholas);
```

The following lines call the makeMembersDance method to make all the parrots dance, use the removeMember method to try to remove the party leader, use the declareNewPartyLeader method to declare a new leader, and finally call the makeMembersSingALyric method to make all the swans sing. The code file for the sample is included in the java_9_oop_chapter_10_01 folder, in the example10_03. java file.

```java
swansParty.makeMembersDance();
try {
    swansParty.removeMember(kevin);
} catch (CannotRemovePartyLeaderException e) {
    System.out.println(
        "We cannot remove the party leader.");
}
try {
    swansParty.declareNewPartyLeader();
} catch (InsufficientMembersException e) {
    System.out.println(
        String.format("We just have %s member",
            e.getNumberOfMembers()));
}
swansParty.makeMembersSingALyric("It will be our swan song");
```

The following lines show the output after we run the preceding code snippets in JShell. Again, we must take into account that there is a pseudo-random selection of the new party leader, and therefore, the results will vary in each execution:

```
Kevin welcomes Brandon

Kevin welcomes Nicholas

Kevin dances alone ^- ^- ^- -^ -^ -^

Brandon dances alone ^- ^- ^- -^ -^ -^

Nicholas dances alone ^- ^- ^- -^ -^ -^

We cannot remove the party leader.

Kevin says: Brandon is our new party leader. ^- ^- ^- -^ -^ -^

Brandon dances with Kevin ^- ^- ^- -^ -^ -^

Kevin sings It will be our swan song OO-OO-OO WHO-HO WHO-HO WHO-WHO WHO-
WHO

Brandon sings It will be our swan song OO-OO-OO WHO-HO WHO-HO WHO-WHO
WHO-WHO

Nicholas sings It will be our swan song OO-OO-OO WHO-HO WHO-HO WHO-WHO
WHO-WHO
```

Test your knowledge

1. The `public class Party<T extends Sociable & Comparable<Sociable>>` line means:

    1. The generic type constraint specifies that `T` must implement either the `Sociable` or `Comparable<Sociable>` interfaces.

    2. The generic type constraint specifies that `T` must implement both the `Sociable` and `Comparable<Sociable>` interfaces.

    3. The class is a subclass of both the `Sociable` and `Comparable<Sociable>` classes.

2. Which of the following lines is equivalent to `List<SocialLion> lionsList = new ArrayList<SocialLion>();` in Java 9:

    1. `List<SocialLion> lionsList = new ArrayList();`

    2. `List<SocialLion> lionsList = new ArrayList<>();`

    3. `var lionsList = new ArrayList<SocialLion>();`

3. Which of the following lines uses the diamond notation to take advantage of Java 9 type inference:

    1. `List<SocialLion> lionsList = new ArrayList<>();`

    2. `List<SocialLion> lionsList = new ArrayList();`

    3. `var lionsList = new ArrayList<SocialLion>();`

4. Java 9 allows us to work with parametric polymorphism through:

    1. Duck typing.

    2. Rabbit typing.

    3. Generics.

5. Which of the following code snippets declares a class whose generic type constraint specifies that `T` must implement both the `Sociable` and `Convertible` interfaces:

    1. `public class Game<T extends Sociable & Convertible>`

    2. `public class Game<T: where T is Sociable & Convertible>`

    3. `public class Game<T extends Sociable> where T: Convertible`

Summary

In this chapter, you learned to maximize code reuse by writing code capable of working with objects of different types, that is, instances of classes that implement specific interfaces or whose class hierarchies include specific superclasses. We worked with interfaces, generics, and constrained generic types.

We created classes capable of working with one constrained generic type. We combined class inheritance and interfaces to maximize the reusability of code. We could make classes work with many different types and we were able to code the behavior of a party that could then be reused to create parties of lions, parrots, and swans.

Now that you have learned the basics about parametric polymorphism and generics, we are ready to work with more advanced scenarios that maximize code reuse with generics in Java 9, which is the topic we are going to discuss in the next chapter.

11
Advanced Generics

In this chapter, we will dive deep into parametric polymorphism and how Java 9 allows us to write generic code with classes that use two constrained generic types. We will:

- Work with more advanced scenarios in which we take advantage of parametric polymorphism
- Create a new interface to be used as a constraint for a second type parameter
- Declare two classes that implement an interface to work with two type parameters
- Declare a class that works with two constrained generic types
- Use a generic class with two generic type parameters

Creating a new interface to be used as a constraint for a second type parameter

So far, we have been working with parties in which the party members were sociable animals. However, it is difficult to enjoy a party without some music. The sociable animals need to hear something in order to make them dance and enjoy their party. We want to create a party of sociable animals and something hearable.

Now, we will create a new interface that we will use as a constraint later when we define another class that takes advantage of generics with two constrained generic types. The following lines show the code for the `Hearable` interface. This interface specifies the requirements that a type must meet in order to be considered as hearable, that is, a generator of music for a party in our application domain. The `public` modifier followed by the `interface` keyword and the interface name, `Hearable`, composes the interface declaration, as follows.

The code file for the sample is included in the `java_9_oop_chapter_11_01` folder, in the `example11_01.java` file.

```java
public interface Hearable {
    void playMusic();
    void playMusicWithLyrics(String lyrics);
}
```

The interface declares two method requirements: `playMusic` and `playMusicWithLyrics`. As we learned in the previous chapters, the interface includes only the method declarations because the classes that implement the `Hearable` interface will be responsible for providing the implementation of the two methods.

Declaring two classes that implement an interface to work with two type parameters

Now, we will declare a class named `Smartphone` that implements the previously defined `Hearable` interface. We can read the class declaration as "the `Smartphone` class implements the `Hearable` interface." The following lines show the code for the new class. The code file for the sample is included in the `java_9_oop_chapter_11_01` folder, in the `example11_01.java` file.

```java
public class Smartphone implements Hearable {
    public final String modelName;

    public Smartphone(String modelName) {
        this.modelName = modelName;
    }

    @Override
    public void playMusic() {
        System.out.println(
            String.format("%s starts playing music.",
                modelName));
        System.out.println(
            String.format("cha-cha-cha untz untz untz",
                modelName));
    }

    @Override
```

```
    public void playMusicWithLyrics(String lyrics) {
        System.out.println(
            String.format("%s starts playing music with lyrics.",
                modelName));
        System.out.println(
            String.format("untz untz untz %s untz untz",
                lyrics));
    }
}
```

The `Smartphone` class declares a constructor that assigns the value of the required `modelName` argument to the `modelName` immutable field. In addition, the class implements the two methods required by the `Hearable` interface: `playMusic` and `playMusicWithLyrics`.

The `playMusic` method prints a message that displays the smartphone model name and indicates that the device starts playing music. Then, the method prints multiple sounds in words. The `playMusicWithLyrics` method prints a message that displays the smartphone model name followed by another message with sounds in words and the lyrics received as an argument.

Now we will declare a class named `AnimalMusicBand` that also implements the previously defined `Hearable` interface. We can read the class declaration as "the `AnimalMusicBand` class implements the `Hearable` interface." The following lines show the code for the new class. The code file for the sample is included in the `java_9_oop_chapter_11_01` folder, in the `example11_01.java` file.

```
public class AnimalMusicBand implements Hearable {
    public final String bandName;
    public final int numberOfMembers;

    public AnimalMusicBand(String bandName, int numberOfMembers) {
        this.bandName = bandName;
        this.numberOfMembers = numberOfMembers;
    }

    @Override
    public void playMusic() {
        System.out.println(
            String.format("Our name is %s. We are %d.",
                bandName,
                numberOfMembers));
        System.out.println(
            String.format("Meow Meow Woof Woof Meow Meow",
                bandName));
```

```
    }

    @Override
    public void playMusicWithLyrics(String lyrics) {
        System.out.println(
            String.format("%s asks you to sing together.",
                bandName));
        System.out.println(
            String.format("Meow Woof %s Woof Meow",
                lyrics));
    }
}
```

The `AnimalMusicBand` class declares a constructor that assigns the value of the required `bandName` and `numberOfMembers` arguments to the immutable field with the same name as these arguments. In addition, the class implements the two methods required by the `Hearable` interface: `playMusic` and `playMusicWithLyrics`.

The `playMusic` method prints a message that introduces the animal music band to the audience and indicates the number of members. Then, the method prints multiple sounds in words. The `playMusicWithLyrics` method prints a message that asks the audience to sing together with the animal music band followed by another message with sounds in words and the lyrics received as an argument.

Declaring a class that works with two constrained generic types

The following lines declare a `PartyWithHearable` subclass of the previously created `Party<T>` class that takes advantage of generics to work with two constrained types. The type constraints declaration is included within angle brackets (`<>`). In this case, we have two generic type parameters: `T` and `U`. The generic type parameter named `T` must implement both the `Sociable` and `Comparable<Sociable>` interfaces, as it happened in the `Party<T>` superclass. The generic type parameter named `U` must implement the `Hearable` interface. Notice that the `extends` keyword that follows the type parameter allows us to add the constraints to the generic type parameters and the same keyword after the angle brackets specifies that the class inherits from the `Party<T>` superclass. This way, the class specifies constraints for both the `T` and `U` generic type parameters, and inherits from `Party<T>`. The code file for the sample is included in the `java_9_oop_chapter_11_01` folder, in the `example11_01.java` file.

```
public class PartyWithHearable<T extends Sociable &
Comparable<Sociable>, U extends Hearable> extends Party<T> {
    protected final U soundGenerator;

    public PartyWithHearable(T partyLeader, U soundGenerator) {
        super(partyLeader);
        this.soundGenerator = soundGenerator;
    }

    @Override
    public void makeMembersDance() {
        soundGenerator.playMusic();
        super.makeMembersDance();
    }

    @Override
    public void makeMembersSingALyric(String lyric) {
        soundGenerator.playMusicWithLyrics(lyric);
        super.makeMembersSingALyric(lyric);
    }
}
```

 When type parameters have constraints in Java, they are also known as **bounded type parameters**. In addition, the type constraint is also known as the **upper bound** for the bounded type parameter because any class that implements the interface used as an upper bound or any subclass of the class indicated as an upper bound can be used for the type parameter.

Now we will analyze many code snippets to understand how the code included in the PartyWithHearable<T, U> class works. The following line starts the class body and declares a protected immutable soundGenerator field of the type specified by U:

```
protected final U soundGenerator;
```

The following lines declare an initializer that receives two arguments, partyLeader and soundGenerator, whose types are T and U. The arguments specify the first party leader that will also become the first member of the party, and the sound generator that will make the party members dance and sing. The constructor calls the constructor defined in its superclass, with partyLeader as an argument, by using the super keyword.

```
public PartyWithHearable(T partyLeader, U soundGenerator) {
    super(partyLeader);
    this.soundGenerator = soundGenerator;
}
```

The following lines declare a `makeMembersDance` method that overrides the method with the same declaration included in the superclass. The code calls the `soundGenetor.playMusic` method and then the `super.makeMembersDance` method, that is, the `makeMembersDance` method defined in the `Party<T>` superclass, by using the `super` keyword:

```
@Override
public void makeMembersDance() {
    soundGenerator.playMusic();
    super.makeMembersDance();
}
```

> When we override a method in a subclass, we can call the method defined in the superclass by using the `super` keyword followed by a dot (`.`) and the method name, and passing the required arguments to the method. The usage of the `super` keyword allows us to call the instance method defined in the superclass that we have overridden. This way, we can add new features to a method and still call the base method.

Finally, the following lines declare a `makeMembersSingALyric` method that overrides the method with the same declaration included in the superclass. The code calls the `soundGenerator.playMusicWithLyrics` method with the received `lyrics` as an argument. Then, the code calls the `super.makeMembersSingALyric` method with the received `lyrics` as an argument, that is, the `makeMembersSingALyric` method defined in the `Party<T>` superclass:

```
@Override
public void makeMembersSingALyric(String lyric) {
    soundGenerator.playMusicWithLyrics(lyric);
    super.makeMembersSingALyric(lyric);
}
```

The following UML diagram shows the interface and the concrete subclasses that we will create, including all the fields and methods.

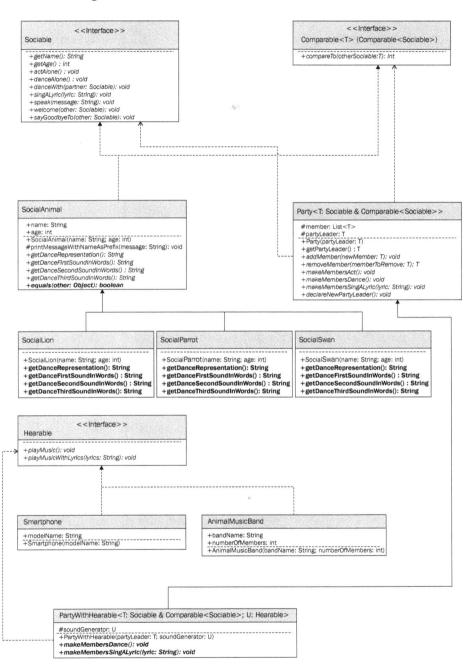

Creating instances of a generic class with two generic type parameters

We can create instances of the PartyWithHearable<T, U> class by replacing both the T and U generic type parameters with any type names that conform to the constraints or the upper bounds specified in the declaration of the PartyWithHearable<T, U> class. We have three concrete classes that implement both the Sociable and Comparable<Sociable> interfaces required by the T generic type parameter: SocialLion, SocialParrot, and SocialSwan. We have two classes that implement the Hearable interface required by the U generic type parameter: Smartphone and AnimalMusicBand.

We can use SocialLion and Smartphone to create an instance of PartyWithHearable<SocialLion, Smartphone>, that is, a party of social lions and a smartphone. Then, we can use SocialParrot and AnimalMusicBand to create an instance of PartyWithHearable<SocialParrot, AnimalMusicBand>, that is, a party of social parrots and an animal music band.

The following lines create a Smartphone instance named android. Then, the code creates a PartyWithHearable<SocialLion, Smartphone> instance named nalaParty and passes nala and android as arguments. We take advantage of type inference and we use the diamond notation we learned in the previous chapter, *Chapter 10, Maximization of Code Reuse with Generics*. This way, we create a party of social lions that use a smartphone, where Nala is the party leader, and Super Android Smartphone is the hearable or music generator. The code file for the sample is included in the java_9_oop_chapter_11_01 folder, in the example11_01.java file.

```
Smartphone android = new Smartphone("Super Android Smartphone");
PartyWithHearable<SocialLion, Smartphone> nalaParty =
    new PartyWithHearable<>(nala, android);
```

The nalaParty instance will only accept a SocialLion instance for all the arguments in which the class definition uses the generic type parameter named T. The nalaParty instance will only accept a Smartphone instance for all the arguments in which the class definition uses the generic type parameter named U. The following lines add the previously created three instances of SocialLion to the party by calling the addMember method. The code file for the sample is included in the java_9_oop_chapter_11_01 folder, in the example11_01.java file.

```
nalaParty.addMember(simba);
nalaParty.addMember(mufasa);
nalaParty.addMember(scar);
```

The following screenshot shows the results of executing the previous code in JShell:

```
jshell> Smartphone android = new Smartphone("Super Android Smartphone");
android ==> Smartphone@184f6be2
|  created variable android : Smartphone

jshell> PartyWithHearable<SocialLion, Smartphone> nalaParty =
   ...>      new PartyWithHearable<>(nala, android);
nalaParty ==> PartyWithHearable@1f7030a6
|  created variable nalaParty : PartyWithHearable<SocialLion, Smartphone>

jshell>

jshell> nalaParty.addMember(simba);
Nala welcomes Simba

jshell> nalaParty.addMember(mufasa);
Nala welcomes Mufasa

jshell> nalaParty.addMember(scar);
Nala welcomes Scar

jshell>
```

The following lines call the `makeMembersDance` method to make the smartphone's playlist invite all the lions to dance and make them dance. Then, the code calls the `removeMember` method to remove a member that isn't the party leader, use the `declareNewPartyLeader` method to declare a new leader, and finally calls the `makeMembersSingALyric` method to make the smartphone's playlist invite all the lions to sing a specific lyric and make them sing this lyric. Remember that we add the `try` keyword before the calls to `removeMember` and `declareNewPartyLeader` because these methods can throw exceptions. The code file for the sample is included in the `java_9_oop_chapter_11_01` folder, in the `example11_01.java` file.

```
nalaParty.makeMembersDance();
try {
    nalaParty.removeMember(mufasa);
} catch (CannotRemovePartyLeaderException e) {
    System.out.println(
        "We cannot remove the party leader.");
}
try {
    nalaParty.declareNewPartyLeader();
} catch (InsufficientMembersException e) {
    System.out.println(
        String.format("We just have %s member",
            e.getNumberOfMembers()));
}
nalaParty.makeMembersSingALyric("It's the eye of the tiger");
```

The following screenshot shows the results of executing the previous code in JShell:

```
jshell> nalaParty.makeMembersDance();
Super Android Smartphone starts playing music.
cha-cha-cha untz untz untz
Nala dances alone *-* ^\/^ (-)
Simba dances alone *-* ^\/^ (-)
Mufasa dances alone *-* ^\/^ (-)
Scar dances alone *-* ^\/^ (-)

jshell> try {
   ...>      nalaParty.removeMember(mufasa);
   ...> } catch (CannotRemovePartyLeaderException e) {
   ...>      System.out.println(
   ...>          "We cannot remove the party leader.");
   ...> }
Mufasa says goodbye to Nala RoarRrooaarrRrrrrrrrooooooaaarrrr

jshell> try {
   ...>      nalaParty.declareNewPartyLeader();
   ...> } catch (InsufficientMembersException e) {
   ...>      System.out.println(
   ...>          String.format("We just have %s member",
   ...>              e.getNumberOfMembers()));
   ...> }
Nala says: Scar is our new party leader. *-* ^\/^ (-)
Scar dances with Nala *-* ^\/^ (-)

jshell> nalaParty.makeMembersSingALyric("It's the eye of the tiger");
Super Android Smartphone starts playing music with lyrics.
untz untz untz It's the eye of the tiger untz untz
Nala sings It's the eye of the tiger Roar Rrooaarr Rrrrrrrrooooooaaarrrr
Simba sings It's the eye of the tiger Roar Rrooaarr Rrrrrrrrooooooaaarrrr
Scar sings It's the eye of the tiger Roar Rrooaarr Rrrrrrrrooooooaaarrrr

jshell>
```

The following lines show the output after we run the preceding code in JShell. However, we must take into account that there is a pseudo-random selection of the new party leader, and therefore, the results will vary in each execution:

```
Nala welcomes Simba

Nala welcomes Mufasa

Nala welcomes Scar

Super Android Smartphone starts playing music.

cha-cha-cha untz untz untz

Nala dances alone *-* ^\/^ (-)

Simba dances alone *-* ^\/^ (-)

Mufasa dances alone *-* ^\/^ (-)

Scar dances alone *-* ^\/^ (-)
```

```
Mufasa says goodbye to Nala RoarRrooaarrRrrrrrrroooooaaarrrr
Nala says: Simba is our new party leader. *-* ^\/^ (-)
Simba dances with Nala *-* ^\/^ (-)
Super Android Smartphone starts playing music with lyrics.
untz untz untz It's the eye of the tiger untz untz
Nala sings It's the eye of the tiger Roar Rrooaarr Rrrrrrrrooooooaaarrrr
Simba sings It's the eye of the tiger Roar Rrooaarr Rrrrrrrrooooooaaarrrr
Scar sings It's the eye of the tiger Roar Rrooaarr Rrrrrrrrooooooaaarrrr
```

The following lines create an `AnimalMusicBand` instance named `band`. Then, the code creates a `PartyWithHearable<SocialParrot, AnimalMusicBand>` instance named `ramboParty` and passes `rambo` and `band` as arguments. As happened in the previous example, we take advantage of type inference and we use the diamond notation we learned in the previous chapter, *Chapter 10, Maximization of Code Reuse with Generics*. This way, we create a party of social parrots that have a music band composed of four animals, where `Rambo` is the party leader, and `Black Eyed Paws` is the hearable or music generator. The code file for the sample is included in the `java_9_oop_chapter_11_01` folder, in the `example11_02.java` file.

```
AnimalMusicBand band = new AnimalMusicBand(
    "Black Eyed Paws", 4);
PartyWithHearable<SocialParrot, AnimalMusicBand> ramboParty =
    new PartyWithHearable<>(rambo, band);
```

The `ramboParty` instance will only accept a `SocialParrot` instance for all the arguments in which the class definition uses the generic type parameter named `T`. The `ramboParty` instance will only accept an `AnimalMusicBand` instance for all the arguments in which the class definition uses the generic type parameter named `U`. The following lines add the previously created three instances of `SocialParrot` to the party by calling the `addMember` method. The code file for the sample is included in the `java_9_oop_chapter_11_01` folder, in the `example11_02.java` file.

```
ramboParty.addMember(rio);
ramboParty.addMember(woody);
ramboParty.addMember(thor);
```

The following screenshot shows the results of executing the previous code in JShell.

```
jshell> AnimalMusicBand band = new AnimalMusicBand(
   ...>      "Black Eyed Paws", 4);
band ==> AnimalMusicBand@3b088d51
|  created variable band : AnimalMusicBand

jshell> PartyWithHearable<SocialParrot, AnimalMusicBand> ramboParty =
   ...>      new PartyWithHearable<>(rambo, band);
ramboParty ==> PartyWithHearable@74650e52
|  created variable ramboParty : PartyWithHearable<SocialParrot, AnimalMusicBand>

jshell>

jshell> ramboParty.addMember(rio);
Rambo welcomes Rio

jshell> ramboParty.addMember(woody);
Rambo welcomes Woody

jshell> ramboParty.addMember(thor);
Rambo welcomes Thor

jshell>
```

The following lines call the makeMembersDance method to make the animal music band invite all the parrots to dance, tell them they are four members in the band and make them dance. Then, the code calls the removeMember method to remove a member that isn't the party leader, use the declareNewPartyLeader method to declare a new leader, and finally calls the makeMembersSingALyric method to make the animal music band invite all the parrots to sing a specific lyric and make them sing this lyric. Remember that we add the try keyword before the calls to removeMember and declareNewPartyLeader because these methods can throw exceptions. The code file for the sample is included in the java_9_oop_ chapter_11_01 folder, in the example11_02.java file.

```
ramboParty.makeMembersDance();
try {
    ramboParty.removeMember(rio);
} catch (CannotRemovePartyLeaderException e) {
    System.out.println(
        "We cannot remove the party leader.");
}
try {
    ramboParty.declareNewPartyLeader();
} catch (InsufficientMembersException e) {
    System.out.println(
        String.format("We just have %s member",
            e.getNumberOfMembers()));
}
ramboParty.makeMembersSingALyric("Turn up the radio");
```

The following screenshot shows the results of executing the previous code in JShell:

```
jshell> ramboParty.makeMembersDance();
Our name is Black Eyed Paws. We are 4.
Meow Meow Woof Woof Meow Meow
Rambo dances alone /|\ -=- % % +=+
Rio dances alone /|\ -=- % % +=+
Woody dances alone /|\ -=- % % +=+
Thor dances alone /|\ -=- % % +=+

jshell> try {
   ...>     ramboParty.removeMember(rio);
   ...> } catch (CannotRemovePartyLeaderException e) {
   ...>     System.out.println(
   ...>         "We cannot remove the party leader.");
   ...> }
Rio says goodbye to Rambo YeahYeeaahYeeeaaaah

jshell> try {
   ...>     ramboParty.declareNewPartyLeader();
   ...> } catch (InsufficientMembersException e) {
   ...>     System.out.println(
   ...>         String.format("We just have %s member",
   ...>             e.getNumberOfMembers()));
   ...> }
Rambo says: Thor is our new party leader. /|\ -=- % % +=+
Thor dances with Rambo /|\ -=- % % +=+

jshell> ramboParty.makeMembersSingALyric("Turn up the radio");
Black Eyed Paws asks you to sing together.
Meow Woof Turn up the radio Woof Meow
Rambo sings Turn up the radio Yeah Yeeaah Yeeeaaaah
Woody sings Turn up the radio Yeah Yeeaah Yeeeaaaah
Thor sings Turn up the radio Yeah Yeeaah Yeeeaaaah

jshell>
```

The following lines show the output after we run the preceding code snippets in JShell. However, we must take into account that there is a pseudo-random selection of the new party leader, and therefore, the results will vary in each execution:

```
Rambo welcomes Rio
Rambo welcomes Woody
Rambo welcomes Thor
Our name is Black Eyed Paws. We are 4.
Meow Meow Woof Woof Meow Meow
Rambo dances alone /|\ -=- % % +=+
Rio dances alone /|\ -=- % % +=+
Woody dances alone /|\ -=- % % +=+
Thor dances alone /|\ -=- % % +=+
Rio says goodbye to Rambo YeahYeeaahYeeeaaaah
Rambo says: Thor is our new party leader. /|\ -=- % % +=+
Thor dances with Rambo /|\ -=- % % +=+
Black Eyed Paws asks you to sing together.
Meow Woof Turn up the radio Woof Meow
Rambo sings Turn up the radio Yeah Yeeaah Yeeeaaaah
Woody sings Turn up the radio Yeah Yeeaah Yeeeaaaah
Thor sings Turn up the radio Yeah Yeeaah Yeeeaaaah
```

Test your knowledge

1. The `PartyWithHearable<T extends Sociable & Comparable<Sociable>, U extends Hearable>` line means:

    1. The generic type constraint specifies that `T` must implement either the `Sociable` or `Comparable<Sociable>` interfaces, and `U` must implement the `Hearable` interface.

    2. The class is a subclass of the `Sociable`, `Comparable<Sociable>`, and `Hearable` classes.

    3. The generic type constraint specifies that `T` must implement both the `Sociable` and `Comparable<Sociable>` interfaces, and `U` must implement the `Hearable` interface.

2. Which of the following lines is equivalent to
   `PartyWithHearable<SocialLion, Smartphone>lionsParty = new`
   `PartyWithHearable<SocialLion, Smartphone>(nala, android);`
   in Java 9:

   1. `PartyWithHearable<SocialLion, Smartphone> lionsParty =`
      `new PartyWithHearable<>(nala, android);`

   2. `PartyWithHearable<SocialLion, Smartphone> lionsParty =`
      `new PartyWithHearable(nala, android);`

   3. `let lionsParty = new PartyWithHearable(nala, android);`

3. When we use a bounded type parameter with the `extends` keyword:

   1. Any class that implements the interface indicated as an upper bound
      can be used for the type parameter. In case the indicated name is a
      name of a class, its subclasses cannot be used for the type parameter.

   2. Any class that implements the interface indicated as an upper bound
      or any subclass of the class indicated as an upper bound can be used
      for the type parameter.

   3. Any subclass of the class indicated as an upper bound can be used
      for the type parameter. In case the indicated name is a name of an
      interface, the classes that implement the interface cannot be used for
      the type parameter.

4. When type parameters have constraints in Java, they are also known as:

   1. Flexible type parameters.

   2. Unbounded type parameters.

   3. Bounded type parameters.

5. Which of the following code snippets declares a class whose generic type
   constraint specifies that `T` must implement the `Sociable` interface and `U`
   must implement the `Convertible` interface:

   1. `public class Game<T: where T is Sociable, U: where U is`
      `Convertible>`

   2. `public class Game<T extends Sociable> where U:`
      `Convertible`

   3. `public class Game<T extends Sociable, U extends`
      `Convertible>`

Summary

In this chapter, you learned to maximize code reuse by writing code capable of working with two type parameters. We worked with more complex scenarios that involve interfaces, generics, and multiple type parameters that have constraints, also known as bounded type parameters.

We created a new interface and then we declared two classes that implemented this new interface. Then, we declared a class that worked with two constrained generic type parameters. We combined class inheritance and interfaces to maximize the reusability of code. We could make classes work with many different types and we were able to code the behavior of a party with different music generators that could then be reused to create parties of lions with a smartphone and parties of parrots with bands of animals.

Java 9 allows us to work with more complex scenarios in which we can specify more restrictions or bounds to the generic type parameters. However, most of the time, we will work with the cases covered by the samples we learned in this chapter and in the previous one.

Now that you have learned advanced usages of parametric polymorphism and generics, we are ready to combine object-oriented programming and functional programming in Java 9, which is the topic we are going to discuss in the next chapter.

12
Object-Oriented, Functional Programming, and Lambda Expressions

In this chapter, we will discuss functional programming and how Java 9 implements many functional programming concepts. We will work with many examples on how to mix functional programming with object-oriented programming. We will:

- Understand functions and methods as first-class citizens
- Work with functional interfaces and lambda expressions
- Create a functional version of array filtering
- Create a data repository with generics and interfaces
- Filter collections with complex conditions
- Use a map operation to transform values
- Combine a map operation with reduce
- Chain many operations with map and reduce
- Work with different collectors

Understanding functions and methods as first-class citizens

Since its first release, Java has been an object-oriented programming language. Starting with Java 8, Java added support for the **functional programming** paradigm and continues to do so in Java 9. Functional programming favors immutable data, and therefore, functional programming avoids state changes.

 The code written with a functional programming style is as declarative as possible, and it is focused on what it does instead of how it must do it.

In most programming languages that provide support to the functional programming paradigm, functions are first-class citizens, that is, we can use functions as arguments for other functions or methods. Java 8 introduced many changes to reduce boilerplate code and make it easy for methods to become first-class citizens in Java and make it easy to write code that uses a functional programming approach. We can easily understand this concept with a simple example such as filtering a list. However, take into account that we will start by writing **imperative code** with methods as first-class citizens, and then, we will create a new version for this code that uses a complete functional approach in Java 9 through a filter operation. We will create many versions of this example because it will allow us to understand how functional programming is possible in Java 9.

First, we will write some code considering that we still don't know about the features included in Java 9 to transform methods into first-class citizens. Then, we will use these features in many examples.

The following lines declare the `Testable` interface that specifies a method requirement that receives a `number` argument of the `int` type and returns a `boolean` result. The code file for the sample is included in the `java_9_oop_chapter_12_01` folder, in the `example12_01.java` file.

```
public interface Testable {
    boolean test(int number);
}
```

The following lines declare the `TestDivisibleBy5` concrete class that implements the previously declared `Testable` interface. The class implements the `test` method with code that returns a `boolean` value indicating whether the received number is divisible by 5 or not. If the result of the modulus, modulo, or remainder operator (`%`) between the number and 5 is equal to `0`, it means that the number is divisible by 5. The code file for the sample is included in the `java_9_oop_chapter_12_01` folder, in the `example12_01.java` file.

```
public class TestDivisibleBy5 implements Testable {
    @Override
    public boolean test(int number) {
        return ((number % 5) == 0);
    }
}
```

The following lines declare the `TestGreaterThan10` concrete class that implements the previously declared `Testable` interface. The class implements the `test` method with code that returns a `boolean` value indicating whether the received number is greater than `10` or not. The code file for the sample is included in the `java_9_oop_chapter_12_01` folder, in the `example12_01.java` file.

```
public class TestGreaterThan10 implements Testable {
    @Override
    public boolean test(int number) {
        return (number > 10);
    }
}
```

The following lines declare the `filterNumbersWithTestable` method that receives a `List<Integer>` in the numbers argument and a `Testable` instance in the tester argument. The method uses an external `for` loop, that is, imperative code to call the `tester.test` method for each `Integer` element in the numbers `List<Integer>`. If the `test` method returns `true`, the code adds the `Integer` element to the `filteredNumbersList<Integer>`, specifically, an `ArrayList<Integer>`. Finally, the method returns the `filteredNumbersList<Integer>` as a result with all the `Integer` objects that satisfied the test. The code file for the sample is included in the `java_9_oop_chapter_12_01` folder, in the `example12_01.java` file.

```
public List<Integer> filterNumbersWithTestable(final List<Integer>
numbers,
    Testable tester) {
    List<Integer> filteredNumbers = new ArrayList<>();
    for (Integer number : numbers) {
        if (tester.test(number)) {
            filteredNumbers.add(number);
        }
    }
    return filteredNumbers;
}
```

The `filterNumbersWithTestable` method works with two `List<Integer>` objects, that is, two `List` of `Integer` objects. We are talking about `Integer` and not the `int` primitive type. `Integer` is a wrapper class for the `int` primitive type. However, the `test` method we declared in the `Testable` interface and then implemented in the two classes that implement this interface receive an argument of the `int` type, and not `Integer`.

Java automatically converts a primitive value into an object of the corresponding wrapper class. Whenever we pass an object as a parameter to a method that expects the value of a primitive type, the Java compiler converts this object to the corresponding primitive type, in an operation known as **unboxing**. In the next line, the Java compiler converts or unboxes the `Integer` object to a value of the `int` type.

```
if (tester.test(number)) {
```

The compiler will execute code that is equivalent to the following line that calls the `intValue()` method that unboxes the `Integer` to an `int`:

```
if (tester.test(number.intValue())) {
```

We won't write a `for` loop to populate a `List` of `Integer` objects. Instead, we will use the `IntStream` class that specializes `Stream<T>` to describe a stream of `int` primitives. These classes are defined in the `java.util.stream` package, and therefore, we must add an `import` statement to be able to use it in our code in JShell. The following line calls the `IntStream.rangeClosed` method with `1` and `20` as the arguments to generate an `IntStream` with `int` values from `1` to `20` (inclusive). The chained call to the `boxed` method converts the generated `IntStream` into a `Stream<Integer>`, that is, a stream of `Integer` objects boxed from the primitive `int` values. The chained call to the `collect` method with `Collectors.toList()` as an argument collects the stream of `Integer` objects into a `List<Integer>`, specifically, an `ArrayList<Integer>`. The `Collectors` class is also defined in the `java.util.stream` package. The code file for the sample is included in the `java_9_oop_chapter_12_01` folder, in the `example12_01.java` file.

```
import java.util.stream.Collectors;
import java.util.stream.IntStream;

List<Integer> range1to20 =
    IntStream.rangeClosed(1,
    20).boxed().collect(Collectors.toList());
```

Boxing and unboxing add overheads and have both performance and memory impacts. In some cases, we might need to rewrite our code to avoid unnecessary boxing and unboxing when we want to achieve the best performance.

It is very important to understand that the `collect` operation will start processing the pipeline to return the desired result, that is, the list generated from the intermediate streams. The intermediate operations aren't executed until we call the `collect` method. The following screenshot shows the results of executing the previous lines in JShell. We can see that `range1to20` is a list of `Integer` that includes the numbers from 1 to 20 (inclusive) boxed into `Integer` objects.

```
jshell>

jshell> import java.util.stream.Collectors;

jshell> import java.util.stream.IntStream;

jshell>

jshell> List<Integer> range1to20 =
  ...>     IntStream.rangeClosed(1, 20).boxed().collect(Collectors.toList());
range1to20 ==> [1, 2, 3, 4, 5, 6, 7, 8, 9, 10, 11, 12, 13, 14, 15, 16, 17, 18, 19, 20]
|  created variable range1to20 : List<Integer>

jshell>
```

The following lines create an instance of the `TestDivisibleBy5` class named `testDivisibleBy5`. Then, the code calls the `filterNumbersWithTestable` method with the `List<Integer>` `range1to20` as the numbers argument and the `TestDivisibleBy5` instance named `testDivisibleBy5` as the `tester` argument. The `List<Integer>` `divisibleBy5Numbers` will have the following values after the code runs: `[5, 10, 15, 20]`. The code file for the sample is included in the `java_9_oop_chapter_12_01` folder, in the `example12_01.java` file.

```
TestDivisibleBy5 testDivisibleBy5 = new TestDivisibleBy5();
List<Integer> divisibleBy5Numbers =
filterNumbersWithTestable(range1to20, testDivisibleBy5);
System.out.println(divisibleBy5Numbers);
```

The following lines create an instance of the TestGreaterThan10 class named testGreaterThan10. Then, the code calls the filterNumbersWithTestable method with range1to20 and testGreaterThan10 as the arguments. The List<Integer> greaterThan10Numbers will have the following values after the code runs: [11, 12, 13, 14, 15, 16, 17, 18, 19, 20]. The code file for the sample is included in the java_9_oop_chapter_12_01 folder, in the example12_01.java file.

```
TestGreaterThan10 testGreaterThan10 = new TestGreaterThan10();
List<Integer> greaterThan10Numbers =
    filterNumbersWithTestable(range1to20, testGreaterThan10);
System.out.println(greaterThan10Numbers);
```

The following screenshot shows the results of executing the previous lines in JShell:

```
jshell> TestDivisibleBy5 testDivisibleBy5 = new TestDivisibleBy5();
testDivisibleBy5 ==> TestDivisibleBy5@6b09bb57
|  created variable testDivisibleBy5 : TestDivisibleBy5

jshell> List<Integer> divisibleBy5Numbers =
   ...>        filterNumbersWithTestable(range1to20, testDivisibleBy5);
divisibleBy5Numbers ==> [5, 10, 15, 20]
|  created variable divisibleBy5Numbers : List<Integer>

jshell> System.out.println(divisibleBy5Numbers);
[5, 10, 15, 20]

jshell>

jshell> TestGreaterThan10 testGreaterThan10 = new TestGreaterThan10();
testGreaterThan10 ==> TestGreaterThan10@eec5a4a
|  created variable testGreaterThan10 : TestGreaterThan10

jshell> List<Integer> greaterThan10Numbers =
   ...>        filterNumbersWithTestable(range1to20, testGreaterThan10);
greaterThan10Numbers ==> [11, 12, 13, 14, 15, 16, 17, 18, 19, 20]
|  created variable greaterThan10Numbers : List<Integer>

jshell> System.out.println(greaterThan10Numbers);
[11, 12, 13, 14, 15, 16, 17, 18, 19, 20]

jshell>
```

Working with functional interfaces and lambda expressions

We had to declare an interface and two classes to make it possible for a method to receive an instance of `Testable` and execute the `test` method implemented by each class. Luckily, Java 8 introduced **functional interfaces** and Java 9 makes it easy for us to supply a compatible **lambda expression** whenever the code requires a functional interface. In a nutshell, we can write less code to achieve the same goal.

 A functional interface is an interface that meets the following condition: it has a single abstract method or a single method requirement. We can create instances of functional interfaces with lambda expressions, method references, or constructor references. We will work with different examples that will allow us to understand lambda expressions, method references, and constructor references and we will see them in action.

The `IntPredicate` functional interface represents a function with one argument of the `int` type that returns a `boolean` result. Boolean-valued functions are known as predicates. This functional interface is defined in `java.util.function`, and therefore, we must include an `import` statement before we use it.

The following lines declare the `filterNumbersWithPredicate` method that receives a `List<Integer>` in the `numbers` argument and an `IntPredicate` instance in the `predicate` argument. The code for this method is the same as the code declared for the `filterNumbersWithTestable` method, with the only difference being that instead of receiving an argument of the `Testable` type named `tester`, the new method receives an argument of the `IntPredicate` type named `predicate`. The code also calls the `test` method with each number retrieved from the list as an argument to evaluate. The `IntPredicate` functional interface defines an abstract method named `test` that receives an `int` and returns a `boolean` result. The code file for the sample is included in the `java_9_oop_chapter_12_01` folder, in the `example12_02.java` file.

```
import java.util.function.IntPredicate;

public List<Integer> filterNumbersWithPredicate(final List<Integer>
numbers,
    IntPredicate predicate) {
    List<Integer> filteredNumbers = new ArrayList<>();
    for (Integer number : numbers) {
```

```
            if (predicate.test(number)) {
                filteredNumbers.add(number);
            }
        }
        return filteredNumbers;
    }
```

The following line declares a variable named `divisibleBy5` with the `IntPredicate` type and assigns a lambda expression to it. Specifically, the code assigns a lambda expression that receives an `int` argument named n and returns a `boolean` value indicating whether the modulus, modulo, or remainder operator (%) between n and 5 is equal to 0. The code file for the sample is included in the `java_9_oop_chapter_12_01` folder, in the `example12_02.java` file.

```
IntPredicate divisibleBy5 = n -> n % 5 == 0;
```

The lambda expression is composed of the following three components:

- n: The argument list. In this case, there is just one argument, and therefore, we don't need to enclose the argument list within parentheses. If we have more than one argument, it is necessary to enclose the list within parentheses. We don't have to specify the types for the arguments.

- ->: The arrow token.

- n % 5 == 0: The body. In this case, the body is a single expression, and therefore, there is no need to enclose it in curly braces ({ }). In addition, there is no need to write the `return` statement before the expression because it is a single expression.

The previous code is equivalent to the following code. The previous code is the shortest version and the next line is the longest version:

```
IntPredicate divisibleBy5 = (n) ->{ return n % 5 == 0 };
```

Imagine that with any of the two versions of the previous code, we are performing the following tasks:

1. Create an anonymous class that implements the `IntPredicate` interface.

2. Declare a test method in the anonymous class that receives an `int` argument and returns a `boolean` with the body specified after the arrow token (->).

3. Create an instance of this anonymous class.

All these things happen under the hood whenever we enter a lambda expression when an IntPredicate is required. When we use lambda expressions for other functional interfaces, similar things will happen with the difference being that the method name, the arguments, and the return type for the method might be different.

 The Java compiler infers the types for the arguments and the return type from the functional interface. Things remain strongly typed and if we make a mistake with types, the compiler will generate the appropriate errors and the code won't compile.

The following lines call the filterNumbersWithPredicate method with the List<Integer> range1to20 as the numbers argument and the IntPredicate instance named divisibleBy5 as the predicate argument. The List<Integer> divisibleBy5Numbers2 will have the following values after the code runs: [5, 10, 15, 20]. The code file for the sample is included in the java_9_oop_chapter_12_01 folder, in the example12_02.java file.

```
List<Integer> divisibleBy5Numbers2 =
    filterNumbersWithPredicate(range1to20, divisibleBy5);
System.out.println(divisibleBy5Numbers2);
```

The following lines call the filterNumbersWithPredicate method with the List<Integer> range1to20 as the numbers argument and a lambda expression as the predicate argument. The lambda expression receives an int argument named n and returns a boolean value indicating whether n is greater than 10. The List<Integer> greaterThan10Numbers2 will have the following values after the code runs: [11, 12, 13, 14, 15, 16, 17, 18, 19, 20]. The code file for the sample is included in the java_9_oop_chapter_12_01 folder, in the example12_02.java file.

```
List<Integer> greaterThan10Numbers2 =
    filterNumbersWithPredicate(range1to20, n -> n > 10);
System.out.println(greaterThan10Numbers2);
```

The following screenshot shows the results of executing the previous lines in JShell.

```
jshell> IntPredicate divisibleBy5 = n -> n % 5 == 0;
divisibleBy5 ==> $Lambda$13/1262822392@731a74c
|  created variable divisibleBy5 : IntPredicate

jshell> List<Integer> divisibleBy5Numbers2 =
   ...>        filterNumbersWithPredicate(range1to20, divisibleBy5);
divisibleBy5Numbers2 ==> [5, 10, 15, 20]
|  created variable divisibleBy5Numbers2 : List<Integer>

jshell> System.out.println(divisibleBy5Numbers2);
[5, 10, 15, 20]

jshell> List<Integer> greaterThan10Numbers2 =
   ...>        filterNumbersWithPredicate(range1to20, n -> n > 10);
greaterThan10Numbers2 ==> [11, 12, 13, 14, 15, 16, 17, 18, 19, 20]
|  created variable greaterThan10Numbers2 : List<Integer>

jshell> System.out.println(greaterThan10Numbers);
[11, 12, 13, 14, 15, 16, 17, 18, 19, 20]

jshell>
```

The Function<T, R> functional interface represents a function where T is the type of the input to the function and R is the type of the result of the function. We cannot specify a primate type such as int for T because it is not a class, but we can use the boxed type, that is, Integer. We cannot use boolean for R, but we can use the boxed type, that is, Boolean. If we want a similar behavior than the IntPredicate functional interface, we can use Function<Integer, Boolean>, that is, a function with one argument of the Integer type that returns a Boolean result. This functional interface is defined in java.util.function, and therefore, we must include an import statement before we use it.

The following lines declare the filterNumbersWithFunction method that receives a List<Integer> in the numbers argument and a Function<Integer, Boolean> instance in the predicate argument. The code for this method is the same as the code declared for the filterNumbersWithCondition method, with the difference being that instead of receiving an argument of the IntPredicate type named predicate, the new method receives an argument of the Function<Integer, Boolean> type named function. The code calls the apply method with each number retrieved from the list as an argument to evaluate, instead of calling the test method.

The Function<T, R> functional interface defines an abstract method named apply that receives a T and returns a result of type R. In this case, the apply method receives an Integer and returns a Boolean that the Java compiler will automatically unbox to boolean. The code file for the sample is included in the java_9_oop_chapter_12_01 folder, in the example12_03.java file.

```
import java.util.function.Function;

public List<Integer> filterNumbersWithFunction(final List<Integer>
numbers,
    Function<Integer, Boolean> function) {
    List<Integer> filteredNumbers = new ArrayList<>();
    for (Integer number : numbers) {
        if (function.apply(number)) {
            filteredNumbers.add(number);
        }
    }
    return filteredNumbers;
}
```

The following lines call the filterNumbersWithFunction method with the List<Integer> range1to20 as the numbers argument and a lambda expression as the function argument. The lambda expression receives an Integer argument named n and returns a Boolean value indicating whether the modulus, modulo, or remainder operator (%) between n and 3 is equal to 0. Java automatically boxes the boolean value generated by the expression into a Boolean object. The List<Integer> divisibleBy3Numbers will have the following values after the code runs: [3, 6, 9, 12, 15, 18]. The code file for the sample is included in the java_9_oop_chapter_12_01 folder, in the example12_03.java file.

```
List<Integer> divisibleBy3Numbers =
    filterNumbersWithFunction(range1to20, n -> n % 3 == 0);
```

Java will run code that is equivalent to the following line. The intValue() function returns an int value for the received Integer instance in n and the lambda expression returns the boolean value generated by the expression evaluation in a new Boolean instance. However, remember that boxing and unboxing happens under the hood.

```
List<Integer> divisibleBy3Numbers =
    filterNumbersWithFunction(range1to20, n -> new Boolean(n.
intValue() % 3 == 0));
```

There are more than 40 functional interfaces defined in `java.util.function`. We just worked with two of them that were capable of working with the same lambda expression. We could dedicate an entire book to analyze all the functional interfaces in detail. We will keep our focus on mixing object-oriented with functional programming. However, it is very important to know that we must check all the functional interfaces defined in `java.util.function` before declaring a customized one.

Creating a functional version of array filtering

The preceding code that declared the `filterNumbersWithFunction` method represents an imperative version of array filtering with an external `for` loop. We can use the `filter` method available for a `Stream<T>` object, in this case, a `Stream<Integer>` object, and achieve the same goal with a functional approach.

The next lines use a functional approach to generate a `List<Integer>` with the numbers included in the `List<Integer>` `range1to20` that are divisible by `3`. The code file for the sample is included in the `java_9_oop_chapter_12_01` folder, in the `example12_04.java` file.

```
List<Integer> divisibleBy3Numbers2 = range1to20.stream().filter(n -> n
% 3 == 0).collect(Collectors.toList());
```

If we want the previous code to run in JShell, we must enter all the code in a single line, which wouldn't be necessary for the Java compiler to successfully compile the code. It is a specific problem with JShell, streams, and lambda expression. This makes the code a bit difficult to understand. Hence, the next lines show another version of the code that uses multiple lines, won't work in JShell, but will make it easier to understand the code. Just take into account that you must enter the code in a single line in the next examples. The code files use single lines. The code file for the sample is included in the `java_9_oop_chapter_12_01` folder, in the `example12_04.java` file.

```
range1to20.stream()
.filter(n -> n % 3 == 0)
.collect(Collectors.toList());
```

The stream method generates a Stream<Integer> from the List<Integer>. A **stream** is a sequence of elements of a specific type that allow us to perform computations or aggregate operations with sequential or parallel executions. In fact, we can chain many stream operations and compose a stream pipeline. These computations have a lazy execution, that is, they won't be computed until there is a terminal operation such as a request to collect the final data into a List of a specific type.

The filter method receives a Predicate<Integer> as an argument and we apply it to the Stream<Integer>. The filter method returns the stream of the elements of the input stream that matches the specified predicate. The method returns a stream with all the elements for whom the Predicate<Integer> evaluates to true. We passed that previously explained lambda expression as an argument for the filter method.

The collect method receives a Stream<Integer> returned by the filter method. We passed Collectors.toList() as an argument to the collect method to perform a mutable reduction operation on the elements of the Stream<Integer> and generate a List<Integer>, that is, a mutable result container. The List<Integer> divisibleBy3Numbers2 will have the following values after the code runs: [3, 6, 9, 12, 15, 18].

Now, we want to follow a functional approach to print each number in the resulting List<Integer>. List<T> implements the Iterable<T> interface that allows us to call the forEach method to perform the action specified as an argument for each element of the Iterable until all the elements have been processed or the action throws an exception. The action argument for the forEach method must be a Consumer<T>, and therefore, in our case, it must be a Consumer<Integer> because we will call the forEach method for the resulting List<Integer>.

A Consumer<T> is a functional interface that represents an operation that accesses a single input argument of type T and returns no result (void). The Consumer<T> functional interface defines an abstract method named accept that receives an argument of type T and returns no result. The following lines pass a lambda expression as an argument to the forEach method. The lambda expression generates a Consumer<Integer> that prints the number received in n. The code file for the sample is included in the java_9_oop_chapter_12_01 folder, in the example12_04.java file.

```
divisibleBy3Numbers2.forEach(n -> System.out.println(n));
```

As a result of the previous line, we will see the following numbers printed in JShell:

3

6

9

12

15

18

The lambda expression that generates the Consumer<Integer> calls the System.out. println method with an Integer as an argument. We can use a method reference instead of a lambda expression to invoke an existing method. In this case, we can replace the previously shown lambda expression with System.out::println, that is, a method reference that invokes the println method for System.out. The Java runtime infers the method type arguments whenever we use a method reference; in this case, the method type argument is a single Integer. The code file for the sample is included in the java_9_oop_chapter_12_01 folder, in the example12_04.java file.

```
divisibleBy3Numbers2.forEach(System.out::println);
```

The code will produce the same results as the previous call to forEach with the lambda expression. The following screenshot shows the results of executing the previous lines in JShell:

```
jshell> List<Integer> divisibleBy3Numbers2 =
   ...>      range1to20.stream().filter(
   ...>          n -> n % 3 == 0).collect(
   ...>          Collectors.toList());
divisibleBy3Numbers2 ==> [3, 6, 9, 12, 15, 18]
|  created variable divisibleBy3Numbers2 : List<Integer>

jshell> divisibleBy3Numbers2.forEach(n -> System.out.println(n));
3
6
9
12
15
18

jshell>

jshell> divisibleBy3Numbers2.forEach(System.out::println);
3
6
9
12
15
18

jshell>
```

We can capture variables that aren't defined within the lambda expression. When a lambda captures variables from the outside world, we can also call them closures. For example, the following lines declare an `int` variable named `byNumber` and assigns 4 to this variable. Then, the next lines use a new version of the combination of stream, filter, and collect to generate a `List<Integer>` with the numbers that are divisible by the number specified in the `byNumber` variable. The lambda expression includes `byNumber` and Java captures this variable from the outside world under the hood. The code file for the sample is included in the `java_9_oop_chapter_12_01` folder, in the `example12_04.java` file.

```
int byNumber = 4;
List<Integer> divisibleBy4Numbers =
    range1to20.stream().filter(
        n -> n % byNumber == 0).collect(
        Collectors.toList());
divisibleBy4Numbers.forEach(System.out::println);
```

As a result of the previous line, we will see the following numbers printed in JShell:

```
4
8
12
16
20
```

If we use a lambda expression that doesn't match a functional interface, the code won't compile and the Java compiler will generate the appropriate errors. For example, the following line tries to assign a lambda expression that returns an `int` instead of either a `Boolean` or a `boolean` to an `IntPredicate` variable. The code file for the sample is included in the `java_9_oop_chapter_12_01` folder, in the `example12_05.java` file.

```
// The following code will generate an error
IntPredicate errorPredicate = n -> 8;
```

JShell will display the following errors, indicating to us that `int` cannot be converted to `boolean`:

```
|  Error:
|  incompatible types: bad return type in lambda expression
|      int cannot be converted to boolean
|  IntPredicate errorPredicate = n -> 8;
|                                      ^
```

Creating a data repository with generics and interfaces

Now we want to create a repository that provides us with entities so that we can apply the functional programming features included in Java 9 to retrieve and process data from these entities. First, we will create an `Identifiable` interface that defines the requirements for an identifiable entity. We want any class that implements this interface to provide a `getId` method that returns an `int` with the value of a unique identifier for the entity. The code file for the sample is included in the `java_9_oop_chapter_12_01` folder, in the `example12_06.java` file.

```
public interface Identifiable {
    int getId();
}
```

The next lines create a `Repository<E>` generic interface that specifies that `E` must implement the recently created `Identifiable` interface in the generic type constraint. The class declares a `getAll` method that returns a `List<E>`. Each class that implements the interface must provide its own implementation for this method. The code file for the sample is included in the `java_9_oop_chapter_12_01` folder, in the `example12_06.java` file.

```
public interface Repository<E extends Identifiable> {
    List<E> getAll();
}
```

The next lines create the `Entity` abstract class, which is the base class for all the entities. The class implements the `Identifiable` interface and defines an immutable `id` protected field of the `int` type. The constructor receives the desired value for the `id` immutable field and initializes the fields with the received value. The abstract class implements the `getId` method that returns the value for the `id` immutable field. The code file for the sample is included in the `java_9_oop_chapter_12_01` folder, in the `example12_06.java` file.

```
public abstract class Entity implements Identifiable {
    protected final int id;

    public Entity(int id) {
        this.id = id;
    }

    @Override
    public final int getId() {
        return id;
    }
}
```

The next lines create the MobileGame class, specifically, a subclass of the previously created Entity abstract class. The code file for the sample is included in the java_9_ oop_chapter_12_01 folder, in the example12_06.java file.

```java
public class MobileGame extends Entity {
    protected final String separator = "; ";
    public final String name;
    public int highestScore;
    public int lowestScore;
    public int playersCount;

    public MobileGame(int id,
        String name,
        int highestScore,
        int lowestScore,
        int playersCount) {
        super(id);
        this.name = name;
        this.highestScore = highestScore;
        this.lowestScore = lowestScore;
        this.playersCount = playersCount;
    }

    @Override
    public String toString() {
        StringBuilder sb = new StringBuilder();
        sb.append("Id: ");
        sb.append(getId());
        sb.append(separator);
        sb.append("Name: ");
        sb.append(name);
        sb.append(separator);
        sb.append("Highest score: ");
        sb.append(highestScore);
        sb.append(separator);
        sb.append("Lowest score: ");
        sb.append(lowestScore);
        sb.append(separator);
        sb.append("Players count: ");
        sb.append(playersCount);

        return sb.toString();
    }
}
```

The class declares many public fields whose values are initialized with the constructor: name, highestScore, lowestScore, and playersCount. The field is immutable but the other three are mutable. We don't use getters or setters in order to keep things simpler. However, it is important to take into account that some frameworks that allow us to work with entities require us to use getters for all the fields and setters when the fields aren't read-only.

In addition, the class overrides the toString method inherited from the java.lang. Object class and that must return a String representation for the entity. The code declared in this method uses an instance of the java.lang.StringBuilder class (sb) to append many strings in an efficient way and finally return the results of calling the sb.toString method to return the generated String. This method uses the protected separator immutable string that determines the separator we use between fields. Whenever we call System.out.println with an instance of MobileGame as an argument, the println method will call the overridden toString method to print the String representation for the instance.

We might also use String concatenation (+) or String.format to write the code for the toString method because we will work with just 15 instances of the MobileGame class. However, it is a good practice to work with StringBuilder whenever we have to concatenate many strings to produce a result and we want to make sure that we will have the best performance when executing the code. In our simple example, any implementation won't have any performance issues.

The following lines create the MemoryMobileGameRepository concrete class that implements the Repository<MobileGame> interface. Notice that we don't say Repository<E> but instead we indicate Repository<MobileGame>, because we already know the value for the E type parameter that we will implement in our class. We aren't creating a MemoryMobileGameRepository<E extends Identifiable>. Instead, we are creating a non-generic concrete class that implements a generic interface and sets the value for the parameter type E to MobileGame. The code file for the sample is included in the java_9_oop_chapter_12_01 folder, in the example12_06.java file.

```
import java.util.stream.Collectors;


public class MemoryMobileGameRepository implements
Repository<MobileGame> {
    @Override
    public List<MobileGame> getAll() {
        List<MobileGame> mobileGames = new ArrayList<>();
```

```
mobileGames.add(
    new MobileGame(1, "Uncharted 4000", 5000, 10, 3800));
mobileGames.add(
    new MobileGame(2, "Supergirl 2017", 8500, 5, 75000));
mobileGames.add(
    new MobileGame(3, "Super Luigi Run", 32000, 300, 90000));
mobileGames.add(
    new MobileGame(4, "Mario vs Kong III", 152000, 1500,
        750000));
mobileGames.add(
    new MobileGame(5, "Minecraft Reloaded", 6708960, 8000,
        3500000));
mobileGames.add(
    new MobileGame(6, "Pikachu vs Beedrill: The revenge",
        780000, 400, 1000000));
mobileGames.add(
    new MobileGame(7, "Jerry vs Tom vs Spike", 78000, 670,
        20000));
mobileGames.add(
    new MobileGame(8, "NBA 2017", 1500607, 20, 7000005));
mobileGames.add(
    new MobileGame(9, "NFL 2017", 3205978, 0, 4600700));
mobileGames.add(
    new MobileGame(10, "Nascar Remix", 785000, 0, 2600000));
mobileGames.add(
    new MobileGame(11, "Little BIG Universe", 95000, 3,
        546000));
mobileGames.add(
    new MobileGame(12, "Plants vs Zombies Garden Warfare 3",
        879059, 0, 789000));
mobileGames.add(
    new MobileGame(13, "Final Fantasy XVII", 852325, 0,
        375029));
mobileGames.add(
    new MobileGame(14, "Watch Dogs 3", 27000, 2, 78004));
mobileGames.add(
    new MobileGame(15, "Remember Me", 672345, 5, 252003));

    return mobileGames;
    }
}
```

The class implements the getAll method required by the Repository<E> interface. In this case, the method returns a List of MobileGame (List<MobileGame>), specifically an ArrayList<MobileGame>. The method creates 15 MobileGame instances and appends them to an ArrayList of MobileGame that the method returns as a result.

The following lines create an instance of the MemoryMobileGameRepository class and call the forEach method for the List<MobileGame> returned by the getAll method. The forEach method calls a body on each element in the list, as is done in a for loop. The closure specified as an argument for the forEach method calls the System.out.println method with the MobileGame instance as an argument. This way, Java uses the toString method overridden in the MobileGame class to generate a String representation for each MobileGame instance. The code file for the sample is included in the java_9_oop_chapter_12_01 folder, in the example12_06.java file.

```
MemoryMobileGameRepository repository = new
MemoryMobileGameRepository()
repository.getAll().forEach(mobileGame -> System.out.
println(mobileGame));
```

The following lines show the output generated after executing the previous code that prints the String returned by the toString() method for each MobileGame instance:

Id: 1; Name: Uncharted 4000; Highest score: 5000; Lowest score: 10; Players count: 3800

Id: 2; Name: Supergirl 2017; Highest score: 8500; Lowest score: 5; Players count: 75000

Id: 3; Name: Super Luigi Run; Highest score: 32000; Lowest score: 300; Players count: 90000

Id: 4; Name: Mario vs Kong III; Highest score: 152000; Lowest score: 1500; Players count: 750000

Id: 5; Name: Minecraft Reloaded; Highest score: 6708960; Lowest score: 8000; Players count: 3500000

Id: 6; Name: Pikachu vs Beedrill: The revenge; Highest score: 780000; Lowest score: 400; Players count: 1000000

Id: 7; Name: Jerry vs Tom vs Spike; Highest score: 78000; Lowest score: 670; Players count: 20000

Id: 8; Name: NBA 2017; Highest score: 1500607; Lowest score: 20; Players count: 7000005

Id: 9; Name: NFL 2017; Highest score: 3205978; Lowest score: 0; Players count: 4600700

Id: 10; Name: Nascar Remix; Highest score: 785000; Lowest score: 0; Players count: 2600000

Id: 11; **Name:** Little BIG Universe; Highest score: 95000; Lowest score: 3; Players count: 546000

Id: 12; **Name:** Plants vs Zombies Garden Warfare 3; Highest score: 879059; Lowest score: 0; Players count: 789000

Id: 13; **Name:** Final Fantasy XVII; Highest score: 852325; Lowest score: 0; Players count: 375029

Id: 14; **Name:** Watch Dogs 3; Highest score: 27000; Lowest score: 2; Players count: 78004

Id: 15; **Name:** Remember Me; Highest score: 672345; Lowest score: 5; Players count: 252003

The following line produces the same results. In this case, the code uses the previously learned reference method to call the `System.out.println` method with each `MobileGame` instance in the `List<MobileGame>` returned by the `getAll` method as an argument. Notice that the line is shorter than the last line for the previous code snippet and the code produces the same result. The code file for the sample is included in the `java_9_oop_chapter_12_01` folder, in the `example12_06.java` file.

```
repository.getAll().forEach(System.out::println);
```

Filtering collections with complex conditions

We can use our new repository to restrict the results retrieved from complex data. We can combine a call to the `getAll` method with stream, filter, and collect to generate a `Stream<MobileGame>`, apply a filter with a lambda expression as an argument, and call the `collect` method with `Collectors.toList()` as an argument to generate a filtered `List<MobileGame>` from the filtered `Stream<MobileGame>`. The `filter` method receives a `Predicate<MobileGame>` as an argument that we generate with a lambda expression and we apply the filter to the `Stream<MobileGame>`. The `filter` method returns the stream of the elements of the input stream that matches the specified predicate. The method returns a stream with all the elements for whom the `Predicate<MobileGame>` evaluates to `true`.

> The next lines show code snippets that use multiple lines, won't work in JShell, but will make it easier to read and understand the code. If we want the code to run in JShell, we must enter all the code in a single line, which wouldn't be necessary for the Java compiler to successfully compile the code. It is a specific problem with JShell, streams, and lambda expression. The code files use single lines to be compatible with JShell.

The following lines declare the new getWithLowestScoreGreaterThan method for the MemoryMobileGameRepository class. Notice that we don't include all the code for the new class in order to avoid repetition. The code file for the sample is included in the java_9_oop_chapter_12_01 folder, in the example12_07.java file.

```
public List<MobileGame> getWithLowestScoreGreaterThan(int
minimumLowestScore) {
    return getAll().stream()
        .filter(game -> game.lowestScore > minimumLowestScore)
        .collect(Collectors.toList());
}
```

The following lines use the MemoryMobileGameRepository instance named repository to call the previously added method and then chain a call to forEach to print all the games whose lowestScore value is greater than 1000:

```
MemoryMobileGameRepository repository = new
MemoryMobileGameRepository()
repository.getWithLowestScoreGreaterThan(1000).forEach(System.
out::println);
```

The following lines show the output generated after executing the previous code:

Id: 4; Name: Mario vs Kong III; Highest score: 152000; Lowest score: 1500; Players count: 750000

Id: 5; Name: Minecraft Reloaded; Highest score: 6708960; Lowest score: 8000; Players count: 3500000

The next code shows another version of the getWithLowestScoreGreaterThan method named getWithLowestScoreGreaterThanV2 that is equivalent and produces the same results. In this case, the lambda expression that generates a Predicate<MobileGame> uses parentheses and specifies the type for the game argument. As shown in the previous code snippet, it is not necessary to do this. However, we can find code written like the next lines, and therefore, it is important to know that this syntax also works fine. The code file for the sample is included in the java_9_oop_chapter_12_01 folder, in the example12_07.java file.

```
public List<MobileGame> getWithLowestScoreGreaterThanV2(int
minimumLowestScore) {
return getAll().stream()
    .filter((MobileGame game) -> game.lowestScore >
minimumLowestScore)
    .collect(Collectors.toList());
}
```

The following lines declare the new `getStartingWith` method for the `MemoryMobileGameRepository` class. The lambda expression passed as an argument to the `filter` method returns the results of calling the `startsWith` method for the game's name with the prefix received as an argument. In this case, the lambda expression is a closure that captures the `prefix` argument and uses it within the lambda expression body. The code file for the sample is included in the `java_9_oop_chapter_12_01` folder, in the `example12_08.java` file.

```
public List<MobileGame> getStartingWith(String prefix) {
    return getAll().stream()
        .filter(game -> game.name.startsWith(prefix))
        .collect(Collectors.toList());
}
```

The following lines use the `MemoryMobileGameRepository` instance named `repository` to call the previously added method and then chain a call to `forEach` to print all the games whose names starts with `"Su"`.

```
MemoryMobileGameRepository repository = new
MemoryMobileGameRepository()
repository.getStartingWith("Su").forEach(System.out::println);
```

The following lines show the output generated after executing the previous code:

Id: 2; Name: Supergirl 2017; Highest score: 8500; Lowest score: 5; Players count: 75000

Id: 3; Name: Super Luigi Run; Highest score: 32000; Lowest score: 300; Players count: 90000

The following lines declare the new `getByPlayersCountAndHighestScore` method for the `MemoryMobileGameRepository` class. The method returns an `Optional<MobileGame>`, that is, a container object which may contain a `MobileGame` instance or it may be empty. If there is a value, the `isPresent` method will return `true` and we will be able to retrieve the `MobileGame` instance by calling the `get` method. In this case, the code calls the `findFirst` method chained to the call to the `filter` method. The `findFirst` method returns an `Optional<T>`, in this case, an `Optional<MobileGame>` with the first element in the `Stream<MobileGame>` generated by the `filter` method. Notice that we aren't sorting the results at any time. The code file for the sample is included in the `java_9_oop_chapter_12_01` folder, in the `example12_09.java` file.

```
public Optional<MobileGame> getByPlayersCountAndHighestScore(
    int playersCount,
    int highestScore) {
    return getAll().stream()
```

```
        .filter(game -> (game.playersCount == playersCount) &&
            (game.highestScore == highestScore))
        .findFirst();
}
```

The following lines use the `MemoryMobileGameRepository` instance named `repository` to call the previously added method. The code calls the `isPresent` method after each call to the `getByPlayersCountAndHighestScore` method to determine whether the `Optional<MobileGame>` has an instance. If the method returns `true`, the code calls the `get` method to retrieve the `MobileGame` instance from the `Optional<MobileGame>`. The code file for the sample is included in the `java_9_oop_chapter_12_01` folder, in the `example12_09.java` file.

```
MemoryMobileGameRepository repository = new
MemoryMobileGameRepository()
Optional<MobileGame> optionalMobileGame1 =
    repository.getByPlayersCountAndHighestScore(750000, 152000);
if (optionalMobileGame1.isPresent()) {
    MobileGame mobileGame1 = optionalMobileGame1.get();
    System.out.println(mobileGame1);
} else {
    System.out.println("No mobile game matches the specified
criteria.");
}
Optional<MobileGame> optionalMobileGame2 =
    repository.getByPlayersCountAndHighestScore(670000, 829340);
if (optionalMobileGame2.isPresent()) {
    MobileGame mobileGame2 = optionalMobileGame2.get();
    System.out.println(mobileGame2);
} else {
    System.out.println("No mobile game matches the specified
criteria.");
}
```

The following lines show the output generated with the previous code. In the first call, there was a mobile game that matched the search criteria. In the second call, there is no `MobileGame` instance that matches the search criteria:

```
Id: 4; Name: Mario vs Kong III; Highest score: 152000; Lowest score:
1500; Players count: 750000
No mobile game matches the specified criteria.
```

The following screenshot shows the results of executing the previous lines in JShell:

```
|    update replaced variable repository, reset to null
|    update overwrote class MemoryMobileGameRepository

jshell>

jshell> MemoryMobileGameRepository repository = new MemoryMobileGameRepository()
repository ==> MemoryMobileGameRepository@7a765367
|  modified variable repository : MemoryMobileGameRepository
|    update overwrote variable repository : MemoryMobileGameRepository

jshell> Optional<MobileGame> optionalMobileGame1 =
   ...>      repository.getByPlayersCountAndHighestScore(750000, 152000);
optionalMobileGame1 ==> Optional[Id: 4; Name: Mario vs Kong III; Highest score: 152000; Lowest score ...
|  created variable optionalMobileGame1 : Optional<MobileGame>

jshell> if (optionalMobileGame1.isPresent()) {
   ...>      MobileGame mobileGame1 = optionalMobileGame1.get();
   ...>      System.out.println(mobileGame1);
   ...> } else {
;  ...>      System.out.println("No mobile game matches the specified criteria.")
   ...> }
Id: 4; Name: Mario vs Kong III; Highest score: 152000; Lowest score: 1500; Players count: 750000

jshell> Optional<MobileGame> optionalMobileGame2 =
   ...>      repository.getByPlayersCountAndHighestScore(670000, 829340);
optionalMobileGame2 ==> Optional.empty
|  created variable optionalMobileGame2 : Optional<MobileGame>

jshell> if (optionalMobileGame2.isPresent()) {
   ...>      MobileGame mobileGame2 = optionalMobileGame2.get();
   ...>      System.out.println(mobileGame2);
   ...> } else {
;  ...>      System.out.println("No mobile game matches the specified criteria.")
   ...> }
No mobile game matches the specified criteria.

jshell>
```

Using a map operation to transform values

The following lines declare a new `getGameNamesTransformedToUpperCase` method for our previously coded `MemoryMobileGameRepository` class. The new method performs one of the simplest map operations. The call to the `map` method transforms a `Stream<MobileGame>` into a `Stream<String>`. The lambda expression passed as an argument to the `map` method generates a `Function<MobileGame, String>`, that is, it receives a `MobileGame` argument and returns a `String`. The call to the `collect` method generates a `List<String>` from the `Stream<String>` returned by the `map` method.

The code file for the sample is included in the `java_9_oop_chapter_12_01` folder, in the `example12_10.java` file.

```
public List<String> getGameNamesTransformedToUpperCase() {
    return getAll().stream()
        .map(game -> game.name.toUpperCase())
        .collect(Collectors.toList());
}
```

The `getGameNamesTransformedToUpperCase` method returns a `List<String>`. The `map` method transforms each `MobileGame` instance in the `Stream<MobileGame>`into a `String` with the `name` field converted to uppercase. This way, the `map` method transforms a `Stream<MobileGame>` into a `List<String>`.

The following lines use the `MemoryMobileGameRepository` instance named `repository` to call the previously added method and generate a list of the game names converted to uppercase strings. The code file for the sample is included in the `java_9_oop_chapter_12_01` folder, in the `example12_10.java` file.

```
MemoryMobileGameRepository repository = new
MemoryMobileGameRepository()
repository.getGameNamesTransformedToUpperCase().forEach(System.
out::println);
```

The following lines show the output generated after executing the previous code:

UNCHARTED 4000

SUPERGIRL 2017

SUPER LUIGI RUN

MARIO VS KONG III

MINECRAFT RELOADED

PIKACHU VS BEEDRILL: THE REVENGE

JERRY VS TOM VS SPIKE

NBA 2017

NFL 2017

NASCAR REMIX

LITTLE BIG UNIVERSE

PLANTS VS ZOMBIES GARDEN WARFARE 3

FINAL FANTASY XVII

WATCH DOGS 3

REMEMBER ME

The following code creates a new `NamesForMobileGame` class with two constructors. The code file for the sample is included in the `java_9_oop_chapter_12_01` folder, in the `example12_11.java` file.

```
public class NamesForMobileGame {
    public final String upperCaseName;
    public final String lowerCaseName;

    public NamesForMobileGame(String name) {
        this.upperCaseName = name.toUpperCase();
        this.lowerCaseName = name.toLowerCase();
    }

    public NamesForMobileGame(MobileGame game) {
        this(game.name);
    }
}
```

The `NamesForMobileGame` class declares two immutable fields of the `String` type: `upperCaseName` and `lowerCaseName`. One of the constructors receives a `nameString` and saves it converted to uppercase in the `upperCaseName` field and saves it converted to lowercase in the `lowerCaseName` field. The other constructor receives a `MobileGame` instance and calls the previously explained constructor with the `name` field for the received `MobileGame` instance as an argument.

The following code adds a new `getNamesForMobileGames` method to the `MemoryMobileGameRepository` class. The new method performs a map operation. The call to the `map` method transforms a `Stream<MobileGame>` into a `Stream<NamesForMobileGame>`. The lambda expression passed as an argument to the `map` method generates a `Function<MobileGame, NamesForMobileGame>`, that is, it receives a `MobileGame` argument and returns an instance of `NamesForMobileGame` by calling the constructor that receives a `name` as an argument. The call to the `collect` method generates a `List<NamesForMobileGame>` from the `Stream<NamesForMobileGame>` returned by the `map` method. The code file for the sample is included in the `java_9_oop_chapter_12_01` folder, in the `example12_11.java` file.

```
public List<NamesForMobileGame> getNamesForMobileGames() {
    return getAll().stream()
        .map(game -> new NamesForMobileGame(game.name))
        .collect(Collectors.toList());
}
```

The following lines use the MemoryMobileGameRepository instance named repository to call the previously added method. The lambda expression passed as an argument to the forEach method declares a body enclosed in curly braces because it requires many lines. This body uses an instance of the java.lang. StringBuilder class (sb) to append many strings with the uppercase name, a separator, and a lower case name. The code file for the sample is included in the java_9_oop_chapter_12_01 folder, in the example12_11.java file.

```
MemoryMobileGameRepository repository = new
MemoryMobileGameRepository()
repository.getNamesForMobileGames().forEach(names -> {
    StringBuilder sb = new StringBuilder();
    sb.append(names.upperCaseName);
    sb.append(" - ");
    sb.append(names.lowerCaseName);
    System.out.println(sb.toString());
});
```

The following lines show the output generated after executing the previous code:

```
UNCHARTED 4000 - uncharted 4000
SUPERGIRL 2017 - supergirl 2017
SUPER LUIGI RUN - super luigi run
MARIO VS KONG III - mario vs kong iii
MINECRAFT RELOADED - minecraft reloaded
PIKACHU VS BEEDRILL: THE REVENGE - pikachu vs beedrill: the revenge
JERRY VS TOM VS SPIKE - jerry vs tom vs spike
NBA 2017 - nba 2017
NFL 2017 - nfl 2017
NASCAR REMIX - nascar remix
LITTLE BIG UNIVERSE - little big universe
PLANTS VS ZOMBIES GARDEN WARFARE 3 - plants vs zombies garden warfare 3
FINAL FANTASY XVII - final fantasy xvii
WATCH DOGS 3 - watch dogs 3
REMEMBER ME - remember me
```

The next code shows another version of the getNamesForMobileGames method named getNamesForMobileGamesV2 that is equivalent and produces the same results. In this case, we replaced the lambda expression that generates a Function<MobileGame, NamesForMobileGame> with the constructor reference method: NamesForMobileGame::new. The constructor reference method is specified with the class name followed by ::new and will create a new instance of the NamesForMobileGame by using the constructor that receives a MobileGame instance as an argument. The code file for the sample is included in the java_9_oop_chapter_12_01 folder, in the example12_12.java file.

```java
public List<NamesForMobileGame> getNamesForMobileGamesV2() {
    return getAll().stream()
        .map(NamesForMobileGame::new)
        .collect(Collectors.toList());
}
```

The following code uses the new version of the method and produces the same results shown for the first version. The code file for the sample is included in the java_9_oop_chapter_12_01 folder, in the example12_12.java file.

```java
MemoryMobileGameRepository repository = new
MemoryMobileGameRepository();
repository.getNamesForMobileGamesV2().forEach(names -> {
    StringBuilder sb = new StringBuilder();
    sb.append(names.upperCaseName);
    sb.append(" - ");
    sb.append(names.lowerCaseName);
    System.out.println(sb.toString());
});
```

Combining a map operation with reduce

The following lines show an imperative code version of a for loop that calculates the sum of all the lowestScore values for the mobile games. The code file for the sample is included in the java_9_oop_chapter_12_01 folder, in the example12_13.java file.

```java
int lowestScoreSum = 0;
for (MobileGame mobileGame : repository.getAll()) {
    lowestScoreSum += mobileGame.lowestScore;
}
System.out.println(lowestScoreSum);
```

The code is very easy to understand. The `lowestScoreSum` variable has a starting value of 0, and each iteration of the `for` loop retrieves a `MobileGame` instance from the `List<MobileGame>` returned by the `repository.getAll()` method and increases the value of the `lowestScoreSum` variable with the value of the `mobileGame.lowestScore` field.

We can combine the map and reduce operations to create a functional version of the previous imperative code to calculate the sum of all the `lowestScore` values for the mobile games. The next lines chain a call to `map` to a call to `reduce` to achieve this goal. Take a look at the following code. The code file for the sample is included in the `java_9_oop_chapter_12_01` folder, in the `example12_14.java` file.

```
int lowestScoreMapReduceSum = repository.getAll().stream().map(game ->
game.lowestScore).reduce(0, (sum, lowestScore) -> sum + lowestScore);
System.out.println(lowestScoreMapReduceSum);
```

First, the code uses the call to `map` to transform a `Stream<MobileGame>` into a `Stream<Integer>` with the values specified in the `lowestScore` stored property boxed into `Integer` objects. Then, the code calls the `reduce` method that receives two arguments: the initial value for an accumulated value, 0, and a combine closure that will be repeatedly called with the accumulated value. The method returns the results of the repeated calls to the combine closure.

The closure specified in the second argument for the `reduce` method receives `sum` and `lowestScore` and returns the sum of both values. Hence, the closure returns the sum of the total accumulated so far plus the `lowestScore` value that is processed. We can add a `System.out.println` statement to display the values for both `sum` and `lowestScore` within the closure specified in the second argument for the `reduce` method. The following lines show a new version of the previous code that adds the line with the `System.out.println` statement that will allow us to dive deep into how the `reduce` operation works. The code file for the sample is included in the `java_9_oop_chapter_12_01` folder, in the `example12_15.java` file.

```
int lowestScoreMapReduceSum2 =
    repository.getAll().stream()
    .map(game -> game.lowestScore)
    .reduce(0, (sum, lowestScore) -> {
        StringBuilder sb = new StringBuilder();
        sb.append("sum value: ");
        sb.append(sum);
        sb.append(";lowestScore value: ");
        sb.append(lowestScore);
        System.out.println(sb.toString());
```

```
            return sum + lowestScore;
        });
    System.out.println(lowestScoreMapReduceSum2);
```

The following lines show the results for the previous lines, where we can see how the value for the sum argument starts with the initial value specified in the first argument for the reduce method (0) and accumulates the sum completed so far. Finally, the lowestScoreSum2 variable holds the sum of all the lowestScore values. We can see that the last value printed for sum and lowestScore are 10910 and 5. The last piece of code executed for the reduce operation computes 10910 plus 5 and returns 10915, which is the result saved in the lowestScoreSum2 variable.

```
sum value: 0; lowestScore value: 10
sum value: 10; lowestScore value: 5
sum value: 15; lowestScore value: 300
sum value: 315; lowestScore value: 1500
sum value: 1815; lowestScore value: 8000
sum value: 9815; lowestScore value: 400
sum value: 10215; lowestScore value: 670
sum value: 10885; lowestScore value: 20
sum value: 10905; lowestScore value: 0
sum value: 10905; lowestScore value: 0
sum value: 10905; lowestScore value: 3
sum value: 10908; lowestScore value: 0
sum value: 10908; lowestScore value: 0
sum value: 10908; lowestScore value: 2
sum value: 10910; lowestScore value: 5
lowestScoreMapReduceSum2 ==> 10915
10915
```

In the previous example, we combined map and reduce to perform a sum. We can take advantage of the reduction methods provided by Java 9 to achieve the same goal with simplified code. In the following code, we take advantage of mapToInt to generate an IntStream; the sum works with int values and doesn't have to unbox Integer to int. The code file for the sample is included in the java_9_oop_chapter_12_01 folder, in the example12_16.java file.

```
    int lowestScoreMapReduceSum3 =
        repository.getAll().stream()
        .mapToInt(game -> game.lowestScore).sum();
    System.out.println(lowestScoreMapReduceSum3);
```

The next lines also produce the same results with a different pipeline that is not as efficient as the previously shown one. The map method has to box the returned int into an Integer and returns a Stream<Integer>. Then, the call to the collect method specifies a call to Collectors.summingInt as an argument. Collectors.summingInt requires int values to compute the sum, and therefore, we pass a method reference to call the intValue method for each Integer in the Stream<Integer>. The following lines use the Collectors.summingInt collector to perform the sum of the int values. The code file for the sample is included in the java_9_oop_chapter_12_01 folder, in the example12_17.java file.

```
int lowestScoreMapReduceSum4 =
    repository.getAll().stream()
.map(game -> game.lowestScore)
.collect(Collectors.summingInt(Integer::intValue));
System.out.println(lowestScoreMapReduceSum4);
```

In this case, we know that the Integer.MAX_VALUE will allow us to hold the accurate result for the sum. However, in some cases, we have to use the long type. The following code uses the mapToLong method to use a long to accumulate the values. The code file for the sample is included in the java_9_oop_chapter_12_01 folder, in the example12_18.java file.

```
long lowestScoreMapReduceSum5 =
    repository.getAll().stream()
    .mapToLong(game -> game.lowestScore).sum();
System.out.println(lowestScoreMapReduceSum6);
```

 Java 9 provides many reduction methods, also known as aggregate operations. Make sure you consider them before writing your own code to perform operations such as count, average, and sum. We can use them to perform arithmetic operations on streams and get the number results.

Chaining many operations with map and reduce

We can chain filter, map, and reduce operations. The following code adds a new getHighestScoreSumForMinPlayersCount method to the MemoryMobileGameRepository class. The code file for the sample is included in the java_9_oop_chapter_12_01 folder, in the example12_19.java file.

```
public long getHighestScoreSumForMinPlayersCount(int minPlayersCount)
{
    return getAll().stream()
        .filter(game -> (game.playersCount >= minPlayersCount))
        .mapToLong(game -> game.highestScore)
        .reduce(0, (sum, highestScore) -> sum + highestScore);
}
```

The new method performs a `filter` chained with a `mapToLong` and finally a `reduce` operation. The call to `filter` generates a `Stream<MobileGame>` with the instance of `MobileGame` whose `playersCount` value is equal or greater than the `minPlayersCount` value received as an argument. The `mapToLong` method returns a `LongStream`, that is, a specialized `Stream<T>` that describes a stream of `long` primitives. The call to `mapToLong` receives the `highestScore` value of the `int` type for each filtered `MobileGame` instance and returns this value converted to `long`.

The `reduce` method receives a `LongStream` from the processing pipeline. The initial value for the accumulated value of the `reduce` operation is specified as the first argument, `0`, and the second argument is a lambda expression with the combine operation that will be repeatedly called with the accumulated value. The method returns the results of the repeated calls to the combine operation.

The lambda expression specified in the second argument for the `reduce` method receives `sum` and `highestScore` and returns the sum of both values. Hence, the lambda expression returns the sum of the total accumulated so far, received in the `sum` argument, plus the `highestScore` value that is processed.

The next lines use the previously created method. The code file for the sample is included in the `java_9_oop_chapter_12_01` folder, in the `example12_19.java` file.

```
MemoryMobileGameRepository repository = new
MemoryMobileGameRepository();
System.out.println(repository.
getHighestScoreSumForMinPlayersCount(150000));
```

JShell will display the following value as a result:

```
15631274
```

As we learned from the previous examples, we can use the sum method instead of writing the code for the reduce method. The next code shows another version of the getHighestScoreSumForMinPlayersCount method named getHighestScoreSumForMinPlayersCountV2 that is equivalent and produces the same results. The code file for the sample is included in the java_9_oop_chapter_12_01 folder, in the example12_20.java file.

```
public long getHighestScoreSumForMinPlayersCountV2(int
minPlayersCount) {
    return getAll().stream()
        .filter(game -> (game.playersCount >= minPlayersCount))
        .mapToLong(game -> game.highestScore)
        .sum();
}
```

The following code uses the new version of the method and produces the same results shown for the first version. The code file for the sample is included in the java_9_oop_chapter_12_01 folder, in the example12_20.java file.

```
MemoryMobileGameRepository repository = new
MemoryMobileGameRepository();
System.out.println(repository.
getHighestScoreSumForMinPlayersCountV2(150000));
```

Working with different collectors

We can follow a functional approach and solve different kinds of algorithms with stream processing pipelines and the help of the diverse collectors provided by Java 9, that is, the diverse static methods provided by the java.util.stream.Collectors class. In the next examples, we will use different arguments for the collect method.

The following lines join all the names for the MobileGame instances to generate a single String with the names separated with a separator ("; "). The code file for the sample is included in the java_9_oop_chapter_12_01 folder, in the example12_21.java file.

```
repository.getAll().stream()
.map(game -> game.name.toUpperCase())
.collect(Collectors.joining("; "));
```

The code passes `Collectors.joining(";" )` as an argument to the `collect` method. The `joining` static method returns a `Collector` that concatenates the input elements into a `String` separated by the delimiter received as an argument. The following shows the results of executing the previous lines in JShell.

UNCHARTED 4000; SUPERGIRL 2017; SUPER LUIGI RUN; MARIO VS KONG III; MINECRAFT RELOADED; PIKACHU VS BEEDRILL: THE REVENGE; JERRY VS TOM VS SPIKE; NBA 2017; NFL 2017; NASCAR REMIX; LITTLE BIG UNIVERSE; PLANTS VS ZOMBIES GARDEN WARFARE 3; FINAL FANTASY XVII; WATCH DOGS 3; REMEMBER ME

The following lines show a new version of the previous code snippet that orders the results by name in ascending order. The code file for the sample is included in the `java_9_oop_chapter_12_01` folder, in the `example12_22.java` file.

```
repository.getAll().stream().sorted(Comparator.comparing(game ->
game.name)).map(game -> game.name.toUpperCase()).collect(Collectors.
joining("; "));
```

The code passes `Comparator.comparing(game -> game.name)` as an argument to the `sorted` method. The `comparing` static method receives a function that extracts the desired sort key from the `MobileGame` and returns a `Comparator<MobileGame>` that compares this sort key using the specified comparator. The code passes a lambda expression as an argument to the `comparing` static method to specify the name as the desired sort key for the `MobileGame` instances. The sorted method receives a `Stream<MobileGame>` and returns a `Stream<MobileGame>` with the `MobileGame` instances sorted according to the provided `Comparator<MobileGame>`. The following shows the results of executing the previous lines in JShell:

FINAL FANTASY XVII; JERRY VS TOM VS SPIKE; LITTLE BIG UNIVERSE; MARIO VS KONG III; MINECRAFT RELOADED; NBA 2017; NFL 2017; NASCAR REMIX; PIKACHU VS BEEDRILL: THE REVENGE; PLANTS VS ZOMBIES GARDEN WARFARE 3; REMEMBER ME; SUPER LUIGI RUN; SUPERGIRL 2017; UNCHARTED 4000; WATCH DOGS 3

Now we want to check the games that have a players' count equal or higher than a specified threshold. We want to check the games that passed and failed. The following lines generate a `Map<Boolean, List<MobileGame>>` whose key specifies whether the mobile games passed or not and the value includes the `List<MobileGame>` that passed or failed. Then, the code calls the `forEach` method to display the results. The code file for the sample is included in the `java_9_oop_chapter_12_01` folder, in the `example12_23.java` file.

```
Map<Boolean, List<MobileGame>> map1 =
repository.getAll().stream()
.collect(Collectors.partitioningBy(g -> g.playersCount >= 100000));
map1.forEach((passed, mobileGames) -> {
    System.out.println(
```

```
        String.format("Mobile games that %s:",
            passed ? "passed" : "didn't pass"));
    mobileGames.forEach(System.out::println);
});
```

The code passes `Collectors.partitioningBy(g -> g.playersCount >= 100000)` as an argument to the `collect` method. The `partitioningBy` static method receives a `Predicate<MobileGame>`. The code passes a lambda expression as an argument to the `partitioningBy` static method to specify that the input elements must be partitioned based on whether the `playersCount` field is greater than or equal to `100000` or not. The returned `Collector<MobileGame>` partitions the `Stream<MobileGame>` and organizes it into a `Map<Boolean, List<MobileGame>>`, performing a downstream reduction.

Then, the code calls the `forEach` method with a lambda expression as an argument that receives the key and value from the `Map<Boolean, List<MobileGame>>` in the `passed` and `mobileGames` arguments. The following shows the results of executing the previous lines in JShell:

```
Mobile games that didn't pass:

Id: 1; Name: Uncharted 4000; Highest score: 5000; Lowest score: 10;
Players count: 3800

Id: 2; Name: Supergirl 2017; Highest score: 8500; Lowest score: 5;
Players count: 75000

Id: 3; Name: Super Luigi Run; Highest score: 32000; Lowest score: 300;
Players count: 90000

Id: 7; Name: Jerry vs Tom vs Spike; Highest score: 78000; Lowest score:
670; Players count: 20000

Id: 14; Name: Watch Dogs 3; Highest score: 27000; Lowest score: 2;
Players count: 78004

Mobile games that passed:

Id: 4; Name: Mario vs Kong III; Highest score: 152000; Lowest score:
1500; Players count: 750000

Id: 5; Name: Minecraft Reloaded; Highest score: 6708960; Lowest score:
8000; Players count: 3500000

Id: 6; Name: Pikachu vs Beedrill: The revenge; Highest score: 780000;
Lowest score: 400; Players count: 1000000

Id: 8; Name: NBA 2017; Highest score: 1500607; Lowest score: 20; Players
count: 7000005

Id: 9; Name: NFL 2017; Highest score: 3205978; Lowest score: 0; Players
count: 4600700

Id: 10; Name: Nascar Remix; Highest score: 785000; Lowest score: 0;
Players count: 2600000
```

Id: 11; **Name:** Little BIG Universe; **Highest score:** 95000; Lowest score: 3; Players count: 546000

Id: 12; **Name:** Plants vs Zombies Garden Warfare 3; Highest score: 879059; Lowest score: 0; Players count: 789000

Id: 13; **Name:** Final Fantasy XVII; Highest score: 852325; Lowest score: 0; Players count: 375029

Id: 15; **Name:** Remember Me; Highest score: 672345; Lowest score: 5; Players count: 252003

The following lines show a new version of the previous code snippet that orders the results for each of the generated partitions by name in ascending order. The line that adds the sorting is highlighted. The code file for the sample is included in the java_9_oop_chapter_12_01 folder, in the example12_24.java file.

```
Map<Boolean, List<MobileGame>> map1 =
repository.getAll().stream()
.sorted(Comparator.comparing(game -> game.name))
.collect(Collectors.partitioningBy(g -> g.playersCount >= 100000));
map1.forEach((passed, mobileGames) -> {
    System.out.println(
        String.format("Mobile games that %s:",
            passed ? "passed" : "didn't pass"));
    mobileGames.forEach(System.out::println);
});
```

The following shows the results of executing the previous lines in JShell:

```
Mobile games that didn't pass:
```

Id: 7; **Name:** Jerry vs Tom vs Spike; Highest score: 78000; Lowest score: 670; Players count: 20000

Id: 3; **Name:** Super Luigi Run; Highest score: 32000; Lowest score: 300; Players count: 90000

Id: 2; **Name:** Supergirl 2017; Highest score: 8500; Lowest score: 5; Players count: 75000

Id: 1; **Name:** Uncharted 4000; Highest score: 5000; Lowest score: 10; Players count: 3800

Id: 14; **Name:** Watch Dogs 3; Highest score: 27000; Lowest score: 2; Players count: 78004

```
Mobile games that passed:
```

Id: 13; **Name:** Final Fantasy XVII; Highest score: 852325; Lowest score: 0; Players count: 375029

Id: 11; **Name:** Little BIG Universe; Highest score: 95000; Lowest score: 3; Players count: 546000

```
Id: 4; Name: Mario vs Kong III; Highest score: 152000; Lowest score:
1500; Players count: 750000

Id: 5; Name: Minecraft Reloaded; Highest score: 6708960; Lowest score:
8000; Players count: 3500000

Id: 8; Name: NBA 2017; Highest score: 1500607; Lowest score: 20; Players
count: 7000005

Id: 9; Name: NFL 2017; Highest score: 3205978; Lowest score: 0; Players
count: 4600700

Id: 10; Name: Nascar Remix; Highest score: 785000; Lowest score: 0;
Players count: 2600000

Id: 6; Name: Pikachu vs Beedrill: The revenge; Highest score: 780000;
Lowest score: 400; Players count: 1000000

Id: 12; Name: Plants vs Zombies Garden Warfare 3; Highest score: 879059;
Lowest score: 0; Players count: 789000

Id: 15; Name: Remember Me; Highest score: 672345; Lowest score: 5;
Players count: 252003
```

Test your knowledge

1. A functional interface is an interface that meets the following condition:

    1. It uses a lambda expression in one of its default methods.

    2. It has a single abstract method or a single method requirement.

    3. It implements the `Lambda<T, U>` interface.

2. You can create an instance of a functional interface with:

    1. Lambda expressions, method references, or constructor references.

    2. Only lambda expressions. Method references and constructor references only work with `Predicate<T>`.

    3. Method references and constructor references. Lambda expressions only work with `Predicate<T>`.

3. The `IntPredicate` functional interface represents a function with:

    1. One argument of the `int` type that returns no result (`void`).

    2. One argument of the `int` type that returns an `Integer` result.

    3. One argument of the `int` type that returns a `boolean` result.

4. When we apply a `filter` method to a `Stream<T>`, the method returns:

    1. A `Stream<T>`.

    2. A `List<T>`.

    3. A `Map<T, List<T>>`.

5. Which of the following code snippets is equivalent to `numbers.forEach(n -> System.out.println(n));`:

    1. `numbers.forEach(n::System.out.println);`

    2. `numbers.forEach(System.out::println);`

    3. `numbers.forEach(n ->System.out.println);`

Summary

In this chapter, we worked with many functional programming features included in Java 9 and combined them with everything we discussed so far about object-oriented programming. We analyzed the differences between imperative code and functional programming approaches for many algorithms.

We worked with functional interfaces and lambda expressions. We understood method references and constructor references. We created a data repository with generics and interfaces and we used it to work with filters, map operations, reductions, aggregate functions, sorting and partitioning. We worked with different stream processing pipelines.

Now that you have learned about functional programming, we are ready to take advantage of modularity in Java 9, which is the topic we are going to discuss in the next chapter.

13
Modularity in Java 9

In this chapter, we will take advantage of one of the new features added to Java 9 to allow us to modularize the source code and easily manage dependencies. We will:

- Refactor existing code to take advantage of object-oriented programming
- Organize object-oriented code with the new modularity in Java 9
- Create modular source code in Java 9
- Compile multiple modules with the Java 9 compiler
- Run modularized code with Java 9

Refactoring existing code to take advantage of object-oriented programming

If we start writing object-oriented code from scratch, we can take advantage of everything we learned in the previous chapters and all the features included in Java 9. As the requirements evolve, we will have to make changes to the interfaces and the classes to further generalize or specialize them, edit them, and create new ones. The fact that we started our project with an object-oriented approach will make it easy to make the necessary adjustments to the code.

Sometimes, we are extremely lucky and we have the chance to follow best practices as soon as we kick off a project. However, many other times we aren't so lucky and we have to work on projects that didn't follow best practices. In these cases, instead of following the same bad practices that generated error-prone, repetitive, and difficult-to-maintain code, we can use the features provided by our favorite IDE and additional helper tools to refactor existing code, and generate object-oriented code that promotes code reuse and allows us to reduce maintenance headaches.

For example, imagine that we have to develop a Web Service that allows us to work with 3D models and render them on a 2D image with a specific resolution. The requirements specify that the first two 3D models that we will have to render with our Web Service are a sphere and a cube. The Web Service must allow us to change the following parameters of a perspective camera that allows us to see a specific part of the 3D world rendered on a 2D screen:

- Position (*X*, *Y*, and *Z* values)
- Direction (*X*, *Y*, and *Z* values)
- Up vector (*X*, *Y*, and *Z* values)
- Perspective field of view in degrees
- Near clipping plane
- Far clipping plane

Imagine that other developers started working on the project and generated a single Java file with a class wrapper that declares two static methods. One of these methods renders a cube and the other method renders a sphere. These methods receive all the necessary arguments to render each 3D figure, including all the necessary parameters to determine the 3D figure's location and size, and configure the perspective camera and a directional light.

The following lines show an example of the declaration of the class named `Renderer` with two static methods: `renderCube` and `renderSphere`. The first one sets up and renders a cube, and the second one sets up and renders a sphere. It is very important to understand that the sample code doesn't follow best practices and we will refactor it. Take into account that the two static methods have a lot of code in common. The code file for the sample is included in the `java_9_oop_chapter_13_01` folder, in the `example13_01.java` file.

```java
// The following code doesn't follow best practices
// Please, do not use this code as a baseline
// We will refactor it to generate object-oriented code
public class Renderer {
    public static void renderCube(int x, int y,
        int z, int edgeLength,
        int cameraX, int cameraY, int cameraZ,
        int cameraDirectionX, int cameraDirectionY, int
            cameraDirectionZ,
        int cameraVectorX, int cameraVectorY, int cameraVectorZ,
        int cameraPerspectiveFieldOfView,
        int cameraNearClippingPlane,
        int cameraFarClippingPlane,
```

```
        int directionalLightX, int directionalLightY, int
            directionalLightZ,
    String directionalLightColor) {
        System.out.println(
            String.format("Created camera at (x:%d, y:%d,
                z:%d)",
                cameraX, cameraY, cameraZ));
        System.out.println(
            String.format("Set camera direction to (x:%d,
                y:%d, z:%d)",
                cameraDirectionX, cameraDirectionY,
                    cameraDirectionZ));
        System.out.println(
            String.format("Set camera vector to (x:%d, y:%d,
                z:%d)",
                cameraVectorX, cameraVectorY, cameraVectorZ));
        System.out.println(
            String.format("Set camera perspective field of view
    to: %d",
                cameraPerspectiveFieldOfView));
        System.out.println(
            String.format("Set camera near clipping plane to:
                %d",
                cameraNearClippingPlane));
        System.out.println(
            String.format("Set camera far clipping plane to:
                %d",
                cameraFarClippingPlane));
        System.out.println(
            String.format("Created directional light at (x:%d,
                y:%d, z:%d)",
                directionalLightX, directionalLightY,
                    directionalLightZ));
        System.out.println(
            String.format("Set light color to %s",
                directionalLightColor));
        System.out.println(
            String.format("Drew cube at (x:%d, y:%d, z:%d) with
    edge length equal to %d" +
                "considering light at (x:%d, y:%d, z:%d) " +
                "and light's color equal to %s",
                x, y, z, edgeLength,
                directionalLightX, directionalLightY,
                directionalLightZ,
                directionalLightColor));
    }
```

```
public static void renderSphere(int x,
    int y, int z, int radius,
    int cameraX, int cameraY, int cameraZ,
    int cameraDirectionX, int cameraDirectionY,
    int cameraDirectionZ,
    int cameraVectorX, int cameraVectorY, int cameraVectorZ,
    int cameraPerspectiveFieldOfView,
    int cameraNearClippingPlane,
    int cameraFarClippingPlane,
    int directionalLightX, int directionalLightY,
    int directionalLightZ,
    String directionalLightColor) {
        System.out.println(
            String.format("Created camera at (x:%d, y:%d,
                z:%d)",
                cameraX, cameraY, cameraZ));
        System.out.println(
            String.format("Set camera direction to (x:%d,
                y:%d, z:%d)",
                cameraDirectionX, cameraDirectionY,
                    cameraDirectionZ));
        System.out.println(
            String.format("Set camera vector to (x:%d, y:%d,
                z:%d)",
                cameraVectorX, cameraVectorY, cameraVectorZ));
        System.out.println(
            String.format("Set camera perspective field of view
    to: %d",
                cameraPerspectiveFieldOfView));
        System.out.println(
            String.format("Set camera near clipping plane to:
                %d",
                cameraNearClippingPlane));
        System.out.println(
            String.format("Set camera far clipping plane to:
                %d",
                cameraFarClippingPlane));
        System.out.println(
            String.format("Created directional light at (x:%d,
                y:%d, z:%d)",
                directionalLightX, directionalLightY,
                    directionalLightZ));
        System.out.println(
            String.format("Set light color to %s",
```

```
                      directionalLightColor));
              // Render the sphere
              System.out.println(
                  String.format("Drew sphere at (x:%d, y:%d z:%d) with
        radius equal to %d",
                      x, y, z, radius));
              System.out.println(
                  String.format("considering light at (x:%d, y:%d,
                      z:%d)",
                      directionalLightX, directionalLightY,
                          directionalLightZ));
              System.out.println(
                  String.format("and the light's color equal to %s",
                      directionalLightColor));
          }
      }
```

Each static method requires a huge number of parameters. Now, let's imagine we have new requirements for our Web Service. We have to add code to render additional shapes, and add different types of cameras and lights. In addition, we have to work in an **IoT (Internet of Things)** project in which we have to reuse shapes in a computer vision application, and therefore, we want to take advantage of the code we have for our Web Service and share the code base with this new project. In addition, we have to work on another project that will run on a powerful IoT board, specifically a member of the Intel Joule series that will run a rendering service and will use its 4K video output capabilities to display the generated graphics. We will use the powerful quad-core CPU included in this board to run the local rendering service and, in this case, we won't be calling the Web Service.

Many applications have to share many pieces of code and our code must be ready for new shapes, cameras, and lights. The code can easily become a really big mess, repetitive, and difficult to maintain. Of course, the previously shown code is already difficult to maintain. Hence, we will refactor the existing code, and we will create many interfaces and classes to create an object-oriented version that we will be able to expand based on new requirements and reuse in our different applications.

So far, we have been working with JShell to run our code samples. This time, we will create one Java source code file for each interface or class. In addition, we will organize these files into the new modules introduced in Java 9. Finally, we will compile these modules and run a console application. You can use your favorite editor or IDE to create the different code files. Remember that you can download the indicated code files and you don't have to type any code.

We will create the following public interfaces, abstract classes, and concrete classes:

- `Vector3d`: This concrete class represents a mutable 3D vector with `int` values for x, y, and z.

- `Rendereable`: This interface specifies the requirements for an element that has a location and can be rendered.

- `SceneElement`: This abstract class implements the `Rendereable` interface, and represents any element that has a location and can be rendered. All the scene elements will inherit from this abstract class.

- `Light`: This abstract class inherits from `SceneElement` and represents a light in the scene that must provide a description of its properties.

- `DirectionalLight`: This concrete class inherits from `Light` and represents a directional light that has a specific color.

- `Camera`: This abstract class inherits from `SceneElement` and represents a camera in the scene.

- `PerspectiveCamera`: This concrete class inherits from `Camera` and represents a perspective camera that has a direction, an up vector, a field of view, a near clipping plane, and a far clipping plane.

- `Shape`: This abstract class inherits from `SceneElement`, and represents a shape in the scene that can be rendered with an active camera and receives multiple lights.

- `Sphere`: This concrete class inherits from `Shape` and represents a sphere.

- `Cube`: This concrete class inherits from `Shape` and represents a cube.

- `Scene`: This concrete class represents the scene with an active camera, shapes, and lights. We can use an instance of this class to compose a scene and render it.

- `Example01`: This concrete class will declare a main static method that will use a `PerspectiveCamera`, a `Sphere`, a `Cube`, and a `DirectionalLight` to create a `Scene` instance and call its render method.

We will declare each of the previously enumerated interfaces, abstract classes, and concrete classes in a file with the `.java` extension and with the same name as the type we declare. For example, we will declare the `Vector3d` class in the `Vector3d.java` file, also known as the Java source file.

It is a good practice and a common convention to declare a single public interface or class in a Java source file with the same name as the type we declare. The Java compiler will generate an error in a case where we declare more than one public type in a Java source file.

Organizing object-oriented code with the new modularity in Java 9

When we have just a few interfaces and classes, hundreds of lines of object-oriented code are easy to organize and maintain. However, as the number of types and lines of code start to increase, it is necessary to follow some rules to organize the code and make it easy to maintain.

A very well-written object-oriented code can generate a maintenance headache if it isn't organized in an effective way. We don't have to forget that a well-written object-oriented code promotes code reuse.

In our example, we will have just a few interfaces, abstract classes, and concrete classes. However, we must imagine that we will have a huge number of additional types to support the additional requirements. Hence, we will end up with dozens of classes related to the mathematical operations required to render the elements that compose a scene, additional types of lights, new types of cameras, classes related to these new lights and cameras, and dozens of additional shapes and their related classes.

We will create many modules to allow us to create units of software that have a name, require other modules, and export a public API that is usable and accessible by other modules. When a module requires other modules, it means that this module depends on the modules listed as requirements. The name for each module will follow the same conventions we usually use for packages in Java.

 Other modules can only access the public types that a module exports. If we declare a public type within a module but we don't include it in the exported API, we won't be able to access it outside of the module. We have to avoid circular dependencies when we create module dependencies.

We will create the following eight modules:

- `com.renderer.math`
- `com.renderer.sceneelements`
- `com.renderer.lights`
- `com.renderer.cameras`
- `com.renderer.shapes`
- `com.renderer.shapes.curvededges`
- `com.renderer.shapes.polyhedrons`
- `com.renderer`

Now, whenever we need to work with lights, we will explore the types declared in the `com.renderer.lights` module. Whenever we need to work with 3D shapes with curved edges, we will explore the types declared in the `com.renderer.shapes.curvededges` module.

Each module will declare the classes and interfaces in a package that will have the same name as the module name. For example, the `com.renderer.cameras` module will declare classes in the `com.renderer.cameras` package. A **package** is a grouping of related types. Each package generates a namespace that declares a scope. Thus, we will work with packages in combination with modules.

The following table summarizes the modules we will create, and the interfaces, abstract classes, and concrete interfaces that we will declare within each module. In addition, the table specifies the list of modules that each module requires.

Module name	Declared public types	Module requirements
`com.renderer.math`	`Vector3d`	-
`com.renderer.sceneelements`	`Rendereable` `SceneElement`	`com.renderer.math`
`com.renderer.lights`	`Light` `DirectionalLight`	`com.renderer.math` `com.renderer.sceneelements`
`com.renderer.cameras`	`Camera` `PerspectiveCamera`	`com.renderer.math` `com.renderer.sceneelements`
`com.renderer.shapes`	`Shape`	`com.renderer.math` `com.renderer.sceneelements` `com.renderer.lights` `com.renderer.cameras`

Module name	Declared public types	Module requirements
com.renderer.shapes. curvededges	Sphere	com.renderer.math com.renderer.lights com.renderer.shapes
com.renderer.shapes. polyhedrons	Cube	com.renderer.math com.renderer.lights com.renderer.shapes
com.renderer	Scene Example01	com.renderer.math com.renderer.cameras com.renderer.lights com.renderer.shapes com.renderer.shapes. curvededges com.renderer.shapes. polyhedrons

It is very important to notice that all the modules also require the java.base module that exports all of the platform's core packages such as java.io, java.lang, java. math, java.net, and java.util, among others. However, every module depends implicitly on the java.base module, and therefore, there is no need to include it in the dependency list when we declare the new modules and specify their required modules.

The next diagram shows the module graph in which the modules are nodes and a dependency of one module on another one is a directed edge. We don't include `java.lang` in the module graph.

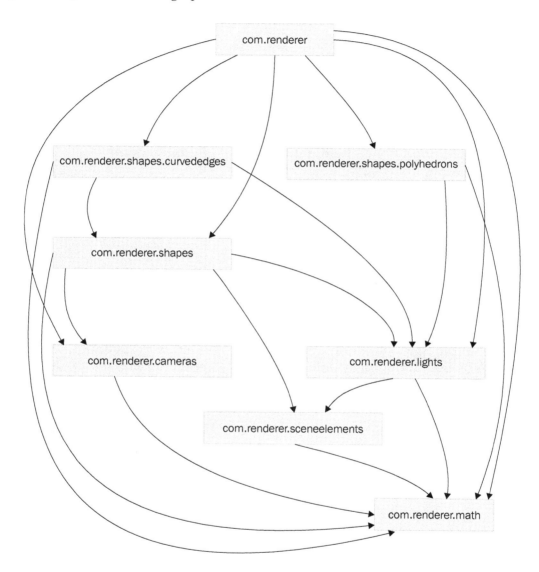

We won't work with any specific IDE to create all the modules. This way, we will understand the directory structure and all the required files. Then, we can take advantage of the features included in our favorite IDE to easily create new modules and their necessary directory structure.

There is a convention that specifies that the source code for the module must be located in a directory with the same name as the module name. For example, the module named com.renderer.math must be located in a directory named com.renderer.math. We have to create a module descriptor for each desired module, that is, a source code file named module-info.java, within the root folder for the module. This file specifies the module name, the modules that are required, and the packages that the module exports. The exported packages will be visible by the modules that require the module.

Then, it is necessary to create subdirectories for each name separated by a dot (.) in the module name. For example, we will create the com/renderer/math directories (com\renderer\math sub-folders in Windows) within the com.renderer.math directory. The Java source files that declare the interfaces, abstract classes, and concrete classes for each module will be located in these sub-folders.

We will create a base directory named Renderer with a sub-folder named src that will include all the source code for our modules. So, we will have Renderer/src (Renderer\src in Windows) as our base directory for the source code. Then, we will create a folder for each module with the module-info.java file and the sub-folders with the Java source code files. The following directory structure shows the final contents we will have within the Renderer/src (Renderer\src in Windows) directory. The file names are highlighted.

```
├──com.renderer
│   │   module-info.java
│   │
│   └──com
│       └──renderer
│               Example01.java
│               Scene.java
│
├──com.renderer.cameras
│   │   module-info.java
│   │
│   └──com
│       └──renderer
│           └──cameras
│                   Camera.java
│                   PerspectiveCamera.java
│
├──com.renderer.lights
│   │   module-info.java
│   │
│   └──com
```

```
|          └───renderer
|              └───lights
|                      DirectionalLight.java
|                      Light.java
|
├───com.renderer.math
|   |   module-info.java
|   |
|   └───com
|       └───renderer
|           └───math
|                   Vector3d.java
|
├───com.renderer.sceneelements
|   |   module-info.java
|   |
|   └───com
|       └───renderer
|           └───sceneelements
|                   Rendereable.java
|                   SceneElement.java
|
├───com.renderer.shapes
|   |   module-info.java
|   |
|   └───com
|       └───renderer
|           └───shapes
|                   Shape.java
|
├───com.renderer.shapes.curvededges
|   |   module-info.java
|   |
|   └───com
|       └───renderer
|           └───shapes
|               └───curvededges
|                       Sphere.java
|
└───com.renderer.shapes.polyhedrons
    |   module-info.java
    |
    └───com
        └───renderer
```

```
└──shapes
    └──polyhedrons
        Cube.java
```

Creating modular source code

Now it is time to start creating the necessary directory structures, and write the code for the `module-info.java` files and the source Java files for each module. We will create the `com.renderer.math` module.

Create a directory named `Renderer` and a `src` sub-directory. We will use `Renderer/src` (`Renderer\src` in Windows) as our base directory for the source code. However, take into account that you don't need to create any folder in a case where you download the source code.

Now create the `com.renderer.math` directory in `Renderer/src` (`Renderer\src` in Windows). Add the following lines to a file named `module-info.java` in the recently created sub-folder. The next lines compose the module descriptor for a module named `com.renderer.math`. The code file for the sample is included in the `java_9_oop_chapter_13_01/Renderer/src/com.renderer.math` sub-folder, in the `module-info.java` file.

```
module com.renderer.math {
    exports com.renderer.math;
}
```

The `module` keyword followed by the module name `com.renderer.math` begins the module declaration. The lines included within the curly braces specify the module body. The `exports` keyword followed by the package name `com.renderer.math` indicates that this module exports all the public types declared within the `com.renderer.math` package.

Create the `com/renderer/math` (`com\renderer\math` in Windows) folders in `Renderer/src` (`Renderer\src` in Windows). Add the following lines to a file named `Vector3d.java` in the recently created sub-folder. The next lines declare the public `Vector3d` concrete class as a member of the `com.renderer.math` package. We will use the `Vector3d` class instead of working with separate values for x, y, and z. The `package` keyword followed by the package name indicates the package in which the class will be included.

The code file for the sample is included in the `java_9_oop_chapter_13_01/Renderer/src/com.renderer.math/com/renderer/math` sub-folder, in the `Vector3d.java` file.

```java
package com.renderer.math;

public class Vector3d {
    public int x;
    public int y;
    public int z;

    public Vector3d(int x,
        int y,
        int z) {
        this.x = x;
        this.y = y;
        this.z = z;
    }

    public Vector3d(int valueForXYZ) {
        this(valueForXYZ, valueForXYZ, valueForXYZ);
    }

    public Vector3d() {
        this(0);
    }

    public void absolute() {
        x = Math.abs(x);
        y = Math.abs(y);
        z = Math.abs(z);
    }

    public void negate() {
        x = -x;
        y = -y;
        z = -z;
    }

    public void add(Vector3d vector) {
        x += vector.x;
        y += vector.y;
        z += vector.z;
    }
```

```
    public void sub(Vector3d vector) {
        x -= vector.x;
        y -= vector.y;
        z -= vector.z;
    }

    public String toString() {
        return String.format(
            "(x: %d, y: %d, z: %d)",
            x,
            y,
            z);
    }
}
```

Now create the `com.renderer.sceneelements` directory in `Renderer/src` (`Renderer\src` in Windows). Add the following lines to a file named `module-info.java` in the recently created sub-folder. The next lines compose the module descriptor for a module named `com.renderer.sceneelements`. The code file for the sample is included in the `java_9_oop_chapter_13_01/Renderer/src/com.renderer.sceneelements` sub-folder, in the `module-info.java` file.

```
module com.renderer.sceneelements {
    requires com.renderer.math;
    exports com.renderer.sceneelements;
}
```

The `module` keyword followed by the module name, `com.renderer.sceneelements` begins the module declaration. The lines included within the curly braces specify the module body. The `requires` keyword followed by a module name, `com.renderer.math`, indicates that this module requires the types exported in the previously declared `com.renderer.math` module. The `exports` keyword followed by the package name, `com.renderer.sceneelements`, indicates that this module exports all the public types declared within the `com.renderer.sceneelements` package.

Create the `com/renderer/sceneelements` (`com\renderer\sceneelements` in Windows) folders in `Renderer/src` (`Renderer\src` in Windows). Add the following lines to a file named `Rendereable.java` in the recently created sub-folder. The next lines declare the public `Rendereable` interface as a member of the `com.renderer.sceneelements` package. The code file for the sample is included in the `java_9_oop_chapter_13_01/Renderer/src/com.renderer.sceneeelements/com/renderer/sceneelements` sub-folder, in the `Rendereable.java` file.

```
package com.renderer.sceneelements;

import com.renderer.math.Vector3d;

public interface Rendereable {
    Vector3d getLocation();
    void setLocation(Vector3d newLocation);
    void render();
}
```

Add the following lines to a file named `SceneElement.java` in the recently created sub-folder. The next lines declare the public `SceneElement` abstract class as a member of the `com.renderer.sceneelements` package. The code file for the sample is included in the `java_9_oop_chapter_13_01/Renderer/src/com.renderer.sceneelements/com/renderer/sceneelements` sub-folder, in the `SceneElement.java` file.

```
package com.renderer.sceneelements;

import com.renderer.math.Vector3d;

public abstract class SceneElement implements Rendereable {
    protected Vector3d location;

    public SceneElement(Vector3d location) {
        this.location = location;
    }

    public Vector3d getLocation() {
        return location;
    }

    public void setLocation(Vector3d newLocation) {
        location = newLocation;
    }
}
```

The `SceneElement` abstract class implements the previously defined `Rendereable` interface. The class represents a 3D element that is part of a scene and has a location specified with a `Vector3d`. The class is the base class for all the scene elements that require a location in the 3D space.

Now create the `com.renderer.lights` directory in `Renderer/src` (`Renderer\` `src` in Windows). Add the following lines to a file named `module-info.java` in the recently created sub-folder. The next lines compose the module descriptor for a module named `com.renderer.lights`. The code file for the sample is included in the `java_9_oop_chapter_13_01/Renderer/src/com.renderer.lights` sub-folder, in the `module-info.java` file.

```
module com.renderer.lights {
    requires com.renderer.math;
    requires com.renderer.sceneelements;
    exports com.renderer.lights;
}
```

The previous lines declare the `com.renderer.lights` module and specifies that the module requires two modules: `com.renderer.math` and `com.renderer.` `sceneelements`. The `exports` keyword followed by the package name, `com.` `renderer.lights`, indicates that this module exports all the public types declared within the `com.renderer.lights` package.

Create the `com/renderer/lights` (`com\renderer\lights` in Windows) folders in `Renderer/src` (`Renderer\src` in Windows). Add the following lines to a file named `Light.java` in the recently created sub-folder. The next lines declare the public `Light` abstract class as a member of the `com.renderer.lights` package. The class inherits from the `SceneElement` class and declares an abstract `getPropertiesDescription` method that must return a `String` with the description for all the properties that the light has. The concrete classes that inherit from the `Light` class will be responsible for providing the implementation for this method. The code file for the sample is included in the `java_9_oop_chapter_13_01/Renderer/src/com.renderer.lights/com/renderer/lights` sub-folder, in the `Light.java` file.

```
package com.renderer.lights;

import com.renderer.sceneelements.SceneElement;
import com.renderer.math.Vector3d;

public abstract class Light extends SceneElement {
    public Light(Vector3d location) {
        super(location);
    }

    public abstract String getPropertiesDescription();
}
```

Add the following lines to a file named `DirectionalLight.java` in the recently
created sub-folder. The next lines declare the public `DirectionalLight` concrete class
as a member of the `com.renderer.lights` package. The code file for the sample is
included in the `java_9_oop_chapter_13_01/Renderer/src/com.renderer.lights/`
`com/renderer/lights` sub-folder, in the `DirectionalLight.java` file.

```
package com.renderer.lights;

import com.renderer.math.Vector3d;

public class DirectionalLight extends Light {
    public final String color;

    public DirectionalLight(Vector3d location,
        String color) {
        super(location);
        this.color = color;
    }

    @Override
    public void render() {
        System.out.println(
            String.format("Created directional light at %s",
                location));
        System.out.println(
            String.format("Set light color to %s",
                color));
    }

    @Override
    public String getPropertiesDescription() {
        return String.format(
            "light's color equal to %s",
            color);
    }
}
```

The `DirectionalLight` concrete class inherits from the previously defined `Light`
abstract class. The `DirectionalLight` class represents a directional light, and
provides an implementation for both the `render` and `getPropertiesDescription`
methods.

Now create the `com.renderer.cameras` directory in `Renderer/src` (`Renderer\src` in Windows). Add the following lines to a file named `module-info.java` in the recently created sub-folder. The next lines compose the module descriptor for a module named `com.renderer.cameras`. The code file for the sample is included in the `java_9_oop_chapter_13_01/Renderer/src/com.renderer.cameras` sub-folder, in the `module-info.java` file.

```
module com.renderer.cameras {
    requires com.renderer.math;
    requires com.renderer.sceneelements;
    exports com.renderer.cameras;
}
```

The previous lines declare the `com.renderer.cameras` module and specifies that the module requires two modules: `com.renderer.math` and `com.renderer.sceneelements`. The `exports` keyword followed by the package name, `com.renderer.cameras`, indicates that this module exports all the public types declared within the `com.renderer.cameras` package.

Create the `com/renderer/cameras` (`com\renderer\cameras` in Windows) folders in `Renderer/src` (`Renderer\src` in Windows). Add the following lines to a file named `Camera.java` in the recently created sub-folder. The next lines declare the public `Camera` abstract class as a member of the `com.renderer.cameras` package. The class inherits from the `SceneElement` class. The class represents a 3D camera. It is the base class for all cameras. In this case, the class declaration is empty, and we only declare it because we know that there will be many types of cameras. In addition, we want to be able to generalize the common requirements for all types of cameras in the future, as we did for the lights. The code file for the sample is included in the `java_9_oop_chapter_13_01/Renderer/src/com.renderer.cameras/com/renderer/cameras` sub-folder, in the `Camera.java` file.

```
package com.renderer.cameras;

import com.renderer.math.Vector3d;
import com.renderer.sceneelements.SceneElement;

public abstract class Camera extends SceneElement {
    public Camera(Vector3d location) {
        super(location);
    }
}
```

Add the following lines to a file named `PerspectiveCamera.java` in the recently created sub-folder. The next lines declare the public `PerspectiveCamera` concrete class as a member of the `com.renderer.cameras` package. The code file for the sample is included in the `java_9_oop_chapter_13_01/Renderer/src/com.renderer.cameras/com/renderer/cameras` sub-folder, in the `PerspectiveCamera.java` file.

```java
package com.renderer.cameras;

import com.renderer.math.Vector3d;

public class PerspectiveCamera extends Camera {
    protected Vector3d direction;
    protected Vector3d vector;
    protected int fieldOfView;
    protected int nearClippingPlane;
    protected int farClippingPlane;

    public Vector3d getDirection() {
        return direction;
    }

    public void setDirection(Vector3d newDirection) {
        direction = newDirection;
    }

    public Vector3d getVector() {
        return vector;
    }

    public void setVector(Vector3d newVector) {
        vector = newVector;
    }

    public int getFieldOfView() {
        return fieldOfView;
    }

    public void setFieldOfView(int newFieldOfView) {
        fieldOfView = newFieldOfView;
    }

    public int nearClippingPlane() {
        return nearClippingPlane;
```

```
    }

    public void setNearClippingPlane(int newNearClippingPlane) {
        this.nearClippingPlane = newNearClippingPlane;
    }

    public int farClippingPlane() {
        return farClippingPlane;
    }

    public void setFarClippingPlane(int newFarClippingPlane) {
        this.farClippingPlane = newFarClippingPlane;
    }

    public PerspectiveCamera(Vector3d location,
        Vector3d direction,
        Vector3d vector,
        int fieldOfView,
        int nearClippingPlane,
        int farClippingPlane) {
        super(location);
        this.direction = direction;
        this.vector = vector;
        this.fieldOfView = fieldOfView;
        this.nearClippingPlane = nearClippingPlane;
        this.farClippingPlane = farClippingPlane;
    }

    @Override
    public void render() {
        System.out.println(
            String.format("Created camera at %s",
                location));
        System.out.println(
            String.format("Set camera direction to %s",
                direction));
        System.out.println(
            String.format("Set camera vector to %s",
                vector));
        System.out.println(
            String.format("Set camera perspective field of view to:
%d",
                fieldOfView));
        System.out.println(
```

```
            String.format("Set camera near clipping plane to: %d",
                nearClippingPlane));
        System.out.println(
            String.format("Set camera far clipping plane to: %d",
                farClippingPlane));
    }
}
```

The `PerspectiveCamera` concrete class inherits from the previously defined `Camera` abstract class. The `PerspectiveCamera` class represents a perspective camera with many getter and setter methods for the camera's properties. The class provides an implementation for the `render` method that displays all the details for the created camera and the values for its different properties.

Now create the `com.renderer.shapes` directory in `Renderer/src` (`Renderer\src` in Windows). Add the following lines to a file named `module-info.java` in the recently created sub-folder. The next lines compose the module descriptor for a module named `com.renderer.shapes`. The code file for the sample is included in the `java_9_oop_chapter_13_01/Renderer/src/com.renderer.shapes` sub-folder, in the `module-info.java` file.

```
module com.renderer.shapes {
    requires com.renderer.math;
    requires com.renderer.sceneelements;
    requires com.renderer.lights;
    requires com.renderer.cameras;
    exports com.renderer.shapes;
}
```

The previous lines declare the `com.renderer.shapes` module and specifies that the module requires four modules: `com.renderer.math`, `com.renderer.sceneelements`, `com.renderer.lights`, and `com.renderer.cameras`. The `exports` keyword followed by the package name, `com.renderer.shapes`, indicates that this module exports all the public types declared within the `com.renderer.shapes` package.

Create the `com/renderer/shapes` (`com\renderer\shapes` in Windows) folders in `Renderer/src` (`Renderer\src` in Windows). Add the following lines to a file named `Shape.java` in the recently created sub-folder. The next lines declare the public `Shape` abstract class as a member of the `com.renderer.shapes` package. The code file for the sample is included in the `java_9_oop_chapter_13_01/Renderer/src/com.renderer.shapes/com/renderer/shapes` sub-folder, in the `Shape.java` file.

```java
package com.renderer.shapes;

import com.renderer.math.Vector3d;
import com.renderer.sceneelements.SceneElement;
import com.renderer.lights.Light;
import com.renderer.cameras.Camera;
import java.util.*;
import java.util.stream.Collectors;

public abstract class Shape extends SceneElement {
    protected Camera activeCamera;
    protected List<Light> lights;

    public Shape(Vector3d location) {
        super(location);
        lights = new ArrayList<>();
    }

    public void setActiveCamera(Camera activeCamera) {
        this.activeCamera = activeCamera;
    }

    public void setLights(List<Light> lights) {
        this.lights = lights;
    }

    protected boolean isValidForRender() {
        return !((activeCamera == null) && lights.isEmpty());
    }

    protected String generateConsideringLights() {
        return lights.stream()
            .map(light -> String.format(
                "considering light at %s\nand %s",
                    light.getLocation(),
                    light.getPropertiesDescription()))
            .collect(Collectors.joining());
    }
}
```

The `Shape` class inherits from the `SceneElement` class. The class represents a 3D shape and is the base class for all the 3D shapes. The class defines the following methods:

- `setActiveCamera`: This public method receives a `Camera` instance and saves it as the active camera.

- `setLights`: This public method receives a `List<Light>` and saves it as the list of lights that must be considered to render the shape.

- `isValidForRender`: This protected method returns a `boolean` value indicating whether the shape has an active camera and at least one light. Otherwise, the shape is not valid for being rendered.

- `generateConsideringLights`: This protected method returns a `String` with the lights that are being considered to render the shape, with their locations and their properties descriptions.

Each subclass of the `Shape` class that will represent a specific 3D shape will provide an implementation for the `render` method. We will code these subclasses in two additional modules.

Now create the `com.renderer.shapes.curvededges` directory in `Renderer/src` (`Renderer\src` in Windows). Add the following lines to a file named `module-info.java` in the recently created sub-folder. The next lines compose the module descriptor for a module named `com.renderer.curvededges`. The code file for the sample is included in the `java_9_oop_chapter_13_01/Renderer/src/com.renderer.curvededges` sub-folder, in the `module-info.java` file.

```
module com.renderer.shapes.curvededges {
    requires com.renderer.math;
    requires com.renderer.lights;
    requires com.renderer.shapes;
    exports com.renderer.shapes.curvededges;
}
```

The previous lines declare the `com.renderer.shapes` module and specifies that the module requires three modules: `com.renderer.math`, `com.renderer.lights`, and `com.renderer.shapes`. The `exports` keyword followed by the package name, `com.renderer.shapes.curvededges`, indicates that this module exports all the public types declared within the `com.renderer.shapes.curvededges` package.

Create the `com/renderer/shapes/curvededges` (`com\renderer\shapes\curvededges` in Windows) folders in `Renderer/src` (`Renderer\src` in Windows). Add the following lines to a file named `Sphere.java` in the recently created sub-folder. The next lines declare the public `Sphere` concrete class as a member of the `com.renderer.shapes.curvededges` package. The code file for the sample is included in the `java_9_oop_chapter_13_01/Renderer/src/com.renderer.shapes.curvededges/com/renderer/shapes/curvededges` sub-folder, in the `Sphere.java` file.

```java
package com.renderer.shapes.curvededges;

import com.renderer.math.Vector3d;
import com.renderer.shapes.Shape;
import com.renderer.lights.Light;

public class Sphere extends Shape {
    protected int radius;

    public Sphere(Vector3d location, int radius) {
        super(location);
        this.radius = radius;
    }

    public int getRadius() {
        return radius;
    }

    public void setRadius(int newRadius) {
        radius = newRadius;
    }

    @Override
    public void render() {
        if (!isValidForRender()) {
            System.out.println(
                "Setup wasn't completed to render the sphere.");
            return;
        }
        StringBuilder sb = new StringBuilder();
        sb.append(String.format(
            "Drew sphere at %s with radius equal to %d\n",
            location,
            radius));
        String consideringLights =
```

```
            generateConsideringLights();
        sb.append(consideringLights);
        System.out.println(sb.toString());
    }
}
```

The `Sphere` class inherits from the `Shape` class and requires a radius value in the constructor in addition to the `Vector3d` instance that specifies the location for the sphere. The class provides an implementation for the `render` method that checks the value returned by the `isValidForRender` method. If the method returns `true`, the sphere is valid for being rendered, and the code builds a message with the sphere radius, its location, and the lights that are being considered when rendering the sphere. The code calls the `generateConsideringLights` method to build the message.

Now create the `com.renderer.shapes.polyhedrons` directory in `Renderer/src` (`Renderer\src` in Windows). Add the following lines to a file named `module-info.java` in the recently created sub-folder. The next lines compose the module descriptor for a module named `com.renderer.polyhedrons`. The code file for the sample is included in the `java_9_oop_chapter_13_01/Renderer/src/com.renderer.polyhedrons` sub-folder, in the `module-info.java` file.

```
module com.renderer.shapes.polyhedrons {
    requires com.renderer.math;
    requires com.renderer.lights;
    requires com.renderer.shapes;
    exports com.renderer.shapes.polyhedrons;
}
```

The previous lines declare the `com.renderer.polyhedrons` module and specifies that the module requires three modules: `com.renderer.math`, `com.renderer.lights`, and `com.renderer.shapes`. The `exports` keyword followed by the package name, `com.renderer.shapes.polyhedrons`, indicates that this module exports all the public types declared within the `com.renderer.shapes.polyhedrons` package.

Create the `com/renderer/shapes/polyhedrons` (`com\renderer\shapes\polyhedrons` in Windows) folders in `Renderer/src` (`Renderer\src` in Windows). Add the following lines to a file named `Cube.java` in the recently created sub-folder. The next lines declare the public `Cube` concrete class as a member of the `com.renderer.shapes.polyhedrons` package. The code file for the sample is included in the `java_9_oop_chapter_13_01/Renderer/src/com.renderer.shapes.polyhedrons/com/renderer/shapes/polyhedrons` sub-folder, in the `Cube.java` file.

```
package com.renderer.shapes.polyhedrons;

import com.renderer.math.Vector3d;
import com.renderer.shapes.Shape;
import com.renderer.lights.Light;
import java.util.stream.Collectors;

public class Cube extends Shape {
    protected int edgeLength;

    public Cube(Vector3d location, int edgeLength) {
        super(location);
        this.edgeLength = edgeLength;
    }

    public int getEdgeLength() {
        return edgeLength;
    }

    public void setEdgeLength(int newEdgeLength) {
        edgeLength = newEdgeLength;
    }

    @Override
    public void render() {
        if (!isValidForRender()) {
            System.out.println(
                "Setup wasn't completed to render the cube.");
            return;
        }
        StringBuilder sb = new StringBuilder();
        sb.append(String.format(
            "Drew cube at %s with edge length equal to %d\n",
            location,
            edgeLength));
        String consideringLights =
            generateConsideringLights();
        sb.append(consideringLights);
        System.out.println(sb.toString());
    }
}
```

The Cube class inherits from the Shape class and requires an edgeLength value in the constructor in addition to the Vector3d that specifies the location for the cube. The class provides an implementation for the render method that checks the value returned by the isValidForRender method. If the method returns true, the cube is valid for being rendered and the code builds a message with the cube's edge length, its location, and the lights that are being considered when rendering the cube. The code calls the generateConsideringLights method to build the message.

Now create the com.renderer directory in Renderer/src (Renderer\src in Windows). Add the following lines to a file named module-info.java in the recently created sub-folder. The next lines compose the module descriptor for a module named com.renderer. The code file for the sample is included in the java_9_oop_chapter_13_01/Renderer/src/com.renderer sub-folder, in the module-info.java file.

```
module com.renderer {
    exports com.renderer;
    requires com.renderer.math;
    requires com.renderer.cameras;
    requires com.renderer.lights;
    requires com.renderer.shapes;
    requires com.renderer.shapes.curvededges;
    requires com.renderer.shapes.polyhedrons;

}
```

The previous lines declare the com.renderer module and specifies that the module requires six modules: com.renderer.math, com.renderer.cameras, com.renderer.lights, com.renderer.shapes, com.renderer.shapes.curvededges, and com.renderer.shapes.polyhedrons. The exports keyword followed by the package name, com.renderer, indicates that this module exports all the public types declared within the com.renderer package.

Create the com/renderer (com\renderer in Windows) folders in Renderer/src (Renderer\src in Windows). Add the following lines to a file named Scene.java in the recently created sub-folder. The next lines declare the public Scene concrete class as a member of the com.renderer package. The code file for the sample is included in the java_9_oop_chapter_13_01/Renderer/src/com.renderer/com/renderer sub-folder, in the Scene.java file.

```
package com.renderer;

import com.renderer.math.Vector3d;
import com.renderer.cameras.Camera;
import com.renderer.lights.Light;
```

```
import com.renderer.shapes.Shape;
import java.util.*;

public class Scene {
    protected List<Light> lights;
    protected List<Shape> shapes;
    protected Camera activeCamera;

    public Scene(Camera activeCamera) {
        this.activeCamera = activeCamera;
        this.lights = new ArrayList<>();
        this.shapes = new ArrayList<>();
    }

    public void addLight(Light light) {
        this.lights.add(light);
    }

    public void addShape(Shape shape) {
        this.shapes.add(shape);
    }

    public void render() {
        activeCamera.render();
        lights.forEach(Light::render);
        shapes.forEach(shape -> {
            shape.setActiveCamera(activeCamera);
            shape.setLights(lights);
            shape.render();
        });
    }
}
```

The Scene class represents the scene to be rendered. The class declares an
activateCamera protected field that holds a Camera instance. The lights protected
field is a List of Light instances, and the shapes protected field is a List of Shape
instances that compose the scene. The addLight method adds the Light instance
received as an argument to the List<Light>lights. The addShape method adds the
Shape instance received as an argument to the List<Shape> shapes.

The render method calls the render method for the active camera and all the lights.
Then, the code performs the following actions for each shape: sets its active camera,
sets the lights, and calls the render method.

Finally, add the following lines to a file named Example01.java in the recently created sub-folder. The next lines declare the public Example01 concrete class as a member of the com.renderer package. The code file for the sample is included in the java_9_oop_chapter_13_01/Renderer/src/com.renderer/com/renderer sub-folder, in the Example01.java file.

```java
package com.renderer;

import com.renderer.math.Vector3d;
import com.renderer.cameras.PerspectiveCamera;
import com.renderer.lights.DirectionalLight;
import com.renderer.shapes.curvededges.Sphere;
import com.renderer.shapes.polyhedrons.Cube;

public class Example01 {
    public static void main(String[] args){
        PerspectiveCamera camera = new PerspectiveCamera(
            new Vector3d(30),
            new Vector3d(50, 0, 0),
            new Vector3d(4, 5, 2),
            90,
            20,
            40);
        Sphere sphere = new Sphere(new Vector3d(20), 8);
        Cube cube = new Cube(new Vector3d(10), 5);
        DirectionalLight light = new DirectionalLight(
            new Vector3d(2, 2, 5), "Cornflower blue");
        Scene scene = new Scene(camera);
        scene.addShape(sphere);
        scene.addShape(cube);
        scene.addLight(light);
        scene.render();
    }
}
```

The Example01 class is the main class for our test application. The class just declares a static method named main that receives an array of String named args as an argument. Java will call this method when we execute the application and will pass the arguments in the args parameter. In this case, the code in the main method doesn't take into account any specified argument.

The main method creates a `PerspectiveCamera` instance with the necessary parameters, and then creates a `Shape` and a `Cube` named `shape` and `cube`. Then, the code creates a `DirectionalLight` instance named `light`.

The next line creates a `Scene` instance with `camera` as the value for the `activeCamera` argument. Then, the code calls the `scene.addShape` method twice with `sphere` and `cube` as arguments. Finally, the code calls `scene.addLight` with `light` as an argument and calls the `scene.render` method to display the messages generated by the simulated render process.

Compiling multiple modules with the Java 9 compiler

Create a sub-folder named `mods` within the base directory named `Renderer`. This new sub-folder will replicate the directory structure that we created in the `Renderer/src` (`Renderer\src` in Windows) folder. We will run the Java compiler to generate a Java class file for each Java source file. A Java class file will contain Java bytecode that can be executed on the **Java Virtual Machine**, also known as the **JVM**. We will have a file with the `.class` extension for each Java source file with the `.java` extension, including the module descriptors. For example, after we successfully use the Java compiler to compile the `Renderer/src/com.renderer.math/com/renderer/math/Vector3d.java` source file, the compiler will generate a `Renderer/mods/com.renderer.math/com/renderer/math/Vector3d.class` file with Java bytecode (known as a Java class file). In Windows, we must use a backslash (\) as the path separator instead of the slash (/).

Now, open a Terminal window on macOS or Linux, or Command Prompt in Windows, and go to the `Renderer` folder. Make sure the `javac` command is included in the path, and that it is the Java compiler for Java 9 and not for previous Java versions that aren't compatible with the modules introduced in Java 9.

In macOS or Linux, run the following command to compile all the modules we have recently created and place the generated Java class files in a directory structure within the `mods` folder. The `-d` option specifies where to place the generated class files and the `--module-source-path` option indicates where to find the input source files for multiple modules.

```
javac -d mods --module-source-path src src/com.renderer.math/module-
info.java src/com.renderer.math/com/renderer/math/Vector3d.java src/com.
renderer.sceneelements/module-info.java src/com.renderer.sceneelements/
com/renderer/sceneelements/Rendereable.java src/com.renderer.
sceneelements/com/renderer/sceneelements/SceneElement.java src/com.
renderer.cameras/module-info.java src/com.renderer.cameras/com/renderer/
cameras/Camera.java src/com.renderer.cameras/com/renderer/cameras/
PerspectiveCamera.java src/com.renderer.lights/module-info.java src/
com.renderer.lights/com/renderer/lights/DirectionalLight.java src/com.
renderer.lights/com/renderer/lights/Light.java src/com.renderer.shapes/
module-info.java src/com.renderer.shapes/com/renderer/shapes/Shape.java
src/com.renderer.shapes.curvededges/module-info.java src/com.renderer.
shapes.curvededges/com/renderer/shapes/curvededges/Sphere.java src/com.
renderer.shapes.polyhedrons/module-info.java src/com.renderer.shapes.
polyhedrons/com/renderer/shapes/polyhedrons/Cube.java src/com.renderer/
module-info.java src/com.renderer/com/renderer/Example01.java src/com.
renderer/com/renderer/Scene.java
```

In Windows, run the following command to achieve the same goal:

```
javac -d mods --module-source-path src src\com.renderer.math\module-
info.java src\com.renderer.math\com\renderer\math\Vector3d.java src\com.
renderer.sceneelements\module-info.java src\com.renderer.sceneelements\
com\renderer\sceneelements\Rendereable.java src\com.renderer.
sceneelements\com\renderer\sceneelements\SceneElement.java src\com.
renderer.cameras\module-info.java src\com.renderer.cameras\com\renderer\
cameras\Camera.java src\com.renderer.cameras\com\renderer\cameras\
PerspectiveCamera.java src\com.renderer.lights\module-info.java src\
com.renderer.lights\com\renderer\lights\DirectionalLight.java src\com.
renderer.lights\com\renderer\lights\Light.java src\com.renderer.shapes\
module-info.java src\com.renderer.shapes\com\renderer\shapes\Shape.java
src\com.renderer.shapes.curvededges\module-info.java src\com.renderer.
shapes.curvededges\com\renderer\shapes\curvededges\Sphere.java src\com.
renderer.shapes.polyhedrons\module-info.java src\com.renderer.shapes.
polyhedrons\com\renderer\shapes\polyhedrons\Cube.java src\com.renderer\
module-info.java src\com.renderer\com\renderer\Example01.java src\com.
renderer\com\renderer\Scene.java
```

The following directory structure shows the final contents we will have within the `Renderer/mods` (`Renderer\mods` in Windows) directory. The Java class files generated by the Java compiler are highlighted.

```
├──com.renderer
│   │   module-info.class
│   │
│   └──com
│       └──renderer
│               Example01.class
│               Scene.class
│
├──com.renderer.cameras
│   │   module-info.class
│   │
│   └──com
│       └──renderer
│           └──cameras
│                   Camera.class
│                   PerspectiveCamera.class
│
├──com.renderer.lights
│   │   module-info.class
│   │
│   └──com
│       └──renderer
│           └──lights
│                   DirectionalLight.class
│                   Light.class
│
├──com.renderer.math
│   │   module-info.class
│   │
│   └──com
│       └──renderer
│           └──math
│                   Vector3d.class
│
├──com.renderer.sceneelements
│   │   module-info.class
│   │
│   └──com
│       └──renderer
│           └──sceneelements
```

```
|                              Rendereable.class
|                              SceneElement.class
|
├────com.renderer.shapes
|    |    module-info.class
|    |
|    └────com
|         └────renderer
|              └────shapes
|                        Shape.class
|
├────com.renderer.shapes.curvededges
|    |    module-info.class
|    |
|    └────com
|         └────renderer
|              └────shapes
|                   └────curvededges
|                             Sphere.class
|
└────com.renderer.shapes.polyhedrons
     |    module-info.class
     |
     └────com
          └────renderer
               └────shapes
                    └────polyhedrons
                              Cube.class
```

Run modularized code with Java 9

Finally, we can use the java command to launch the Java application. Go back to the Terminal window on macOS or Linux, or a Command Prompt in Windows, and make sure you are in the Renderer folder. Make sure the java command is included in the path, and that it is the java command for Java 9 and not for previous Java versions that aren't compatible with the modules introduced in Java 9.

In macOS, Linux or Windows, run the following command to load the compiled modules, resolve the `com.renderer` module, and run the `main` static method for the `Example01` class declared in the `com.renderer` package. The `--module-path` option specifies the directory in which the modules can be found. In this case, we just specify the `mods` folder. However, we may include many directories separated by a semicolon (`;`). The `-m` option specifies the initial module name to resolve followed by a slash (/) and the name of the main class to execute.

```
java --module-path mods -m com.renderer/com.renderer.Example01
```

The following lines show the generated output after executing the previous command that runs the `main` static method for the `Example01` class.

```
Created camera at (x: 30, y: 30, z: 30)
Set camera direction to (x: 50, y: 0, z: 0)
Set camera vector to (x: 4, y: 5, z: 2)
Set camera perspective field of view to: 90
Set camera near clipping plane to: 20
Set camera far clipping plane to: 40
Created directional light at (x: 2, y: 2, z: 5)
Set light color to Cornflower blue
Drew sphere at (x: 20, y: 20, z: 20) with radius equal to 8
considering light at (x: 2, y: 2, z: 5)
and light's color equal to Cornflower blue
Drew cube at (x: 10, y: 10, z: 10) with edge length equal to 5
considering light at (x: 2, y: 2, z: 5)
and light's color equal to Cornflower blue
```

In previous Java versions we could aggregate many Java class files, and their associated metadata and resources into a compressed file with the `.jar` extension, known as a **JAR (Java Archive)** file. We can also package modules as modular JARs that include the `module-info.class` file within the compressed file in the top-level folder.

In addition, we can use the Java linking tool (`jlink`) to create a customized runtime image with only the modules that are required for our application. This way, we can take advantage of whole-program optimizations and generate a custom runtime image that will run on top of the JVM.

Test your knowledge

1. By default, a module requires:

    1. The `java.base` module.

    2. The `java.lang` module.

    3. The `java.util` module.

2. There is a convention that specifies that the source code for a Java 9 module must be located in a directory with:

    1. The same name as the main class exported by the module.

    2. The same name as the module name.

    3. The same name as the main type exported by the module.

3. Which of the following source code files is a module descriptor:

    1. `module-def.java`

    2. `module-info.java`

    3. `module-data.java`

4. Which of the following keywords must be followed by the module name in the module descriptor:

    1. `name`

    2. `module-name`

    3. `module`

5. The `exports` keyword followed by a package name in the module descriptor indicates that the module exports:

    1. All the classes declared within the package.

    2. All the types declared within the package.

    3. All the public types declared within the package.

Summary

In this chapter, we learned to refactor existing code to take full advantage of object-oriented code with Java 9. We have prepared the code for future requirements, reduce maintenance costs, and maximized code reuse.

We learned to organize object-oriented code. We created many Java source files. We declared interfaces, abstract classes, and concrete classes in different Java source files. We took advantage of the new modularity features included in Java 9 to create many modules that have dependencies on different modules and exported specific types. We learned to declare modules, compile them to Java bytecode, and launch an application outside of JShell.

Now that you have learned to write object-oriented code in Java 9, you are ready to use everything you learned in real-life desktop applications, mobile apps, enterprise applications, Web Services, and web applications. These applications will maximize code reuse, simplify maintenance, and they will be always ready for future requirements. The fact that you can use JShell to easily prototype new interfaces and classes will boost your productivity as an object-oriented Java 9 developer.

Exercise Answers

Chapter 1, JShell – A Read-Evaluate-Print-Loop for Java 9

Questions	Answers
1	1
2	3
3	2
4	1
5	2

Chapter 2, Real-World Objects to UML Diagrams and Java 9 via JShell

Questions	Answers
1	3
2	2
3	1
4	3
5	3
6	1
7	2

Chapter 3, Classes and Instances

Questions	Answers
1	3
2	1
3	3
4	2
5	2
6	3
7	1

Chapter 4, Encapsulation of Data

Questions	Answers
1	2
2	1
3	2
4	1
5	3

Chapter 5, Mutable and Immutable Classes

Questions	Answers
1	2
2	3
3	2
4	1
5	2

Chapter 6, Inheritance, Abstraction, Extension, and Specialization

Questions	Answers
1	2
2	2
3	1
4	3
5	3

Chapter 7, Members Inheritance and Polymorphism

Questions	Answers
1	2
2	1
3	3
4	1
5	2

Chapter 8, Contract Programming with Interfaces

Questions	Answers
1	2
2	1
3	3
4	2
5	2

Chapter 9, Advanced Contract Programming with Interfaces

Questions	Answers
1	3
2	3
3	1
4	3
5	3

Chapter 10, Maximization of Code Reuse with Generics

Questions	Answers
1	2
2	2
3	1
4	3
5	1

Chapter 11, Advanced Generics

Questions	Answers
1	3
2	1
3	2
4	3
5	3

Chapter 12, Object-Oriented, Functional Programming, and Lambda Expressions

Questions	Answers
1	2
2	1
3	3
4	1
5	2

Chapter 13, Modularity in Java 9

Questions	Answers
1	1
2	2
3	2
4	3
5	3

Index

overridability of members,
    controlling in 178-184
subclassing of classes
    controlling 184-190
superclass 144

U

UAV (Unmanned Aerial Vehicle) 5
UML diagrams
    classes, organizing with 51, 52
UML (Unified Modeling Language) 46
unboxing 294
upper bound 279

V

values
    transforming, map operation used 315-319
    transforming, with getters 103-105
    transforming, with setters 103-105
variables
    recognizing 44-46
    working with 13-16

W

Windows
    required software, installing on 3
WonderCat character 200

www.ingramcontent.com/pod-product-compliance
Lightning Source LLC
Chambersburg PA
CBHW081505050326
40690CB00015B/2931